D0018990

RETURN TO
THE GOSPEL
OF THE WATER
AND THE SPIRIT

RETURN TO THE GOSPEL OF THE WATER AND THE SPIRIT

PAUL C. JONG

Hephzibah Publishing House

A Division of THE NEW LIFE MISSION

SEOUL, KOREA

Return to the gospel of the water and the Spirit

Copyright © 2001 by Hephzibah Publishing House

All rights reserved. No part of this publication may be reproduced, stored in a retrieval system, or transmitted in any form or by any means—electronic, mechanical, photocopying, recording, or otherwise—without the prior written permission of the publisher and copyright owners.

Scripture quotations used in this book are from the *New King James Version*.

ISBN 89-8314-038-0

Design by Min-soo Kim

Illustration by Young-ae Kim

Printed in Korea

Hephzibah Publishing House

A Division of THE NEW LIFE MISSION

48 Bon-dong Dongjack-gu

Seoul, Korea 156-060

Email : newlife@bjnewlife.org

Hephzibah Publishing House is a ministry of THE NEW LIFE MISSION founded by Rev. Paul C. Jong in 1991.

THE NEW LIFE MISSION is a non-denominational, nonprofit organization whose main purpose is to preach the words of God to every one. It aims to train disciples of Jesus to spread the gospel of being born again of water and the Spirit.

It has built mission-oriented churches worldwide and published dozens of spiritual books and tapes in many languages.

For more information please call 1-718-463-0838, 82-391-653-6465 or browse its website http://www.bjnewlife.org

THANKS

I thank the Lord for allowing us to preach the gospel of the water and the Spirit through the church of God in this age of darkness. I am sure that the Lord blesses us as we preach the gospel of the water and the Spirit to all the souls in this world through this book, so that they may all be born again.

I also thank the Lord for giving us workers and the ability to carry out the work of God. I would like to express my sincere appreciation to Mrs. Jungpil Sul for translating, to Ross Wallace for proofreading, to sister Lee Sangmin for editing, and to Rev. Samuel J. Kim and Rev. John K. Shin. I would like to express heartfelt thanks to all the other workers of the gospel who helped in the publication of this book.

This book, a sequel to my first book, reveals more clearly the gospel of the water and the Spirit and the origin and the reality of the false gospel. I hope and pray that it will help lead you back to the true gospel of the water and the Spirit.

I pray to God that all souls in this world may come to believe in the gospel of the water and the Spirit and be born again, so that the will of God may be done in this world. I thank the Lord again. ✉

PAUL C. JONG

The kingdom of heaven

Jesus answered, "Most assuredly, I say to you, unless one is born of water and the Spirit, he cannot enter the kingdom of God" (John 3:5).

PREFACE

CHRISTIANITY HAS LOST THE LIGHT

This is the era when all souls are in pain are full of regrets. All this spiritual pain comes from the spiritual deprivation which mankind is faced with at the moment. According to the Bible, the reason the wickedness and evil was such a great force in the time of Noah lies in the fact that; *"The sons of God saw the daughters of men, that they were beautiful; and they took wives for themselves of all whom they chose" (Genesis 6:2).*

When the children of God, the born again of words of truth, left the knowledge of the true and complete gospel and took into their hearts the words of false Christians who compromised the truth with man's thoughts, numerous pseudo gospel churches were born. Therefore God said, *"My Spirit shall not strive with man forever, for he is indeed flesh" (Genesis 6:3).*

Jesus called His born again disciples "the light of the world" because they received the light of life only Jesus could give. But Christians today do not have this light of life. The light still shines in the darkness, but the darkness refuses to receive it.

Consequently, contemporary Christianity has fallen to a status of a mere religion. Therefore, although there are more Christians today than ever before, not all of them are saved. They are always studying and learning the Bible, but they never reach the knowledge of the truth and are wallowing in a mire of a hypocritical life of religion, while their hearts wander in ignorance and chaos. Most present day Christians are ignorant of how to be born again and what this blessing means.

All these wasted efforts stem from errors in theology. In the history of Christianity, many religious leaders have interpreted and systematized the word of God according to their own thoughts and the motivation of their flesh.

They have divided Christianity into many denominations, increased their followers and reined them in with the regimental system of their denominations. They have justified their false teachings with theology and trained their followers through the secular and popular system called theological doctrines.

As a result, no one can be redeemed of his sins under this patton of Christianity but can only suffer and lament under the unbearable burden of his sins. They are the ones who have the form of godliness but deny its power (2 Timothy 3:5). How godly they look from the outside!

But present day Christianity is "full of extortion and self-indulgence" (Matthew 23:25). It is all because of the devil who has sowed seeds of deception. Heretical Christianity disguises itself as orthodoxy. It antagonizes those who seek righteousness and stands in the way of the true words of life.

THE BIBLICAL DEFINITION OF HERESY AND ITS ORIGIN

Heretics within the Christian Church are those who

believe in Jesus as their Savior but not in the words of the truth of the gospel. They follow the lies of the devil and are never redeemed of their transgressions, but are held in captivity by their own sinfulness. The true gospel is "the gospel of the water and the Spirit." Anyone who does not have "the faith of being born again of the salvation of the water and the Spirit" is a heretic in the eyes of God.

The true gospel is that Jesus Christ, the only begotten Son of God, came to this world in the flesh of a man and was baptized by the representative of humankind, John the Baptist at the Jordan. He took away all the sins of the world, carried them to the Cross and was crucified to save all people from their sins and the final judgment.

Therefore the Bible says, *"For God so loved the world that He gave His only begotten Son, that whoever believes in Him should not perish but have everlasting life" (John 3:16).* It is the will of God that we believe the truth that Jesus Christ entirely washed away all the sins of the world with His baptism and blood on the Cross in order to make us children of God.

However, today, most Christians believe that they can be saved by believing only in the Cross of Jesus, disregarding His baptism. They claim that all sins were washed away by the Son of God, Jesus, when He bled and died on the Cross. This is the pseudo gospel that is far from the true gospel that makes us truly born again of water and the Spirit. Therefore, Christianity, having been swept up in the current of theological fallacy, has become heretical.

The devil, seizing his opportunity when Adam believed his lies and stepped away from the words of God, has led humankind away from the true life into the false gospel.

Satan has long held people tightly in the mire of lies and false gospel, thus condemning us to destruction, sin, and death. In the same way, the devil tempts whoever accepts his lies as truth, causes them to fall into heresy, detains them in heresy and refuses to allow them to learn the truth.

This is just like the sinful works of the first king of the northern kingdom of Israel, Jeroboam. He was afraid that his people might return to the south kingdom, where the temple was, so he changed the sacrificial system that God gave the Israelites for their redemption.

He made golden calves and forced his people to worship them, turning Christianity into a heretic religion. He instituted festivals for the Israelites on the dates of his own choosing, like the festival held in Judah. He also appointed priests from among those who were not the sons of Levi, thus turning all his people away from the true ritual of atonement. Therefore Christianity has been fundamentally altered and stayed that way until now. It is such a lamentable thing.

Did Jesus truly save us from sin only through His blood on the Cross? If someone believes only in Christ's crucifixion, can his sins be washed away clean? No. The disciples of Jesus never said that the blood of Jesus was the whole gospel. John testified that he saw and touched Jesus Christ, the word of life, the true light. He testified that Jesus Christ came by "water and blood."

Jesus Christ came to this world to become the sin offering for all of us, and for this purpose He was baptized by John the Baptist at the Jordan and took on to Himself all the sins of the world. He then paid the wages of sin with His blood on the Cross. This is the true gospel. The Bible tells us that Jesus "came not only by water, but by water and blood," and it is the Spirit who bears witness that Jesus is God, and these three, "the Spirit, the water, and the blood agree as one" (1 John 5:6-8). Only those who share the beliefs of the disciple John have true faith that can overcome the world.

COME NOW, LET US REASON TOGETHER

Can we take one out of these three and still be saved? Never. The Spirit, the water, and the blood are one. Any one of these could never stand as the complete gospel and we could never become sinless if we removed one of these three. If people did not believe in the baptism of Jesus through which all their sins were passed on to Jesus, could they become completely without sin?

God is calling to us. *"'Come now, and let us reason together,' says the Lord, 'though your sins are like scarlet, they shall be as white as snow; though they are red like crimson, they shall be as wool. If you are willing and obedient, you shall eat the good of the land; but if you refuse and rebel, you shall be devoured by the sword;' For the mouth of the Lord has spoken" (Isaiah 1:18-20).*

Now, let us reason together with the written words of God. Has His Son, Jesus Christ, not washed away all our sins? How did He do so? Jesus Christ, who is God, came to this world in the flesh of a man and washed away all our sins with His baptism and death on the Cross.

For those who gladly obey the word of truth, God allows the blessings of the Millennium and everlasting life in the kingdom of heaven. But those who refuse to accept His love and salvation, or fail to come to Him with faith, shall be judged and thrown into the lake of fire for all eternity.

Therefore, in order to stay clear of temptation and the condemnation of heresy in this evil day and age, we should all follow the true gospel. We can overcome the lies of the devil and the filth of this world only by heeding the word of truth, believing it with all our heart, and confessing that we are born again of water and the Spirit. Jesus said, *"If you abide in My word, you are My disciples indeed. And you shall know the truth, and the truth shall make you free" (John 8:31-32).* Only when we are born again of "water and the Spirit," can we overcome the world and become free of all the sins, chaos, and emptiness within us.

When the true light shines, darkness recedes. Light and darkness cannot coexist. No matter how deeply buried in darkness this age is, no matter how chaotic and empty you are, the moment you take your heart into "the gospel of being born again of water and the Spirit," your heart will be filled with the light of truth. *"For it is the God who commanded light to shine out of darkness who has shone in our hearts to give the light of the knowledge of the glory of God in the face of Jesus Christ" (2 Corinthians 4:6).*

LET US RETURN TO "THE GOSPEL OF THE WATER AND THE SPIRIT"

I talked about the gospel as it is written in the Bible in my previous book, "Have You Truly Been Born Again of Water and the Spirit?" This book, the sequel to it, focuses on comparing the true gospel to the false ones that are rampant today. In so doing, I hope to steer true Christians away from the fallacy of theological theories, while providing deeper insight into the truth of "the gospel of the water and the blood" that appears throughout the Bible. And by providing the historical roots and reality of the false gospel and heretical teachings that are contrary to the truth of God, I hope to lead you to realize clearly the gospel of truth.

My fellow servants of God and I want to preach the gospel of the water and the Spirit to the ends of the earth till the day Jesus comes again in glory. Therefore we are going to publish more spiritual books in English, dealing with the subject from various angles.

Salvation from sin is already complete. The gate of Heaven is open. Whoever heeds the word of truth, confirms it in the Bible and believes in "the gospel of the water and the Spirit" can protect himself from the false gospel of the devil and be saved from all his sins. He can receive God's blessings and enter the kingdom of heaven. As the people of Israel led by Moses were freed from slavery in Egypt, I hope and pray that you will read these two books and have faith in the words of salvation and become children of God.

The Lord is calling us earnestly, saying, *"Everyone who thirsts, come to the waters; and you who have no money, come, buy and eat. Yes, come, buy wine and milk without money and without price" (Isaiah 55:1).* Let us all turn back to "the gospel of the water and the Spirit!" Let us avoid the upcoming judgment of God and enter the world of His grace and amazing blessings! ✉

CONTENTS

SERMON 1

The Meaning of the Original Gospel of Being Born Again

For as many of you as were baptized into Christ have put on Christ (Galatians 3:27).

The Meaning of the Original Gospel of Being Born Again

<John 3:1-6>

"There was a man of the Pharisees named Nicodemus, a ruler of the Jews. This man came to Jesus by night and said to Him, 'Rabbi, we know that You are a teacher come from God; for no one can do these signs that You do unless God is with him.' Jesus answered and said to him, 'Most assuredly, I say to you, unless one is born again, he cannot see the kingdom of God.' Nicodemus said to Him, 'How can a man be born when he is old? Can he enter a second time into his mother's womb and be born?' Jesus answered, 'Most assuredly, I say to you, unless one is born of water and the Spirit, he cannot enter the kingdom of God. That which is born of the flesh is flesh, and that which is born of the Spirit is spirit.'"

WHAT IS THE MEANING OF BEING BORN AGAIN ACCORDING TO THE BIBLE?

In this world, there are many who want to be born again by simply believing in Jesus. However, I would like to tell you firstly that being born again is not up to us, in other words, it is something which cannot come about as a result through our deeds alone.

Is being born again related to physical emotion and change?

No. Being born again is related to spiritual change. It is for a sinner to be born again as a sinless man.

Most Christians have this misconception. They believe that they are sure to be reborn. They believe so for the following reasons, amongst others. Some try for salvation by building many new churches, some devote themselves to preaching Christ as missionaries among peoples not yet reached by His Word in remote places, and still others refuse to get married and spend all their energy doing what they believe is the work of God.

This is not all. There are also people who donate large amount of money to their church, or maybe they sweep the floor of their church every day. All in all, they devote their time and property to the church. And they believe all these efforts will earn them the crown of life. They hope that God will recognize their efforts and allow them to be born again.

The point is that there are many devoted people who want to be born again. They are to be found everywhere. They work hard, hoping that someday God will bless them and allow them to be born again. They are found in many different kinds of religious institutions, seminaries, and sanatoriums. It is very unfortunate that they do not know the truth about being born again.

They all think in terms of their deeds, "If I do this perfectly, I will be born again." Therefore they put all their efforts into these works, believing that they are building the foundation necessary to be born again, and thinking, "I, too, shall be born again someday, like Rev. Wesley!" Reading John 3:8, they interpret the verse to mean that no one can tell where the blessing of being born again comes from or where it is going.

Therefore they can only work hard in hopes that Jesus will allow them to be born again some day. There are many who think, "If I keep trying like this, Jesus will allow me to be born again some day. I will become born again without even being aware of it. Some morning I will simply wake up born again and know that I am destined for Heaven." How fruitless such hopes and faith are!

We can never be born again that way! We can never be born again by staying away from alcohol and cigarettes, or by attending church diligently. As Jesus said, we have to "be born again of water and the Spirit" to enter the kingdom of God. And the water and the Spirit are God's only conditions for being born again.

Unless one is born again of water and the Spirit, all one's efforts to be righteous before Jesus are in vain. One can never be born again with offerings, donations, or devotion. One may think that because only God knows who are the born again, he cannot know whether he is born again or not.

It might be a comfort to think this way, but being born again cannot be hidden under the table. One would definitely know it oneself, and others would feel it also.

We would probably not feel it physically, but we would definitely feel it very well spiritually. The truly born again are those believers reborn through the word of God, the words of water, blood and the Spirit. However, those who are not born again will not understand it just as Nicodemus could not.

Therefore we have to listen to the words of the truth, the redemption through the baptism and blood of Jesus. As we listen and learn the word of God, we can find the truth therein. Therefore it is very important to open our minds and listen carefully.

"The wind blows where it wishes, and you hear the sound of it, but cannot tell where it comes from and where it goes. So is everyone who is born of the Spirit" (John 3:8).

When a person who is not born again reads this passage, he thinks, "Ah! Jesus said that I cannot know when I am born again! Nobody knows!" And the thought gives comfort. But this is not true. We may not know where the wind comes from or where it goes, but God knows all.

Even among the born again, there are some who do not realize it in the beginning. This is understandable. But within such a person's heart, there is the gospel: the words of redemption through the baptism and blood of Jesus.

This is the testimony to being born again. Those who hear the gospel and realizes, "Oh, then I am without sin. Then, I have been saved and born again." When they believe and keep the gospel of the water and the Spirit in their heart, they become righteous, a child of God.

Someone might be asked, "Are you born again?" and he would answer, "Not yet." "Then, are you saved?" "Yes, I believe I am saved." But he makes a contradictory statement, doesn't he? He does so because he thinks that when a person is born again, he should also be changed in his flesh.

Such people regard being born again as something like a radical change in lifestyle. But the truth is that they do not understand the gospel of being born again of water and the Spirit.

There are so many who do not understand the meaning of being born again. It is such a pity. It is not only laymen, but most of the church leaders who are operating under this delusion. The hearts of those of us who are born again mourn for these people.

When we feel this way, how much more pain does it cause Jesus our God in Heaven? Let us all be born again by believing in the gospel of being born again of the baptism of Jesus and His blood on the Cross.

To be born again and to be saved means the same thing. However, there are many who do not know this truth. To be born again means that the sin in one's heart has been washed away through belief in the gospel of the water and the Spirit. It means to become righteous through faith in the baptism of Jesus and His sacrifice on the Cross.

Before being born again, people are sinners, but after, they are completely without sin literally, born again as a new person. They have become a child of God by believing in the gospel of salvation.

Being born again means wearing the clothes of the baptism of Jesus, dying on the Cross with Jesus, and being resurrected with Him. It means that one has become righteous through the words of the baptism and the Cross of Jesus.

When one is born from the womb of one's mother, he is a sinner. But when he has heard the true gospel of being born again of water and the Spirit, he is then born again and becomes righteous.

Outwardly such a person seems no different, but is born again inside, in spirit. This is what it means to be born again. But there are so few who know this truth; not even one out of ten thousand. Can you agree with me that there are so few who understand the true meaning of being born again?

Those who believe the gospel of the water and the Spirit and are born again can distinguish the truly born again from common Christians.

IT IS JESUS WHO CONTROLS THE WIND

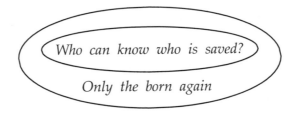

Who can know who is saved?

Only the born again

"The wind blows where it wishes, and you hear the sound of it, but cannot tell where it comes from and where it goes. So is everyone who is born of the Spirit." Jesus was talking about those who have not been born again. The born again know about being born again, but Nicodemus did not. God knows who is born again, and the born again also know it.

However, those who are not born again do not know how a person can be born again just as they do not know where the wind comes from and where it goes.

Are you able to understand this? Who moves the wind? God does. Who created the wind? God in Heaven did. Who controls the climate on earth, channels the wind and water?

And who puts breath of life into all living things? In other words, who created all life in this world and made it thrive? It was none other than Jesus Christ. And Jesus is God.

When we don't know the words of the gospel of the water, the blood and the Spirit, we cannot be born again and we cannot teach others spiritually, either. Jesus told us that unless one is born of water and the Spirit, one cannot be born again.

We must believe in the gospel of the water and the Spirit, the powerful gospel that makes us born again. The Spirit enters and dwells in the minds of all those who believe in the gospel of the water and the Spirit.

Jesus Christ was baptized to take away all the sins of humankind, and He bled on the Cross to pay for these sins. He has instilled the salvation of being born again in the hearts of all humankind. When we believe in this gospel, the Spirit enters our soul. This is the salvation of being born again. When we believe in the washing away of all sins through the baptism of Jesus and His blood, we are truly born again.

In Genesis 1:2, it is written, *"The earth was without form, and void; and darkness was on the face of the deep. And the Spirit of God was hovering over the face of the waters."* It is written that the Spirit of God was hovering over the face of the waters. The Spirit of God was moving outside the earth's surface.

It means that the Spirit cannot enter the hearts of sinners. The heart of the one who is not born again is in chaos, it is filled with the darkness of sin. Therefore the Spirit of God is not able to dwell in the heart of such a person.

God sent down the light of His gospel to illuminate

the hearts of sinners. God said, *"Let there be light,"* and there was light. Then, and only then, could the Spirit of God dwell in the hearts of all people.

Therefore, in the hearts of the born again, those who believe in the gospel of the water and the Spirit, dwells the Spirit of God. That is the meaning of their being "born again." They are born again in their hearts because they listened to the words of the salvation of the water and the Spirit and they believed it!

How can someone be born again? Jesus explained it to Nicodemus, the Pharisee, saying, *"Unless one is born of water and the Spirit, he cannot enter the kingdom of God."* Nicodemus said, "How can we be born again of water and the Spirit? Can we enter our mother's womb again and then be born again?" Obviously, he took it literally and couldn't figure out how a man could be born again.

Jesus said to him, "You are a teacher, and you don't even know what it means?" Jesus told him that unless one is born again of water and the Spirit, he cannot enter the kingdom of Heaven nor even see it. Jesus told Nicodemus the truth of being born again.

It is true that there are many people who believe in Jesus without being born again. Most Christians like Nicodemus are not really born again.

Nicodemus was a spiritual leader of Israel at that time, similar to the leaders of the church today. In modern terms, he was comparable to a state congressman. By religious standards he was a teacher, a rabbi of the Hebrews, He was a religious leader of the Jews. He was also an accomplished scholar.

In Israel in those days, there was no institution comparable to the schools of today, so all the people went to the temple or the synagogues to study under "the learned men." They were the teachers of the people. Just as today, there were many false teachers then too. And they were teaching people without having been born again themselves.

Nowadays there are so many religious leaders, church officials, teachers, preachers, elders and deacons, who have not been born again. Like Nicodemus, they do not know the truth of being born again. Many even think that we have to enter our mother's womb a second time to be born again. They know that they have to be born again, but they do not know how.

And because of their ignorance, like a blind man touching an elephant to try vainly to perceive with their hands alone, their instruction is based on their own personal feelings and experiences. They preach of worldly values in church. Owing to this, many faithful people are prevented from being born again.

Being born again has nothing to do with our good deeds. We are born again through belief in the words of the water, the blood and the Spirit that God gave us. It is God's gospel that changes us from being a sinner to being righteous.

Jesus spoke these words, *"If I have told you earthly things and you do not believe, how will you believe if I tell you heavenly things?"* Indeed, people did not believe when Jesus told them the truth that atonement for all our sins was completed through His baptism. What didn't they believe? They didn't believe that their redemption was made possible through the baptism of Jesus and His death on the Cross. This is what He meant when He said people wouldn't believe Him if He told them about "heavenly things."

To cleanse us of all our sins, Jesus was baptized by John the Baptist and died on the Cross, and then was resurrected from the dead to pave the way for sinners to be born again.

Therefore Jesus explained it to Nicodemus by quoting the Old Testament. *"No one has ascended to heaven but He who came down from heaven, that is, the Son of Man who is in heaven. And as Moses lifted up the serpent in the wilderness, even so must the Son of Man be lifted up, that whoever believes in Him should not perish but have eternal life"* *(John 3:13-15).* As Moses lifted up the serpent in the wilderness, even so must the Son of Man be lifted up to allow whoever believes in Him to have eternal life.

What did Jesus mean when He said, *"As Moses lifted up the serpent in the wilderness, even so must the Son of Man be lifted up?"* He quoted this passage from the Old Testament to illustrate how His baptism and blood would bring atonement for all the sins of humankind.

For Jesus to die on the Cross, for Him to be lifted up, He first had to take away the sin of the world by being baptized by John the Baptist. Because Jesus was without sin, He could not be crucified on the Cross. In order for Him to be crucified on the Cross, He had to be baptized by John the Baptist and thus take all the sins of the world upon Himself.

Only by taking on our sins and paying for them with His blood, could He save all sinners from damnation. Jesus gave us the salvation of being born again of water and the Spirit.

Therefore those who believe in Jesus as their Savior wear the clothes of His baptism, die with Him, and are born again with Him. Later, Nicodemus came to understand this.

AS THE SERPENT WAS LIFTED UP

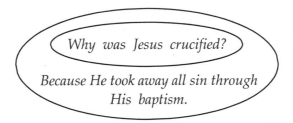

Why was Jesus crucified?

Because He took away all sin through His baptism.

Do you know the story of how Moses lifted up the bronze serpent in the wilderness? The story is written in Numbers chapter 21. It says that the souls of the Israelites became very discouraged after the Exodus from Egypt, causing them to speak out against God and against Moses.

As a result, the Lord sent fiery serpents among the people, which entered their tents and bit and killed them. After they were bitten, their bodies began to swell up and many died.

When the people began to die, Moses, their leader, prayed to God. "Lord, please save us." God told him to make a fiery serpent with brass and set it on a pole. He told him that whoever looked at it would live. Moses did as he was told and proclaimed God's words to the people.

Anyone who believed in his words and looked up at the bronze serpent was healed. In the same way, we have to be healed of the poisoned bites of the devil. The people of Israel listened to Moses and looked up at the bronze serpent on the pole, and thus they were healed.

The revelation of the serpent on the pole was that

damnation for all humankind's sins was brought upon Jesus Christ through His baptism and death on the Cross. He took it upon Himself to pay the penalty for the sins of all the sinners in the world. Thus, He ended all punishment for our sins.

Jesus Christ came into this world to save all people, who were destined to die from "the venom of the serpent," the temptations of Satan. To pay for all of our sins, He had to be baptized and die on the Cross before being resurrected to save those who believed in Him.

Just as the Israelites in the Old Testament were spared when they looked up at the serpent on the pole, today all who believe in Jesus and have faith that He paid for our sins through His baptism and blood can be saved and born again.

Jesus paid in full for all the sins of the world through His baptism by John the Baptist at the Jordan, His death on the Cross, and His resurrection from the dead. Now, all those who believe in Him can be blessed with salvation through His mercy.

"No one has ascended to heaven but He who came down from heaven, that is, the Son of Man who is in heaven" (John 3:13). As compensation for our sins, Jesus was baptized and bled on the Cross and opened the gates of Heaven for us. *"I am the way, the truth, and the life. No one comes to the Father except through Me,"* said Jesus in John 14:6.

Because Jesus was baptized and crucified on the Cross to open the gates of the Heaven for us, all who believe in salvation through Him are saved. Jesus has already paid for our sins, so whoever believes in the truth of the water, the blood and the Spirit can enter the kingdom of Heaven.

Jesus saved us with the gospel of the water and the

Spirit. Being born again comes from having faith in the baptism and blood of Jesus and in the fact He is God.

"*And as Moses lifted up the serpent in the wilderness, even so must the Son of Man be lifted up*" *(John 3:14).* What does this verse mean? Why did Jesus have to be crucified? Did He commit sins like us? Was He as weak as we are? Was He as incomplete as we are? No, He wasn't.

Then, why did He have to be crucified? It was to save us and compensate for all our sins. He was baptized and crucified to save all of us from all our sins.

This is the truth of salvation, of being born again of water and the Spirit. Jesus gave new life to all those who believed in His baptism and His death on the Cross, which was the compensation for our sins.

THE MEANING OF WATER AND THE SPIRIT

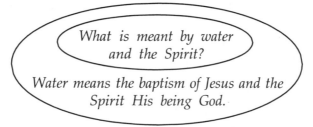

What is meant by water and the Spirit?

Water means the baptism of Jesus and the Spirit His being God.

The Bible tells us that when we believe in the baptism of Jesus and His blood on the Cross, we have been born again. Becoming children of God, being born again, is achieved through the written words of God, the gospel of the water, the blood and the Spirit which is the compensation for our sins.

According to the Bible, "the water"' means the baptism of Jesus (1 Peter 3:21), and "the Spirit" means that Jesus is God. And this is the truth of being born again, that Jesus came to this world in the flesh of humankind to pay for our sins through His baptism and blood.

He took away all our sins through His baptism and paid the wages of sin by dying on the Cross. By being baptized and bleeding on the Cross, He saved all those who believe in Him.

We have to realize that the baptism and the blood of Jesus represent our salvation in that they saved us from our sins. Only those who have been born again of water and the Spirit can see and enter the kingdom of Heaven. Jesus saved us with the water of His baptism, His blood and the Spirit. Do you believe in this?

Jesus is the heavenly High Priest who came down to this world to pay for the sins of the world. He was baptized, bled on the Cross and was resurrected, thus becoming the Savior to all those who believe in Him.

Jesus said in John 10:7, *"I am the door of the sheep."* Jesus stands at the door of heaven. Who opens the door for us? It is Jesus Christ.

He turns His face away from those who believe in Him without knowing the truth of His salvation. He doesn't allow those who do not believe in His baptism, blood and the Spirit to be born again. He turns His face away from anyone who does not believe in His written word, who refuses to accept His holiness, and who will not recognize Him as God.

The written truth is that He came to this world in the flesh, was baptized, and died on the Cross to compensate for all the sins of the world, that He died at the Cross to receive judgment on our behalf, that He was resurrected on the third day after the crucifixion. Anyone refusing to believe in this truth is cast out by Him and will perish. As it is written, *"The wages of sin is death."*

Those however, who believe in the blessing of redemption through His baptism and blood, those who have become holy in their hearts, are allowed to enter the kingdom of Heaven. This is the true gospel of being born again, the gospel which came to us by water, blood and the Spirit. To be born again of water and the Spirit is the heavenly gospel. Only those who believe in the baptism and the blood of Jesus can be born again. Those who believe in the gospel of the water, the blood and the Spirit are without sin; they are the ones who are truly born again.

Today, just as Nicodemus wasn't aware of the truth, most people believe in Jesus without knowing the true gospel. What an upstanding member of society Nicodemus was! However, he heard the true gospel from Jesus, and later, when Jesus was crucified, he was the one who came to bury His body. By that time Nicodemus had fully come to believe.

Nowadays, there are too many of us who do not know the truth about the water and the Spirit of Jesus. Moreover, there are so many people who do not accept the truth when they have a chance to hear the true gospel. It is such a pity.

Jesus made it possible for all of us to be born again. What made us born again? It was the water, the blood and the Spirit. Jesus took away our sins when He was baptized. He died on the Cross and then was resurrected from the dead.

And He gives all to those who believe in Him the blessing of being born again. Jesus is the Savior who allows all those who believe in Him to be born again. Pray that you will always be with Jesus, the one who created Heaven and earth and all things in between.

John 3:16 says, *"That whoever believes in Him should not perish but have everlasting life."* We have earned everlasting life by believing in Jesus. We have been born again by believing in the water and the Spirit. It is the truth that if we believe in the gospel of salvation, the baptism and the blood of Jesus, and that Jesus is the Savior and God, we can be saved.

But if we don't believe in this truth, we will be thrown into hell for eternity. That is why Jesus told Nicodemus, *"If I have told you earthly things and you do not believe, how will you believe if I tell you heavenly things?"*

What did God do for us? The salvation through Jesus allowed us to be born again. Jesus saved us from the world, the devil and the sins of the world. To save the sinners of this world from the judgment of sin, He took away all our sins through His baptism, was crucified on the Cross and was then resurrected from the dead.

It is our choice whether we believe in this salvation or not. The salvation of being born again comes from faith in salvation through the baptism and the blood of Jesus.

It is said that there are two blessings that God bestowed on us. One is the general blessing, which includes all things of nature, including the sun and the air. This is known as the general blessing because it is given to all people whether they are sinners or the righteous.

Then, what is this special blessing? The special blessing is being born again of water and the Spirit, which saves all sinners from death for their sins.

THE SPECIAL BLESSING

What is the special blessing of God?

That He made us born again though His baptism, crucifixion, and resurrection

It is written in John 3:16, *"For God so loved the world that He gave His only begotten Son, that whoever believes in Him should not perish but have everlasting life."* This describes the special blessing of God: Jesus came down to this world in the flesh of a man and washed away all our sins by being baptized and crucified for us. This is the special blessing of God, the truth, that we have been saved from all sins.

It is a fact that Jesus has saved us and changed us from sinners into the righteous. You can have the special blessing of God simply by believing in this truth. Do you all believe?

All your faith would be in vain if you refused this special blessing of God no matter how faithfully you lived throughout your life.

I preach all the time and I have never forgotten to preach that belief in the baptism of Jesus and His Cross are the only way to be born again. Any book of the Bible reveals that the blessing of being born again through Jesus is "the special blessing of God" that we are talking about. There is nothing that illustrates the blessing of God better than the salvation of sinners through the baptism of Jesus and His crucifixion.

The baptism of Jesus and His crucifixion are the special

blessing of God. The false preachers in this world have nothing to say about this. These false preachers appear in the clothes of the angels of light, armed with the morals of Christianity and humanity. Yes, this is true. The miracles they perform, the healing of the sick are all evil things if they have nothing to do with the special blessing of God.

It is this special blessing of God which gave us sinners the gospel of atonement. With His special blessing, God allowed us to be born again. He made us new through His baptism, blood, death and resurrection. He made us His children, free from sin.

Do you believe in this? — Yes. — Have you been truly blessed? — Yes. — The baptism of Jesus and His blood, death and resurrection are the special blessing that God gave us through the water and the Spirit. This is the gospel of the special blessing. Praise the Lord for saving us through His special blessing.

It is such a pity that so many faithful Christians today are not aware of the special blessing of God, the gospel of baptism and blood, of being born again of water and the Spirit. They try blindly to find ways in their own theology and religious morals. How ignorant they are!

Christianity has been with us so long and it has been nearly five hundred years since the Reformation, but still, there are so many in Korea and in the rest of the world who are ignorant about the truth of being born again and the special blessing of God.

I hope however, and believe that He will let them know the truth now because we are in the ear which is close to the end of this world.

Sinners have to be born again and accept the truth of the water and the Spirit in order to become righteous and enter the kingdom of Heaven. Many Christians are trying hard to be born again.

However, if they try without knowing the true meaning of being born again, their faith is in vain. They say that they have to be born again to enter the kingdom of Heaven, but they do not have a clue about the truth of being born again.

They just assume that since they believe so faithfully, since they feel the fire in their hearts, that they can be born again. But trying to be born again based on personal feelings or fervent religious deeds can only lead to incorrect faith.

THE WORD OF GOD WHICH LEADS US TO BE TRULY BORN AGAIN

What is the difference between faith and religion?

Faith is to believe what Jesus did to save us, while religion is to rely on one's own thoughts and works.

It is written clearly in 1 John 5:4-8 that we can be born again only by believing in the water, the blood and the Spirit. If we are to be born again, we should keep in mind that we can be born again only through the written word of God, the word of truth. We should know that visions, speaking in tongues or sensational experiences can never lead us to be born again.

Jesus said in John chapter 3 that one cannot enter the kingdom of Heaven unless one is born again of water and the Spirit. If one is to be born again, one generally has to believe in Jesus twice. First, one tends to believe in Jesus in the religious way, recognizing his sins through the law of God. The first time someone believes in Jesus, it is through the law of God and the realization of what a terrible sinner he really is.

We should not believe in Jesus in accordance with one of the many religions of this world. Christianity is not just another religion. It is the only way to gain eternal life through faith.

Anyone who believes in Jesus as a religion will end up empty-handed. He will be left with a heart full of sin, chaos and emptiness. Isn't this the truth? You would not want to end up a hypocrite like the Pharisees in the Bible.

Everyone wants to become a born-again-Christian. However, when one believes in Christianity as a religion, he ends up being a hypocrite with a heart full of sin. We must come to know the truth of being born again.

Anyone who believes in Christianity as a religion without being born again is sure to end up with confusion and emptiness in his heart. If one believes in Jesus but is not born again, his belief is incorrect. Therefore he ends up as a phony, trying hard to appear holy before everyone but failing miserably.

As long as you believe in Christianity as a religion, you will always be a sinner, a hypocrite, and live out your days lamenting your sins. If you want to be freed from your sins, you have to believe in the written truth, the gospel of the water, the blood and the Spirit.

FINDING OUT THE SECRET OF REDEMPTION THROUGH THE BAPTISM OF JESUS

What makes us born again?

The baptism of Jesus, His death on the Cross, and His resurrection

The Bible tells us that anyone can be born again through the word of God, which never changes. Now, let us look at the words of the apostle Peter in 1 Peter 3:21. *"There is also an antitype which now saves us, namely baptism."*

In the Bible, it is recorded that the baptism of Jesus is the antitype which saves us. All who believe in Jesus should know, not about our own baptism, but the baptism of Jesus. The baptism of Jesus gives us sinners new life. Believe it, and you will be born again and gain the blessing of salvation.

By understanding that salvation is gained through belief in the baptism of Jesus, we can be saved, become righteous and earn everlasting life. In other words, when we believe in the truth of salvation through the words of God, our sins will be cleansed for all time.

To be born again is to be born a second time. Most of us usually begin by believing in Jesus as a religion, and then we become born again through faith when we realize the truth. The name Jesus means *"For He will save His people from their sins" (Matthew 1:21)*.

When we believe in Jesus and know exactly what He

has done for all humankind, we are freed of our sins and are born again as brand new people. At first we believe in Jesus as a religion, then, when we hear and believe in the gospel of the baptism of Jesus and His blood, we are born again.

What is the truth which makes us born again? First, it is the baptism of Jesus, then the blood He shed on the Cross, and finally His resurrection from the dead. Being born again means believing in Jesus as our God, our Savior. Let us see how the people of the Old Testament were born again.

The Compensation for Sin in the Old Testament: the Laying on of Hands and the Offering of Blood

What is the gospel of being born again in the Old Testament? First, let us read Leviticus chapter 1 and what it says about being born again.

In Leviticus 1:1-5, *"Now the Lord called to Moses, and spoke to him from the tabernacle of meeting, saying, "Speak to the children of Israel, and say to them: 'When any one of you brings an offering to the Lord, you shall bring your offering of the livestock—of the herd and of the flock. If his offering is a burnt sacrifice of the herd, let him offer a male without blemish; he shall offer it of his own free will at the door of the tabernacle of meeting before the Lord. Then he shall put his hand on the head of the burnt offering, and it will be accepted on his behalf to make atonement for him. He shall kill the bull before the Lord; and the priests, Aaron's sons, shall bring the blood and sprinkle the blood all around on the altar that is by the door of the tabernacle of meeting.'"*

God tells us in Leviticus how the Israelites could be united with God through the sacrificial system. It is the truth that we should all know and understand. Therefore let us review these words.

God called Moses and spoke to him from the tabernacle of meeting. It was about atoning for the sins of the Israelites. When the people of Israel committed sins of disobedience of the law of God, they were able to atone for their sins by offering livestock without blemish to God.

These sacrificial animals had to be those specified by God and they had to be without blemish. Also, they had to be offered according to the ritual set down by God. The form of the sacrifice was as follows.

If anyone sinned in time of the Old Testament, he had to offer a sacrifice before God for the remission of sin. First, the sacrifice had to be without blemish, and then the sinner had to lay his hands on it in order to pass his sins on to its head.

After it was killed, its blood had to be put on the horns of the altar, and the rest of it was poured on to the ground. This was the ritual of the holy tabernacle which God had given His people as the blessing of redemption.

The law and commandments of God consist of 613 articles prescribing what they "should do," or "should not do." God gave the law and His commandments to the people of Israel. Although the people knew that the law and the commandments of God were right, they could not live up to them because everyone was born with twelve kinds of sins inherited from Adam.

Therefore, they lost the ability to do right before God.

The Israelites lost the ability to become righteous. Rather, they could not help but keep committing sins, even while trying very hard to stay free from sin. It is the destiny of all humankind to be born and die as sinners.

But God, in His infinite mercy, gave His people the sacrificial system through which they could atone for their sins. He provided the ritual of the holy tabernacle so that the people of Israel and all the people of the world could be redeemed of their sins. He revealed through the sacrificial system His righteous love for all humankind. He showed the world the way to salvation.

God gave the people the sacrificial system and ordained the house of Levi to minister the sacrifice. Among the 12 tribes of Israel, only the house of Levi was ordained to minister the sacrifice for the people of Israel.

Moses and Aaron were of the house of Levi. And the Bible records the laws and regulations governing the sacrifice of the holy tabernacle, the gospel of atonement by the laying on of hands.

Therefore, when we really understand the sacrificial ritual of the Levites, we can be born again ourselves. That is why we have to study the word of God regarding the sacrifice of the holy tabernacle. This is the most important part of the Old Testament. Finally, when we come to the New Testament, we have the blessings of being born again through the water and the Spirit.

ATONEMENT FOR SIN IN THE OLD TESTAMENT

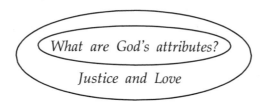

What are God's attributes?

Justice and Love

God called Moses, of the house of Levi, to the holy tabernacle of meeting and ordained his brother Aaron as the high priest. Aaron was to pass the sins of the people on to the sin offerings.

This is what God said to Moses as recorded in Leviticus 1:2. *"Speak to the children of Israel, and say to them: 'When any one of you brings an offering to the Lord, you shall bring your offering of the livestock — of the herd and of the flock.'"* God specifies here the sacrificial offerings. If any one of the people sought atonement for his sins, he had to offer a bull or a sheep from his livestock.

God also told them, *"If his offering is a burnt sacrifice of the herd, let him offer a male without blemish; he shall offer it of his own free will at the door of the tabernacle of meeting before the Lord"* (Leviticus 1:3).

The sacrifice was accepted by God in place of the life of the person who was supposed to die for his sins. The Israelites could pass on their sins by laying their hands on the heads of the animals. The sacrificial animals had to be offered of the person's own free will. Now, let us see what verse 4 says.

"Then he shall put his hand on the head of the burnt offering, and it will be accepted on his behalf to make atonement for him."

The offering would thus be accepted by God. When a sinner put his hands on the head of the burnt offering, his sins were passed on to the head of the animal. Therefore a sinner had to lay his hands on the head of the offering before God, so then He would accept it and grant atonement for his sins.

The person making the offering then killed the animal and put the blood on the horns of the altar and poured the rest on the ground before the altar. In order to pay for his sins and become free of them, one had to offer the sacrifice according to the laws set down by God.

It is written in Leviticus 1:5, *"He shall kill the bull before the Lord; and the priests, Aaron's sons, shall bring the blood and sprinkle the blood all around on the altar that is by the door of the tabernacle of meeting."* Inside the tabernacle, by the door, was the altar of burnt offerings with horns on the four corners.

After laying his hands on the head of the burnt offering to pass on his sins, the sinner had to kill the sacrificial animal, and the priest sprinkled its blood on the horns. The horns of the altar refer to the judgment for sins. Thus, putting blood on these horns meant that the animal had shed blood to pay for sins on behalf of the sinner. When God looked at the blood on the horns of the altar, He expiated the sins of the sinner.

Why did the sin offering have to bleed? Because *"the wages of sin is death" (Romans 6:23)* and because the life of the flesh is in the blood. Therefore it is written in Hebrews, *"Without shedding of blood there is no remission" (Hebrews 9:22).* Thus, the shedding of blood of the sin offering fulfilled the law of God, which says that the wages of sin is death.

By all rights, the offered blood should have come from

the sinner, but the sin offering bled in his place for the atonement. The priest then put the blood on the horns of the altar to signify that the wages of the sin was paid.

If we read Revelations 20:11-15 in the New Testament, we can see that the horns signify the Book of Judgment. Therefore to put blood on the horns is to put blood on the Book of Judgment. It is to testify that judgment for the sins was fulfilled by laying on hands and the blood of the sin offering.

SINS ARE RECORDED IN TWO PLACES

All the sins of humankind before God are recorded in two places. One is the tablets of their hearts, and the other is the Book of Judgment opened before God.

It is written in Jeremiah 17:1, *"The sin of Judah is written with a pen of iron; with the point of a diamond it is engraved on the tablet of their heart, and on the horns of your altars."*

In Leviticus 17:11, it says, *"For the life of the flesh is in the blood."* The blood is the life of the flesh, and our sins can be paid for only with this blood. Therefore, blood was put on the horns of the altar. According to the law, almost all things are purged with blood, and without shedding of blood there is no remission (Hebrews 9:22).

"And he shall skin the burnt offering and cut it into its pieces. The sons of Aaron the priest shall put fire on the altar, and lay the wood in order on the fire. Then the priests, Aaron's sons, shall lay the parts, the head, and the fat in order on the wood that is on the fire upon the altar; but he shall wash its entrails and its legs with water. And the priest shall burn all on the altar as a burnt sacrifice, an offering made by fire, a sweet aroma

to the Lord" (Leviticus 1:6-9).

Then the priests cut the burnt offering into pieces and placed them onto the fire on the altar. This ritual was meant to present that when people sinned before God, they had to die in that way and bleed and be thrown into the fires of hell. However, judgment was carried out through the sin offering, so that the people could atone for their sins.

The sacrifice of burnt offerings was the ritual of the judgment of the righteous law of God. God incorporated both His laws, the law of righteousness and the law of love, into the ritual of atonement for all humankind.

Because God is righteous, He had to judge and sentence them to death. But, because He also loved His people, He allowed them to pass their sins on to the sin offering. In the New Testament, because our Lord loved us so, He was baptized and crucified to become the sin offering for us sinners. The baptism of Jesus and His death on the Cross blotted out all the sins of the world.

ATONEMENT FOR A DAY'S SIN IN THE OLD TESTAMENT

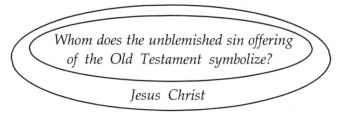

Whom does the unblemished sin offering of the Old Testament symbolize?

Jesus Christ

Let us read from Leviticus 4:27. *"If anyone of the common people sins unintentionally by doing something against any of the commandments of the Lord in anything which ought not to be done, and is guilty, or if his sin which he has committed comes to his knowledge, then he shall bring as his offering a kid of the goats, a female without blemish, for his sin which he has committed. And he shall lay his hand on the head of the sin offering, and kill the sin offering at the place of the burnt offering. Then the priest shall take some of its blood with his finger, put it on the horns of the altar of burnt offering, and pour all the remaining blood at the base of the altar. He shall remove all its fat, as fat is removed from the sacrifice of the peace offering; and the priest shall burn it on the altar for a sweet aroma to the Lord. So the priest shall make atonement for him, and it shall be forgiven him"* (Leviticus 4:27-31).

The descendants of Adam, the people of Israel, and all the people of the world were born into this world full of sin. Therefore our hearts are filled with sin. There are all kinds of sins inside the heart of a person: evil thoughts, adulteries, fornications, murders, thefts, covetousness, and foolishness.

When a sinner wanted to atone for a day's sins, he had to bring an animal without blemish to the holy tabernacle. He then had to lay his hands on the head of the animal to pass on his sins, kill the sacrifice and give its blood to the priest to be offered before God. The priest would then carry out the rest of the sacrifice so that the sinner could be forgiven for his sins.

Without the law and commandments of God, people wouldn't know if they had sinned or not. When we look at ourselves through the law and the commandments of God, we recognize our sins. Our sins are not judged by our standards, but by the law and commandments of God.

The common people of Israel sinned, not because they wanted to, but because they were born with all kinds of sin in their hearts. The sins man commits because of his weaknesses are called transgressions. Sin includes all the transgressions and iniquities of humankind.

All men are incomplete beings. As the people of Israel were also incomplete, they were sinners and committed sins. All of our transgressions and iniquities can be categorized in the following way. When we have evil thoughts in our minds, they are called sins, and when we act them out, they are called trespasses. The sins of the world include both kinds.

In the Old Testament, sins were passed on to the head of the sin offering by the laying on of hands. Afterwards, the sinner was without sin and therefore had no need to die for his sins. The sacrificial system is thus the shadow of the just judgment and love of God.

Because God created us from the earth, we were mere dust in the beginning. Putting blood on the horns of the altar and pouring the rest at the base of the altar meant that the Israelites had compensated for their sins and erased all sins from the tablets of their hearts.

"The priest shall burn the fat on the altar for a sweet aroma to the Lord." The fat in the Bible means the Holy Spirit. Therefore, in order to atone for our sins, we have to do it in the way God ordained. We also have to take into our hearts the atonement of our sins in the way God deemed proper.

God told the people of Israel that the sin offerings should be a lamb, goat, or calf. The sin offerings of the Old Testament were the chosen ones. The calf is a clean animal. The reason the sin offerings had to be without blemish was that they were revealing Jesus Christ who was conceived by the Holy Spirit to become the sin offering for all humankind.

The people of the Old Testament passed on their sins by laying their hands on the head of the unblemished sin offering. The priests ministered the sacrifice to compensate for their sins. This was how the people of Israel atoned for their sins.

THE RITUAL OF THE DAY OF ATONEMENT

Why did the people of Israel need to offer the sacrifice on the Day of Atonement?

Because they continued to sin until death. Daily sin offerings couldn't sanctify them before God.

However, as they had to make a sacrifice every time they committed a sin, it was impossible to supply all the sacrifices they needed to atone for their sins. So, gradually, they became negligent. It seemed like an endless task to atone for their sins every day and they came to feel that they could do away with this ritual altogether.

No matter how hard we try, we can never offer sacrifice enough for all our sins. Therefore the true compensation for our sins has to be given through our heartfelt belief in the law of salvation that God prepared for us.

Because of our weakness, no matter how hard we try to live by the law of God, we only become more aware of how incomplete and weak we are. Therefore God gave the people of Israel a way to atone for the whole year's sins all at once (Leviticus 16:17-22).

It is written in Leviticus, *"In the seventh month, on the tenth day of the month, you shall afflict your souls, and do no work at all, whether a native of your own country or a stranger who dwells among you. For on that day the priest shall make atonement for you, to cleanse you, that you may be clean from all your sins before the Lord. It is a sabbath of solemn rest for you, and you shall afflict your souls. It is a statute forever"* *(Leviticus 16:29-31).*

Thus, the people of Israel had peace of mind once a year when the high priest ministered the sacrifice of atonement on the tenth day of the seventh month for all sins the people had committed during the year. With their sins washed away, their minds were at peace on that day.

On the tenth day of the seventh month, the high priest Aaron, as the representative of all Israel, had to minister the sacrifice of atonement. At this time, the other priests could not enter the holy tabernacle. First of all, Aaron had to minister the sacrifice of atonement for himself and his house before he could do it for the rest of the people of Israel because he and his house had also sinned.

He ministered the sacrifice for the people like this. *"He shall take the two goats and present them before the Lord at the door of the tabernacle of meeting. Then Aaron shall cast lots for the two goats: one lot for the Lord and the other lot for the scapegoat. And Aaron shall bring the goat on which the Lord's lot fell, and offer it as a sin offering. But the goat on which the lot fell to be the scapegoat shall be presented alive before the Lord, to make atonement upon it, and to let it go as the scapegoat into the wilderness"* *(Leviticus 16:7-10).*

After he had performed the ritual of atonement for his house and himself, Aaron "cast lots for the two goats." One lot was for the Lord and the other was for the scapegoat, "*Azazel.*"

First, one of the two goats was offered to the Lord. Here, the high priest laid his hands on the goat on behalf of the people to pass on the sins they had committed during the year.

The blood was taken to the mercy seat inside the Most Holy Place and sprinkled seven times. The people of Israel were forgiven for all their sins over the past year. Instead of the people of Israel dying for their sins, the high priest Aaron passed the sins on to the head of the sin offering and let it take the judgment for them. Then he sacrificed the other live goat before God. That was the sacrifice which was carried for the people.

FOR THE PEOPLE

In front of all the people, Aaron laid his hands on the second goat and confessed before God. "Lord, the people of Israel have committed murder, adultery, theft, covetousness, deceit . . . and they have bowed before idols. They have not kept the Sabbath holy, they have called Your name in vain, and they have broken all the articles of Your Laws and commandments." Then he took away his hands. With this, all the sins of the people for the whole year were passed on to the sin offering.

Let's read Leviticus 16:21. "*And Aaron shall lay both his hands on the head of the live goat, confess over it all the iniquities of the children of Israel, and all their transgressions, concerning all their sins, putting them on the head of the goat, and shall send it away into the wilderness by the hand of a suitable man.*"

The scapegoat would then wander around in the wilderness and die with the sins of the people of Israel on its head. The scapegoat, *"Azazel"* in Hebrew, means "to put out." It means that the sin offering was cast out before the Lord, in place of all the people of Israel.

Therefore, the sins of Israel were passed on to the scapegoat through the laying on of Aaron's hands. In this way the Israelites were forgiven for their sins. When they saw the high priest laying his hands on the goat and saw it led into the wilderness, all the people of Israel who believed in the ritual of atonement were sure of the atonement for their sins. All the rituals of the Old Testament were the shadow of 'the gospel of the being born again' of the New Testament.

In the Old Testament, the laying on of hands and the blood of the sacrifice was the gospel of salvation from sin. It remained basically the same in the New Testament.

THE GOSPEL OF REDEMPTION IN THE NEW TESTAMENT

In the New Testament, how were all the sins of the people expiated?

It is written in Matthew 1:21-25, *"And she will bring forth a Son, and you shall call His name Jesus, for He will save His people from their sins. So all this was done that it might be fulfilled which was spoken by the Lord through the prophet, saying; 'Behold, the virgin shall be with child, and bear a Son, and they shall call His name Immanuel,' which is translated, 'God with us.' Then Joseph, being aroused from sleep, did as the angel of the Lord commanded him and took to him his wife, and did not know her till she had brought forth her firstborn Son. And he called His name Jesus."*

Our Lord Jesus came down to this world in the name of Immanuel to save all humankind from sin. Therefore He was named Jesus. Jesus came to take away all the sins of the world. He came in the flesh of a human being to become humankind's Savior. He fulfilled our salvation and freed us forever from sin.

THE GOSPEL OF BEING BORN AGAIN

And how did Jesus free us from all our sins? He did it through His baptism. Let us look at Matthew 3:13.

"Then Jesus came from Galilee to John at the Jordan to be baptized by him. And John tried to prevent Him, saying, 'I need to be baptized by You, and are You coming to me?' But Jesus answered and said to him, 'Permit it to be so now, for thus it is fitting for us to fulfill all righteousness.' Then he allowed Him. When he had been baptized, Jesus came up immediately from the water; and behold, the heavens were opened to Him, and He saw the Spirit of God descending like a dove and alighting upon Him. And suddenly a voice came from heaven, saying, 'This is My beloved Son, in whom I am well pleased'" (Matthew 3:13-17).

In the New Testament, when Jesus turned 30 years old, He came to John the Baptist at the Jordan. He was baptized by him and took away the sins of all sinners. By doing so, He fulfilled the righteousness of God.

WHY WAS JESUS BAPTIZED AT THE JORDAN?

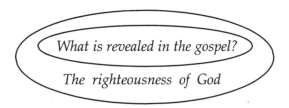

What is revealed in the gospel?

The righteousness of God

Let us now take a look at the scene when the heavenly High Priest met the last high priest of mankind. Here, we can see the righteousness of God through the baptism which secured atonement for all the sins of the world.

John the Baptist, the one who baptized Jesus, was the greatest among those born of women. Jesus had testified in Matthew 11:11, *"Among those born of women there has not risen one greater than John the Baptist."* Just as the sins of the people were expiated when the high priest Aaron laid his hands on the head of the sin offering on the Day of Atonement, in the New Testament, all the sins of the world were expiated when Jesus was baptized by John the Baptist.

The gospel of being born again is the gospel of complete atonement for all our sins, past, present and future. Therefore the gospel of redemption through the baptism of Jesus was the gospel God set down for the fulfillment of His righteousness, which saved all the people of the world. Jesus was baptized in the most proper way to atone for the sins of the world.

What does fulfilling "all righteousness" mean? It means God washed away all the sins of the world in the most proper way. Jesus was baptized to wash away all the sins of humankind. *"For in it the righteousness of God is revealed from faith to faith"* (Romans 1:17).

The righteousness of God was shown in His decision

to send His own Son Jesus to this world to wash away all the sins of the world through His baptism by John the Baptist and His death on the Cross.

In the New Testament, the righteousness of God was expressed through the baptism of Jesus and His blood. We became righteous because Jesus took away all the sins of humankind almost two millennia ago at the Jordan. When we accept the salvation of God in our hearts, the righteousness of God is truly fulfilled.

"But Jesus answered and said to him, 'Permit it to be so now, for thus it is fitting for us to fulfill all righteousness.' Then he allowed Him. When He had been baptized, Jesus came up immediately from the water; and behold, the heavens were opened to Him, and He saw the Spirit of God descending like a dove and alighting upon Him. And suddenly a voice came from heaven, saying, 'This is My beloved Son, in whom I am well pleased'" (Matthew 3:15-17).

This passage reveals that God Himself testified to the fact that the baptism of His Son fulfilled all the righteousness of salvation. He was telling us, "Jesus, who was baptized by John the Baptist, now is truly My Son." God testified that His Son was baptized for the atonement of all humankind. He did so, so that the holy work of His Son, Jesus, would not be in vain.

Jesus is the Son of God and also the Savior of the sinners of the world. *"In whom I am well pleased,"* said God. It is the truth that Jesus obeyed the will of the Father and took away all the sins of humankind through His baptism.

The word baptism means "to be washed, to pass to, to be buried." Because all our sins were passed on to Jesus when He was baptized, all we have to do is believe in the gospel to be saved from all the sins of the world.

The fulfillment of all the prophecies of salvation in the Old Testament was accomplished through the baptism of Jesus in the New Testament. Therefore the prophecies in the Old Testament have finally found counterparts in the New Testament. Just as the people of Israel atoned for their sins once a year in the Old Testament, the sins of the people were passed on to Jesus and expiated forever in the New Testament.

Leviticus 16:29 is the antitype of Matthew 3:15. Jesus was baptized to take on all the sins of the world. Thanks to His baptism, all who believe in His eternal forgiveness of sin are saved; all their sins were erased from the tablets of their hearts.

If you do not recognize and believe in your heart the truth of the baptism of Jesus and His death on the Cross, you can never be cleansed of your sins no matter how pious a life you live. Only through the baptism of Jesus is the word of God fulfilled and our sins erased. True salvation is achieved through the redemption of all our sins, in other words, through the baptism of Jesus.

With this in mind, what will you do? Will you accept this salvation into your heart? Or will you not? This is not the word of man, but that of God Himself. Jesus died on the Cross because He had taken away all your sins through His baptism. Don't you agree that the crucifixion of Jesus was the result of His baptism?

It is written in Romans 8:3-4, *"For what the law could not do in that it was weak through the flesh, God did by sending His own Son in the likeness of sinful flesh, on account of sin; He condemned sin in the flesh, that the righteous requirement of the law might be fulfilled in us who do not walk according to the flesh but according to the Spirit."*

Because we as work beings cannot keep the law and commandments of God owing to the weakness of the flesh, Jesus took away all the sins of the flesh by taking them on to Himself. This is the truth of the baptism of Jesus. The baptism of Jesus foreordained His death on the Cross. This is the wisdom of the original gospel of God.

If you have been believing only in the death of Jesus on the Cross, turn back now and accept in your heart the gospel of salvation through the baptism of Jesus. Then, and only then, can you truly become a child of God.

THE ORIGINAL GOSPEL

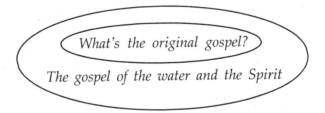

What's the original gospel?

The gospel of the water and the Spirit

The original gospel is the gospel of the atonement of sins. This is the gospel of the baptism of Jesus, His death and resurrection that God revealed to us. Jesus Christ washed away sin all at one time by being baptized at the Jordan and through this gave salvation to all those who believe in this truth. Owing to our faith, all our sins of the future also have been washed away.

Now, whoever believes in the baptism of Jesus and His blood on the Cross is saved from all the sins of the world forever. Do you believe? If your answer is "Yes, I do," then you will truly become righteous.

Let us briefly summarize the events that happened after

Jesus was baptized. In John 1:29, it is written, *"Behold! The Lamb of God who takes away the sin of the world!"*

John the Baptist testified that Jesus was the Lamb of God who took away the sin of the world. John the Baptist had passed on to Jesus all the sins of the world when he baptized Him at the Jordan. Additionally, because John the Baptist himself baptized Jesus, he could testify, *"Behold! The Lamb of God who takes away the sin of the world!"* Jesus was baptized and took away the sins of the world, and this is the gospel of being born again.

Adam → Abraham → The baptism → Present → The end
of Jesus   of the world
4000 B.C.   2000 B.C.   30 A.D.   2000 A.D.   ? A.D.

≪ = = = = All the sins of the world = = = = ≫

"Behold! The Lamb of God who takes away the sin of the world!" (John 1:29). Jesus took away all the sins of the world through His baptism.

The sins you committed from birth until your tenth birthday are included in the sins of the world. Do you believe that those sins were passed on to Jesus? — Yes, I do. — What about your transgressions from the age of 11 to 20? Do you believe that those sins were also passed on to Jesus? — Yes, I do. —

Are the sins you will commit in the future among the sins of the world? — Yes, they are also included. — Then, were they passed on to Jesus? — Yes, they were. — Do you really believe that all your sins have been passed on to Jesus? — Yes, I do. — Do you believe that all the sins of the world were passed on to Jesus through His baptism?

—Yes, I do.—

Do you truly want to be saved from the sins of the world? If you do, believe in the gospel of the baptism of Jesus and His blood on the Cross. Once you believe, you have been saved. Do you believe this? This is the true salvation of being born again. The baptism of Jesus and His blood is the original gospel of being born again. It is the blessing from God for all the sinners of the world.

To believe in the salvation of being born again through the baptism of Jesus and His blood on the Cross, to look up to His love is to have true faith and to be truly born again. The signs of being born again are the water and blood of Jesus. You have only to accept the words of truth written in the Bible.

RELIGION AND FAITH

What witness do we have in the hearts of the born again?

That Jesus blotted out all our sins with His baptism and blood

The meaning of religion is to believe in Jesus according to one's own thoughts, rejecting the pure word of God. However, salvation from sin is apart from one's own thoughts. Faith is to believe all the words of the Old and New Testament, denying one's own thoughts. It is to take it as it was written in the Bible and accept salvation through the water and the blood: the baptism of Jesus and His death on the Cross. One can be saved by taking into his heart the wisdom of the original gospel.

Without the baptism of Jesus there is no passing on of our sins, and without the shedding of blood there is no remission of sins. All our sins were passed on to Jesus before He took them to the Cross and shed blood for us. When we believe in the baptism of Jesus and His blood on the Cross, in being born again through the gospel, we become free of all the sins of the world.

True faith is to believe that Jesus Christ completely cleansed us of all our sins when He was baptized; it is to believe that He took the judgment for all our sins on the Cross. We have to believe in the righteous salvation of God. God loved all of us so much that He saved us through the baptism of Jesus and His blood on the Cross. When we believe in this gospel, we are saved from all our sins, freed from judgment and become righteous before God.

"Lord, I believe. I am undeserving of salvation but I believe in the gospel of the baptism of Jesus, His crucifixion and resurrection." We have only to thank the Lord for the blessing of the gospel of being born again. To believe in the original gospel of being born again is the true faith.

The truth of being born again is this; *"So then faith comes by hearing, and hearing by the word of God" (Romans 10:17). "And you shall know the truth, and the truth shall make you free" (John 8:32).* We have to know the truth exactly and we have to believe in the water, the blood, and the Spirit that bears witness to it (1 John 5:5-8).

"The truth shall make you free." These are the words of Jesus about the water and the blood. Have you been set free? Are we the religious or the faithful? Jesus wants only

those who have faith in the gospel of being born again of water and the Spirit.

If you believe in the gospel of the baptism of Jesus and His blood, you are without sin in your heart. However, if you believe in Jesus merely as a part of a religion, you are still living in sin because you do not have complete faith in the salvation of Jesus. Religious people try to obtain redemption for their sins every-time they pray in repentance.

Thus, such people can never be saved from their sins completely. Even if they repented throughout their life, it could never replace the complete remission of sins through the baptism of Jesus and His death on the Cross. Let us be saved by believing in the gospel of Jesus, which washed away all the sins of the world, even those of the future.

I will tell you again repenting every day can never substitute for the gospel of being born again. All Christians should now believe in the remission of sins through the gospel of being born again.

We can never repent for our sins completely. False repentance cannot lead one to God, but only consoles his soul. False repentance is a one-sided confession which never takes into account the will of God. This is not something that God expects from us.

What is true repentance? It is to return to God. To come back to the word of the salvation of Jesus and believe in the word the way it was written. The gospel that saves us is the gospel of the baptism of Jesus, His crucifixion and resurrection. When we believe in this gospel completely, we are then saved and earn everlasting life.

This is the wisdom of the gospel of being born again; it is to believe in the baptism of Jesus and His blood and the gospel of the kingdom of God that allows us to be born again.

When Jesus told us that we should be born again of water and the Spirit, He meant that we should be born again by believing in His baptism and blood on the Cross. Then we are able to enter and dwell in the kingdom of God. We have to believe in His word. The two things that bear witness to the remission of our sins, the baptism of Jesus and His blood on the Cross, are the words that allow us to be born again.

Do you now believe in the gospel of being born again, and of the remission of sins? The faith in the baptism of Jesus and His blood on the Cross saves us from all the sins of the world. We can be born again with this faith. Since the Bible tells us that Jesus washed away the sins of all the sinners in the world, why shouldn't we believe and be born again?

Those who believe in the two things that bear witness to our being born again, the baptism of Jesus and His crucifixion, are the truly born again. And he who believes in the Son of God has the witness in himself (1 John 5:3-10). When you believe in Jesus, you should not leave out the gospel of the water, the blood and the Spirit.

Just as Commander Naaman washed at the Jordan seven times to be healed completely from leprosy (2 Kings chapter 5), we should believe that Jesus washed away all the sins of the world once and for all at the Jordan and as a result gave us everlasting salvation.

Because Jesus loved us, we can be saved from all the sins of the world and have everlasting life by believing in the gospel of the remission of sin. Let us all believe in the gospel of being born again and obtain God's salvation. ⊠

SERMON 2

Pseudo Christians and

Heretics within Christianity

But there were also false prophets among the people, even as there will be false teachers among you, who will secretly bring in destructive heresies, even denying the Lord who bought them, and bring on themselves swift destruction. And many will follow their destructive ways, because of whom the way of truth will be blasphemed. By covetousness they will exploit you with deceptive words; for a long time their judgment has not been idle, and their destruction does not slumber (2 Peter 2:1-3).

Pseudo Christians and Heretics within Christianity

<Isaiah 28:13-14>

"But the word of the Lord was to them, 'Precept upon precept, precept upon precept, line upon line, line upon line, here a little, there a little,' that they might go and fall backward, and be broken and snared and caught. Therefore hear the word of the Lord, you scornful men, who rule this people who are in Jerusalem."

BIBLICAL HERESY

How does the Bible define the word "heretic?"

The Bible defines a heretic as one who has sin in his heart even though he believes in Jesus.

There are many pseudo newswriters these days, especially in developing countries. They pretend to be newswriters but usually extort money from their victims, threatening to expose something their victims have done. The word pseudo means something that looks genuine but is not the real thing. In other words, it refers to something whose true self is completely different from its outside appearance.

The words "heretic" and "pseudo" are used quite often, especially in Christian churches.

There are few clear-cut definitions of what a heretic is and what it is to be termed "pseudo," nor are there many who teach these concepts in strict accordance with the Bible.

Under these circumstances, I feel duty bound to disclose what the Bible defines as "heresy" and shed some light on the subject. I also want to point out some examples of heresy in everyday life and thus allow us to think about it together. Anyone who believes in God has to think about heresy at least once in their lives.

Titus 3:10-11 defines a heretic as a divisive person who is warped and engaged in sinning, one being self-condemned. A heretic is someone who condemns himself as a sinner. Therefore those who believe in Jesus but have sin in their hearts are heretics before God.

Jesus took away all sins through His baptism. But heretics refuse to believe in the true gospel that brings salvation to sinners and thus condemn themselves to join the ranks of sinners.

Are you a heretic? We have to think about this if we want to live an upright and truly faithful life.

Are you not condemning yourself as a sinner even though you believe in Jesus if you have not yet heard the gospel of the water and the Spirit? If you consider yourself a sinner, then you are doing a disservice to Jesus by slighting His perfect salvation and the gospel of the water and the Spirit.

To call oneself a sinner before God is to admit that one is not a child of God. Those who confess to Jesus, "Lord, I am a sinner," have to reconsider their own faith.

How can you believe in Jesus and still claim to be a sinner when Jesus took away all the sins of the world and saved you completely from eternal damnation? How can you deny His free gift of salvation and define yourself as a sinner when Jesus took away all your sins through His baptism and was judged thoroughly for them on the Cross?

Such people are heretics because they volunteer to be sinners apart from the word of God. You have to know the gospel of the water and the Spirit to avoid committing heresy before God.

Anyone who believes in Jesus but is not born again is a heretic because he still has sin in his heart.

Because God took away all the sins of the world including our own, we are heretics before God if we ignore this blessing of salvation. Because God is holy, we are heretics if we have sin in our hearts. If we really want to become righteous, we have to believe in the gospel of the baptism of Jesus and His blood on the Cross.

THE ORIGIN OF HERESY IN THE BIBLE

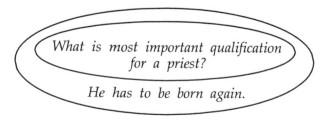

What is most important qualification for a priest?

He has to be born again.

Let's look at 1 Kings 12:25-26. *"Then Jeroboam built*

Shechem in the mountains of Ephraim, and dwelt there. Also he went out from there and built Penuel. And Jeroboam said in his heart, 'Now the kingdom may return to the house of David.'" Jeroboam was one of Solomon's subordinates. When Solomon became corrupt in his later years, Jeroboam rebelled against the king, and later he became the king of the ten tribes of Israel in the time of Rehoboam, the son of Solomon.

Jeroboam's first concern when he became king of Israel was that his people might return to Judah where there was temple.

Therefore, he came up with an idea to prevent this from happening. He made two golden calves in Bethel and Dan and commanded his people to worship them. 1 Kings 12:28 says, *"Therefore the king asked advice, made two calves of gold."* One he set up in Bethel, and the other in Dan and told his people to worship them, despite the fact doing so was a terrible sin. He even arbitrarily appointed priests to lead the worship.

"After this event Jeroboam did not turn from his evil way, but again he made priests from every class of people for the high places; whoever wished, he consecrated him, and he became one of the priests of the high places" (1 Kings 13:33). That is the origin of heresy.

Even now, heretics appoint to the priesthood anyone who volunteers to do the work of God. Anyone who graduates from a theological seminary can become a minister, an evangelist, a missionary and elder even if he is not born again of water and the Spirit.

How can someone who is not born again become a minister? If such a person is appointed as a priest, the church that elects him becomes a factory for the production of heretics.

Let us think again about the origin of heresy. First, Jeroboam substituted golden calves for God in order to maintain his political power. Second, he consecrated anyone who volunteered to become a priest. In other words, he consecrated ordinary people as priests. The same practice continues even now.

The history of heresy continued on well after the time of Jeroboam. Those who are not born again of water and the Spirit should never be allowed to become priests.

Can anyone who only graduates from a theological seminary become a minister or an evangelist? Is it correct for them to serve God despite the fact they have not been approved by God? Never. Only those who have been acknowledged by God should be allowed to become His servants. Those who are acknowledged by God are those who are born again of water and the Spirit.

It is recorded in 1 Kings 12:25-26 and 1 Kings chapter 13 that the sin of Jeroboam provoked the wrath of God. We should all know this story, and if someone is not familiar with it, he should go back to the Bible and find out.

Think again if you are substituting golden calves for God in your ministry. Do you, by any chance, put emphasis on earthly blessings lest your followers may return to the gospel of being born again of water and the Spirit?

Do you tell your followers that they can be cured of disease if they believe in Jesus? Do you tell them that they will be blessed in wealth? Do you appoint those who are not born again to be ministers or staff members of your church and claim that your denomination is the only orthodox one? If so, you are committing the sin of Jeroboam before God and provoking His wrath.

HERETICS WORSHIP A GOD OF GOLDEN CALVES

Even today, there are so many heretics who worship golden calves. They say that God blessed Solomon when he offered a thousand burnt offerings to God. I Kings 3:3-5 says, *"And Solomon loved the Lord, walking in the statutes of his father David, except that he sacrificed and burned incense at the high places. Now the king went to Gibeon to sacrifice there, for that was the great high place: Solomon offered a thousand burnt offerings on that altar. At Gibeon the Lord appeared to Solomon in a dream by night; and God said, 'Ask! What shall I give you?'"*

They swindle money out of their followers under the fraudulent promise of "a thousand burnt offerings of Solomon." Those foolish followers are extorted of their money. And those who worship golden calves as their God are deprived of their money, which is used as contributions to build tremendous church buildings. It is not because their churches are too small, but because they want to extort money from their followers.

Setting up golden calves for their congregations to worship was only an excuse heretics came up with to extort money from them. We who believe in God should never be taken for fools. If you offer your money in worship of golden calves, it is not offered to God, but ends up in the pockets of pseudo priests who are full of greed like Jeroboam. You should never fall into the traps of such heretics.

Then why was God pleased with the thousand burnt offerings of Solomon? Because Solomon knew his own sins, acknowledged that he had to die for them and offered sacrifices in accordance with the faith. He offered a thousand burnt offerings in gratitude for the salvation of God. Solomon offered a thousand burnt offerings every day, thinking of the redemption of the water and the Spirit.

Now, you should remember the true meaning of heresy so that you will never be deceived by pseudo priests.

THOSE WHO MINISTER WITHOUT BEING BORN AGAIN ARE HERETICS

What do heretics say about being born again?

They say they are born again of visions, dreams, and various kinds of spiritual experiences

There are those who teach others to be born again when they themselves have not been reborn in the faith. They are all heretics. They tell others to be born again when they are incapable of rebirth because they do not know about the gospel of the water and the Spirit. We can only laugh.

Pseudo priests preach a false gospel, distorting the gospel of the water and the Spirit. They tell people to wash away their own sins every day.

They say, "Go and pray in the mountains, try fasting, devote yourself to the work of God, pray at the break of dawn, be obedient, offer a lot of money for building churches, but be mindful that you take care of your own sins."

Once, I heard someone testifying that he was born again. He said that in a dream, he was standing in a line and when his turn came, Jesus called his name. He said it was the testimony for his being born again. But is his conviction a correct one? Jesus did not say so.

In John 3, He says, *"Unless one is born of water and the Spirit, he cannot enter the kingdom of God."* God says that only those who are born again of water and the Spirit can become true priests. Anyone who believes that he is born of dreams, fantasies, spiritual ecstasies, or prayers for repentance is a heretic.

These days, many people do not believe in the written word of God and uphold their denominational doctrines instead of being born again of water and the Spirit. Those who refuse to preach the gospel of being born again of water and the Spirit are pseudo Christians and heretics.

REFORMERS AND EXISTING CHRISTIANITY

When did the true gospel begin to be mixed in with and distorted by other religions?

From the time when the Roman Emperor Constantine proclaimed the Milan Edict in 313 A.D.

When were the denominations of Christianity formed? When did the different denominations such as Presbyterian, Methodist, Baptist, Lutheran, Holiness, and Full Gospel begin? The Reformation occurred only about 500 years ago.

Early Christians were those who followed Jesus when He was in this world. "Christians" means "those who follow Christ."

The first Christians were the apostles and their disciples. The apostles and the Fathers of the church followed the true gospel till 313 A.D. However, after the Milan Edict of Constantine the Great, Christians and Gentiles began to mix together. The result was the Dark Ages that lasted for more than 1000 years.

Later, in early 16th century, Martin Luther proclaimed the Reformation, saying, *"Only the righteous shall live by faith."* A little later, between 1500 ~ 1600, Reformers like John Calvin and John Knox led the movement away from Catholicism. This was all that the Reformation achieved.

The Reformation was simply an effort to establish new churches separate from the Roman Catholic Church. Reformers did not attempt to make any fundamental denial of Catholicism itself.

Their purpose was not to promote faith in being born again of water and the Spirit, but to free themselves from the oppression and corruption of the Roman Catholic Church. The Roman Catholic Church called this movement Protestantism. It means the protesters.

At the time, the Roman Catholic Church urged people to buy Indulgences, saying they could send their dead ancestors to Heaven when they bought such Indulgences with large sums of money. Luther did not realize that

Catholicism was fundamemtally wrong. He was only trying to stop the Roman Catholic Church from selling Indulgences to finance construction of Saint Peter's Cathedral.

As a result, we can see many remnants of the Catholic Church in the modern Protestant Church: infant baptism, the prayers of repentance which are similar to confession under the Roman Catholic Church, holy rituals, recognition only of those who graduate from theological seminaries as ministers, majestic and grandiose churches. All these are the remnants of the Roman Catholic Church.

Counting from the Reformation in the early 1500's, the history of the Protestantism is only about 500 years old. This year is the 481st anniversary of the Reformation. You may not realize that Martin Luther protested against his mother church only 481 years ago. Protestantism cannot thus lay sole claim to legitimacy in light of its comparative youth. The reformation of Christianity is still going on. And it should go on continuously.

However, there is one thing we should keep in mind. We should never forget that only those who are born again of water and the Spirit can enter the kingdom of Heaven. Let us preach that! Do you preach the gospel of Jesus, the gospel of being born again of water and the Spirit? If not, you are not a servant of God. It is the gospel of "being born again of water and the Spirit" that God wants us to believe. It is what Jesus taught Nicodemus in John chapter 3.

Does the Bible talk only about the gospel of being born again of water and the Spirit, or does it talk about other things such as working for the good of society and living a holy life? Of course the latter is important, too. However, you can do that after you are born again of water and the Spirit. The will of God is for us to believe in the gospel.

TEACHINGS OF HERETICS

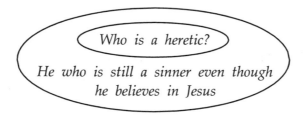

Who is a heretic?

He who is still a sinner even though he believes in Jesus

When did pseudo Christian, heretical faith begin to prosper in the world?

The people of Israel worshiped one God until they were separated into two kingdoms at the time of Jeroboam as written in 1 Kings chapter 12-13. From that time, before Christ came to this world, heretical faith began to prosper. There are also so many heretics practicing these days.

The Bible talks about their pseudo Christian teachings in Isaiah chapter 28 and Titus 3:10-11. The Bible says that heretics are those who believe in Jesus but still have sin in their hearts. Anyone who is like that is a heretic.

And they teach, as written in Isaiah 28:9-10, *"Whom will he teach knowledge? And whom will he make to understand the message? Those just weaned from milk? Those just drawn from the breasts? For precept must be upon precept, precept upon precept, line upon line, line upon line, here a little, there a little."*

Heretics add precept upon precept, line upon line. What does this mean? It means "Be careful, be careful, be careful of those who say they are born again through their faith in Jesus." They just tell you to be careful no matter what. They tell you not to listen, not to go, lest you might fall into heresy.

However, if they are so sure that theirs is the orthodox faith, why can they not repel those who say their beliefs differ from the word of God? It is so pitiful. They claim to be the orthodox Christians, but they do not have the words to overcome what they call heresy. The true Christian can win over any heretic with the word of God.

These days, would-be orthodox Christians denounce the born again as "heretics" just because their beliefs are different. How can we be heretics when we believe in the gospel of the water and the Spirit?

If those called heretics preach the gospel of the water and the Spirit, they are true orthodox Christians. Likewise, if would-be orthodox Christians do not preach the gospel of the water and the Spirit, they are heretics.

The difference between "orthodoxy" and "heresy" lies in whether they preach the gospel of the water and the Spirit and whether they believe in Jesus and have sin in their hearts or not. How can they be heretics if they believe in the word of God and are born again of water and the Spirit?

Is it heresy to believe in the baptism of Jesus and His blood on the Cross and to be completely cleansed of sin? Is it "orthodox" not to believe in the gospel of the water and the Spirit?

There are so many denominationalists who have drifted away from the Bible and yet claim to be the "orthodox" Christians. They drift away from being born again of water and the Spirit as specified in the Bible because they preach only the blood on the Cross, denying the baptism of Jesus (the water).

What is the difference between the Roman Catholic Church and the Protestant Church these days? Just as reformers rebelled against the Roman Catholic Church, just as they came out of the Roman Catholic Church and built Protestantism, we should also rebel against blind Christians and pseudo priests. Only then can we open our eyes to the true gospel, have true faith, and be completely saved through the gospel of the water and the Spirit.

What do we have to do to avoid becoming heretics?

We have to be born again of water and the Spirit.

The Bible tells us that only those who believe in the gospel of the baptism of Jesus and His blood on the Cross follow the true faith. Jesus said as such to Nicodemus in John 3:1-12.

Heretics always urge their followers to be devout in their faith. They urge them to pray at the break of dawn and to work harder. It is like urging blind men to run.

No matter how hard you pray, it is of no use if you are not born again of water and the Spirit. When we say that those who are born again of water and the Spirit are the righteous, heretics counter with Romans 3:10, *"There is none righteous, no, not one."* With this verse, they label believers as heretics.

In reality, however, it is they who are heretics. The true meaning of the verse is not as simple as its sounds. These heretics have not read the whole Bible. The apostle Paul said that there is not a righteous man in the world. He was only quoting a verse from the Old Testament which says there was no one righteous in the world before Jesus Christ came and delivered all humankind from their sins with the salvation of God. However, those who are saved by Jesus have become righteous.

We can see the truth if we read the whole chapter. Heretics only warn their followers to be careful of those whose faith is different from theirs. Except for churches that they recognize as orthodox ones, they prohibit their followers from worshipping elsewhere. So their congregations dare not go to churches that preach the gospel of the water and the Spirit.

They become deaf to the true gospel and cannot be born again. These are the teachings of false leaders who are in fact raising the sons and daughters of hell. They will be judged by God for this. Heretics have to turn back to God.

Who are the heretics? Are they the ones redeemed by believing in the gospel of the water and the Spirit, or are they the ones who claim to believe in Jesus but fail to be born again of water and the Spirit?

Titus 3:11 says that those who believe in Jesus but remain *"self-condemned"* are heretics.

They teach their followers not to go to the revival meetings at which the gospel of being born again of water and the Spirit is preached, saying it is dangerous. How can the "orthodox" be afraid of conflicting beliefs? They are afraid because they do not have the truth on their side. *"For precept must be upon precept, precept upon precept."* The teachings of heretics are like that.

Heretical priests quote a little from this book, a little from that book, from the words of philosophers, from literature, and mix them in with their own thoughts and make everything sound appealing.

They believe their followers to be ignorant and they try to educate them with worldly teachings. The true church preaches the word of God and educates believers with the word of God. People do not come to church to be educated in the ways of the world. Rather, they come to church to hear of heavenly things that cannot be heard in the world. They come to hear the word of Jesus.

People enter their church as sinners but they want to emerge from the church as righteous believers who have no sin. What do heretic priests teach them? They tell their followers not to go to the revival meetings in which the servants of God preach the true gospel. They prevent their followers from being born again of water and the Spirit.

It is so foolish. They may be able to deceive their followers but they can never deceive God.

> *Can pseudo priests make their followers born again of water and the Spirit?*
>
> *No. Only the born again can make others born again.*

Heretics, if you are true servants of God, can you not hear the Spirit reproach you? You have to turn back. You should stop obstructing your followers from attending the revival meetings in which the true servants of God preach the gospel of being born again of water and the Spirit.

Heretics educate their followers with theology alone, so when they encounter other theories, they are beaten.

It is so pitiful. Pseudo priests are good at ministering without the word of God. They preach, consult, and minister based only on their own misguided convictions. Those who minister and preach without the word of God are heretics and hirelings (John 10:13).

Pseudo ministers are heretics because their inward and outward selves are different. Some people define churches that do not fit into the established denominations as heretical churches. However, some of those churches do not want to belong to any denomination because most churches are operating so far away from the true teachings of the Bible.

Heretics tell their followers to be redeemed even though they themselves have never solved the problem of their sins. They are committing the sin of Jeroboam. If there is anyone who still has sin in his heart but tries to do the works of God, he has to realize that his sins and the holiness of God are utterly incompatible. He must know he is a heretic.

Therefore, if anyone who preaches or has duties in the church is still a sinner, he ought to realize that he is a heretic. He is a heretic because he does not know the gospel of Christ's salvation, the gospel of being born again of water and the Spirit. If one learns the Bible from a heretic and teaches others in the same way, he becomes a heretic.

We can know the tree by its fruit. Those who have become righteous by believing in the baptism of Jesus and His blood can only bear the righteous while those who are still sinners are doomed to bear sinners. *"Even so, every good tree bears good fruit, but a bad tree bears bad fruit"* (Matthew 7:17).

What Do Heretical Priests Preach in Their Sermons?

What do heretical priests preach
in their sermons?

Worldly theology and man's thoughts

False priests watch out for this and that. Why are they so careful! They have to watch out lest their lies be disclosed because they do not have the sound faith of being born again of water and the Spirit.

Heretics take a little here and a little there. They deceive people and teach without knowing the true meaning of the gospel.

"Precept upon precept, precept upon precept, line upon line, line upon line, here a little there a little" (Isaiah 28:13).

Line upon line, they say, "This word means so and so in Greek and so and so in Hebrew. And there are such and such theories." They also warn people to be careful if they encounter a theory of salvation expressed in purely black-and-white terms. They say, "Martin Luther said this and John Calvin said that while John Knox said such and such, and we think they all make sense in their own ways."

They neither know what they are talking about nor what they believe in. One who has true faith can express the truth in black-and-white terms. True believers can clearly tell the difference between the born again and those who are not born again. We clearly preach the gospel of being born again of water and the Spirit.

But heretics are in a world of chaos. Their faith is like a bat. Just as a bat prefers the inside of a cave during the day and the outside world only at night, heretics like this theory and that, believe in this and that. They never know what the truth is. When a heretical priest goes to hell, his followers accompany him to the bitter end. So many people end up in hell because they believe in false prophets.

Is your minister born again of water and the Spirit? Does he preach the words of the gospel of being born again as it is written in the Bible? If he does, you are indeed fortunate, and if he does not, you will be damned. If you are not born again, you must listen to the gospel of the water and the Spirit, read books that explain it, and be born again.

Heretics dislike the gospel of being born again of water and the Spirit. They preach that, "Jesus Christ came to blot out our sins, and He did just that. He is still washing away our sins today and will continue to do so in the future." How can this be true? They say they are righteous but they go right on sinning. They are righteous one moment, sinners the next.

Theirs is a false theology. It is untrue. Anyone who is righteous now and a sinner later is a heretic, a false prophet. Anyone who condemns himself, who corrupts himself is the same.

THE CURSE OF GOD IS ON THE FOLLOWERS OF HERETICS

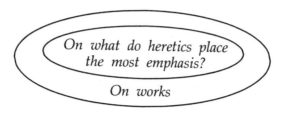

On what do heretics place the most emphasis?

On works

Heretics are not consistent. Therefore they cannot lead their followers to be born again of water and the Spirit when their followers go to them and ask them how to be born again. Rather, they give their followers the ridiculous idea that people can be born again of fantasy and that are not be aware when they are born again. It is so ridiculous.

Jesus said in John chapter 3, *"Unless one is born of water and the Spirit, he cannot enter the kingdom of God."* These days however, righteous people who are born again are called presumptuous heretics.

Heretical priests say they cannot call themselves righteous because they are humble. They tell their followers, "Do not attend any revival meetings at which the preacher plans to speak about the blessing of being born again of water and the Spirit. If you are born again, you will become a heretic. You will be denounced by this church. If you want to be with us, stay a sinner, and God will make you righteous when the time comes." That is what they say. What they really mean is that it is up to you to decide to be born again or not.

Heretics tell their followers, "You have to stay with us, but being born again is your responsibility. So, try on your own. Just stay as you are now, and go before God when the time comes, then you will find out the truth. I don't know what will happen after that. But this is an orthodox church, so you have to stay with us." Do you think this is true?

These heretical priests take a little from here and a little from there and make up their own theories. Then it becomes the only truth for them. They do not know about the word of God which tells us about the water and the Spirit.

Heretics interpret the Bible according to their own thoughts. We have to interpret the Bible according to the words per se, but they interpret it their own way. That is why there are so many theologians and denominations in Christianity.

Because there are so many heretical denominations and theologians, there are a countless number of heretical books. Pseudo priests cite a little from this book and a little from that book when they preach. True priests however, preach from the Bible alone.

Heretics extort money from their followers in many cunning ways. They eat and live well in this world and end up in hell because they failed to be born again. This is the end that God has prepared for them.

God endures them in the beginning. But to those who steadfastly refuse to accept the blessing of being born again of water and the Spirit, He will send them to hell.

God will judge heretics. Heretics believe in God very fervently and consume volumes and volumes of Bible commentary and theological works in the beginning. But then little by little they begin to preach from the precepts of man, so that their followers can never be born again.

Heretics tend also to place far greater emphasis on their

earthly works. Any minister who does not preach the gospel of being born again of water and the Spirit is a heretic before God.

They pressure their followers to no end. They coerce them to attend 40-day all-night prayers, 100-day early morning prayers, mountain prayers, to fast on a regular basis, to make contributions for building churches, a thousand burnt offerings, contributions for revival meetings . . . and they even draw up a graph to show how much each believer has contributed. Just by looking at the fruits of their works, we can see that they are heretics.

The curse of God befalls their followers, too. Ministers who preach without being born again and their followers are all under the curse of God.

HERETICS TRY TO READ THE MINDS OF THEIR FOLLOWERS

Why do heretics try to read the minds of their followers?

Because they are not born again, but minister with hypocrisy and without the Spirit in their hearts.

Heretic priests cry every day. They have to be sure to please senior deacons and deaconesses, elders, ordinary deacons and even laymen. It is how they get on every day.

They behave as hypocrites every day. "Ho∼ly and

Mer~ciful. . . ." They are full of sin but they have to speak of holy things, so they become more hypocritical with every passing day.

A preacher once said, "It is a curse to minister without the Spirit inside." What this means is that it is heretical to do the work of God without being redeemed; it is a cursed life. If you are one of these heretics, you have to be born again of water and the Spirit.

Anyone who believes in Jesus but is not born again is a heretic. In addition to this, everyone has to turn back to the gospel of being born again of water and the Spirit. Only the righteous who are born again of water and the Spirit can preach the gospel to others.

HERETICS CRY OUT FOR PEACE ALONE

How do heretic priests satisfy their followers?

They always cry out for peace, saying their followers can enter into the kingdom of Heaven even though they are sinners.

Isaiah 28:14-15 says, *"Therefore hear the word of the Lord, you scornful men, who rule this people who are in Jerusalem, because you have said, 'We have made a covenant with death, and with Sheol we are in agreement. When the overflowing scourge passes through, it will not come to us, for we have made lies our refuge, and under falsehood we have hidden ourselves.'"*

Who are the scornful men here? They are those who preach the word of God, mixing in their own mistaken beliefs. Whatever a preacher's thoughts are, whatever theology says, he has to offer a true interpretation of the Bible. But heretical priests preach the Bible in the way they see fit. These are the scornful men.

"We have made a covenant with death, and with Sheol we are in agreement. When the overflowing scourge passes through, it will not come to us."

Heretics say that the scourge will not pass through them. They tell people not to worry. Destruction and hell are awaiting them, but they say not to worry, destruction and hell do not exist for them. So you have to stay away from such heretics if you wish to live.

Heretics say that you don't have to be born again of water and the Spirit. Is it true? No, absolutely not. You cannot enter the kingdom of Heaven unless you are born again of water and the Spirit.

Is it all right not to enter the kingdom of Heaven? This is the same as asking if it is all right to burn in hell. Needless to say, the answer to both questions is no. Let us all believe in the gospel of being born again of water and the Spirit and enter the kingdom of Heaven together.

Heretical priests seduce people, saying that because they believe in Jesus, it is all right for them to remain sinners and that they will not go to hell.

Does Jesus take care of you even if you are a sinner? Can a sinner go to Heaven? Can you avoid going to hell even though you are a sinner? Is it written in the Bible that you don't have to go to hell when you believe in Jesus, even though you have sin in your heart?

Heretics say that they have made a covenant with

death, so that death will not come to them. They say a believer can avoid being condemned to hell even if he has sin in his heart. Do you think it really happens this way?

Heretics inspire people with confidence, saying that death and hell do not await them. Heretical priests appoint those who are not born again to be deacons, elders, ministers. But they have to know that they will all end up in hell because they do not believe in the gospel of the water and the Spirit. What they should do is to instill in their followers the belief in the gospel of the water and the Spirit.

Are believers, even if they are sinners, still eligible for entry into Heaven? Can a sinner go to Heaven? Does the Bible say that sinners can go to Heaven? No. Can there be a righteous man with sin? No. These are the teachings of heresy and pseudo theology.

The Bible says, *"The wages of sin is death"* (Romans 6:23). It is the law of God. He sends all sinners directly to hell. In contrast to this terrible fate, however, all those who are born again of water and the Spirit are welcomed into Heaven.

"When the overflowing scourge passes through, it will not come to us, for we have made lies our refuge, and under falsehood we have hidden ourselves." Heretical priests speak words to that effect and firmly believe that they will not go to hell even though they have sin in their hearts. Because they are hiding behind a false and untrue theology, God can not do anything to help them. They believe in their theology alone. Because they believe in their theology instead of God's word, they are heretics and sinners destined for hell. How sad it is that there are so many of them.

HERETICS ARE INTERESTED ONLY IN MONEY

What's the aim of heretical priests?

To extort as much money as possible from their followers

Heretics and pseudo priests are only interested in money. They are covetous. "How much money will this person offer if he comes to my church?" They think about the tithe he will pay. This is just like worshipping a golden calf. "Please let me become successful, let me make a lot of money, Lord." Pseudo priests teach people to pray like that.

They say, "If you believe in Jesus, you will make a lot of money, you will conceive when you are barren, and you will be successful in your business."

So many people are deceived by these pseudo priests, and they are extorted of their money and go to hell for their troubles. How unfair this is! If someone who has come under the spell of heresy comes to his senses, he will be surprised to find out how much money he has contributed to his deceivers. He will reproach himself for his own foolishness in following and working so hard for them.

Heretics are especially fervent practitioners of what they consider a legitimate religion. Their followers devote themselves to early morning prayers, mountain prayers, special contributions, tithe, weekly offerings. There are so many reasons to take money from their followers.

Their followers work so hard, but they still have sin in their hearts because no one has taught them the gospel of the water and the Spirit. Some ask them about it, but they never get a straight answer. Anyone who is not born again of water and the Spirit is a heretic.

PITIFUL HERETICS AND THEIR FOLLOWERS

Who are the most pitiful in the world?

Those who minister without being born again of water and the Spirit

"Oh, you pitiful heretics! You should work on your redemption first!" The paramount sign of pseudo faith is to worship the golden calves of Jeroboam. The first thing heretics did in Old Testament times was to build a temple and stock it with golden calves (1 Kings 12:25-33).

These days, they build large churches and extort money from their followers. They tell their followers to get loans from banks to contribute for the construction of a grand church. They work up the emotions of the congregation and pass around the collection dishes. Money, rings, gold watches fill the dish in no time. Heretics work this way. It is the same in every one of the heretic churches.

Outwardly, they seem to be interested in spiritual things, but in reality they are interested only in money. I advise you to stay away from churches that care only about money. Please do not go to churches where only the rich are treated cordially. It is wrong to announce the amount of each congregation's offerings because they do it in hopes of attracting more money.

Heretics say tempting words to their followers.

"You will be blessed if you believe in Jesus."

"Devote yourself to the works of God. The more you do, the more blessed you shall be."

"If you serve as an elder, you will be materially blessed."

As a result, their followers vie with each other to become elders. If there weren't any compensation, who would want to serve as an elder? And the elders are expected to contribute financially as well.

Are they elected based on how deeply they believe in the doctrine of the denomination, how prominent they are in society and how much money they can contribute to the church? It is true.

Heretics care only about money. They are interested in building large churches. They do not care if their followers go to hell as long as they offer a lot of money.

Heretics are those who work for bread. They snare their people with fancy titles. They issue the titles to their followers at random (Ezekiel 13:17-19). This is meant to tie them to the church and increase its wealth. Heretics do not preach the gospel of the water and the Spirit. They just try to enrich themselves.

Even someone who has attended a church for only a few months can become a deacon. Moreover, if he is well acquainted with the doctrine and has a sound financial background, he is elevated to elder. This is all in the shameful tradition of the sin of Jeroboam, who replaced God with a golden calf.

Heretics worship golden calves. They do not help their

people to be born again. They only take money from their followers by tempting them with promises of secular blessings. They do not care if their followers are condemned to hell as long as their church is on sound financial ground.

HERETICS LACK CONVICTION IN THEIR SERMONS

Heretics like to say "probably" or "maybe" frequently because they lack conviction in what they are saying. They do not have faith in the word of God and they do not truly believe in what they preach. Their belief system does not lie within the faith in the word of God. They say, "It could be said that. . . ." They never speak clearly and with conviction. It would be better if they did not teach their followers anything rather than teaching lies.

Heretics cannot lead people to be born again of water and the Spirit. They just condemn more people to hell.

HERETICS PLAY THE ROLE OF FALSE PROPHETS

What constitutes blasphemy against the Spirit?

To believe in Jesus while living as a sinner who doesn't believe in His baptism

Matthew chapter 7 tells us about those who believe in Jesus but still end up in hell. Heretics will protest before God on the last day. As it is written in the Bible, *"Many will say to Me in that day, 'Lord, Lord, have we not prophesied in Your name, cast out demons in Your name, and done many wonders in Your name?' And then I will declare to them, 'I never knew you; depart from Me, you who practice lawlessness!'"* (Matthew 7:22-23).

They do not believe that Jesus washed away all the sins of man; they do not believe in the gospel of the water and the Spirit.

They practice lawlessness. What does this mean? It means they tell people to believe in Jesus when they still have sin in their hearts. You may wonder what is so wrong with this but it is a serious sin against God.

When a sinner preaches to other people the necessity of believing in Jesus, he cannot lead them to be born again because he was not himself born again of water and the Spirit. Therefore heretics only produce sinners who believe in Jesus. It is a sin against the Spirit to practice lawlessness.

Heretics neither believe in the word of God nor preach the gospel as it is written. They just extort money from their followers. They are sinners even though they believe in Jesus. They try to lead others when they are not born again themselves. In this way, they practice lawlessness.

HERETICS ARE BUT PALE IMITATIONS OF THE RIGHTEOUS

How do we distinguish between those who have been born again and those who have not?

We can distinguish by testing whether they have sin or not.

Do not be deceived by those false preachers who say they are sinners. Do not offer them your money. Do not give your hard-earned money to those sinners.

Why would you give money to those preachers who cannot help you with your sins? If you want to give your money to a church, at least wait until your sins are blotted out through the gospel of the water and the Spirit.

Just as there are imitations in art, there are also imitations in life. There are, for example, imitative religions that cannot wash away all sins in the heart. How can you identify an imitative religion? An imitation is something that looks genuine from the outside but is in fact quite different from the real thing.

You have to decide for yourself. Who are the true preachers? Who are the heretics? What is the orthodox faith? The orthodox believe in Jesus and His redemptive power. They have no sin in their hearts. But heretics have sin in their hearts.

Are all people such as these heretics? It may well be so. However, let us go back to the Bible. Anyone who believes in Jesus and is not born again is a heretic. It is clear that the born again are the orthodox. Therefore, those who are not born again are heretics. Heretics are those who believe in Jesus but still have sin in their hearts.

Heretics are imitations of the righteous. They may know that the way to become sanctified is by believing in Jesus but unfortunately they still have sin in their hearts. They believe themselves to be sinners. They claim that they can still go to Heaven and they say that they worship God. It sounds very much like they are righteous, but let us not be deceived by imitations.

THE JUDGMENT OF GOD AWAITS HERETICS

Why was the pure gospel changed?

Because false priests and heretics mixed people's mistaken beliefs in with the pure gospel.

"*Therefore the Lord says, the Lord of hosts, the Mighty One of Israel, 'Ah, I will rid Myself of My adversaries, and take vengeance on My enemies. I will turn My hand against you, and thoroughly purge away your dross, and take away all your alloy. I will restore your judges as at the first, and your counselors as at the beginning. Afterward you shall be called the city of righteousness, the faithful city.' Zion shall be redeemed with justice, and her penitents with righteousness. The destruction of transgressors and of sinners shall be together, and those who forsake the Lord shall be consumed. For they shall be ashamed of the terebinth trees which you have desired; and you shall be embarrassed because of the gardens which you have chosen. For you shall be as a terebinth whose leaf fades, and as a garden that has no water. The strong shall be a tinder, and the work of it as a spark; both will burn together, and no one shall quench them"* (Isaiah 1:24-31).

God tells us that if we believe in human beings, we shall be ashamed because of human beings. He tells us that we shall be ashamed because of the church we have chosen for ourselves, and this shame will be like a tree whose leaves fade like a garden that has no water.

He tells us that false priests and their followers who believe in the precepts of humankind rather than the word of God will become tinder and their works spark. Both will burn in hell. False preachers and heretics who have not been redeemed as well as sinners and enemies of the righteous shall be judged with the flame of God.

Churches built on theology alone may look grand outside, but they are empty inside. Any church that is not founded on belief of the word of God and the gospel of being born again of water and the Spirit is like a garden that has no water.

It may be a tree, but it is a dead tree which is unable to bear fruit. When a well does not have water, it is no longer a well.

"The strong shall be a tinder, and the work of it as a spark; both will burn together, and no one shall quench them." Those who do not have the Spirit may look strong to others, but in the eyes of God, they are like tinder bound for the fires of hell.

The Lord asks, *"Watchman, what of the night?"* (Isaiah

21:11) The righteous who have eternal life should preach the gospel of the water and the Spirit in the dark of the night.

God is light and Satan is darkness. God leads people to righteousness and Satan leads people to false temples of chaos and false theology.

In the time of the prophet Isaiah, the people's faith was as chaotic as it is now. They mixed up the word of God with the theologies and precepts of human world. They misled the people of Israel with the chaotic products of humankind so much that God decided to get rid of them all.

"And take away all your alloy. I will restore your judges as at the first, and your counselors as at the beginning." The offerings which will never be accepted by God are like alloy, a mixture of God's truth and humankind's theories.

God never accepts offerings that are mixed. They may look pure to the human eye, but if they are mixed in with humankind's mistaken beliefs they are mixed with impurities and thus not acceptable to God.

God scolded the people of Israel, especially heretics, pseudo preachers and sinners.

If we read Exodus or Numbers, we can see that God did not scold them at first. God helped the people of Israel and bestowed blessings on them. But after Joshua's death, from Judges, the people of Israel were invaded.

However, they chose to go their own way. At that time, God sent the prophet Jeremiah and told Israel to surrender to Babylon.

Jeremiah told the people to surrender to Babylon. This has a spiritual meaning, symbolizing the fact that the righteous tell those who follow heretics to surrender to the gospel of the water and the Spirit.

GOD REPROVES HERETICS

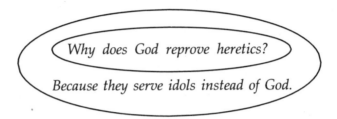

Why does God reprove heretics?

Because they serve idols instead of God.

Why did the servants of God scold the people of Israel? Because they changed the sacrificial system, appointed ordinary people to be priests, and changed the dates of sacrifices.

They changed the Day of Atonement from the tenth day of the seventh month to the fifth day of the eighth month and appointed priests from outside the Levites. They thus blocked the way to being born again.

God scolded the false preachers. Those who served golden calves instead of God became heretic priests.

In fact, God didn't scold them just for worshiping idols. Do not you and I sometimes worship idols, too? We sin so often, but our iniquities are not considered to be grave sins only because we are in the grace of God. But replacing God with golden calves cannot be forgiven. And the same goes for changing the sacrificial system and appointing ordinary people to the priesthood.

What terrible sins these are! They are the gravest of sins. How can one be pardoned for exchanging God for golden calves! It is written in the Bible that it was the sin of Jeroboam which brought on the wrath of God.

Just as God showed His wrath in the Old testament, He now destroys sinners who are against Him. God told Israel that He would curse those who did not turn away from worshiping golden calves.

HERETICS OFFER SACRIFICES OUTSIDE THE LAW

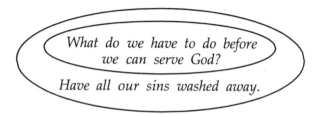

What do we have to do before we can serve God?

Have all our sins washed away.

The kings and heretical priests of Israel were against God and they appointed those who disregarded the sacrificial system to the priesthood. Jeroboam, the king with a warped mind, ordained someone who was not from the house of Levi as a priest.

Only those who were from the house of Levi could become priests and work in the tabernacle. More precisely, priests had to be from the house of Aaron. This was the eternal law of God. But Jeroboam ordained priests from outside the house of Levi and had them offer sacrifices to golden calves. We should know how this brought on the wrath of God.

Even today, those who are not born again can become ministers, elders, and deacons in the church. This goes against the law of God and invites His wrath. Is God pleased with lawless sacrifices? Heretics have to destroy their golden calves and return to God and be born again.

Isaiah 1:10-17 says, *"Hear the word of the Lord, you rulers of Sodom; give ear to the law of our God, you people of Gomorrah: 'To what purpose is the multitude of your sacrifices to Me?' says the Lord. 'I have had enough of burnt offerings of rams and the fat of fed cattle. I do not delight in the blood of bulls, or of lambs or goats. When you come to appear before Me, who has required this from your hand, to trample My courts? Bring no more futile sacrifices; insense is an abomination to Me. The New Moons, the Sabbaths, and the calling of assemblies—I cannot endure iniquity and the sacred meeting. Your New Moons and your appointed feasts My soul hates; they are a trouble to Me, I am weary of bearing them. When you spread out your hands, I will hide My eyes from you; even though you make many prayers, I will not hear. Your hands are full of blood. Wash yourselves, make yourselves clean; put away the evil of your doings from before My eyes. Cease to do evil, learn to do good; seek justice, rebuke the oppressor; defend the fatherless, plead for the widow.'"*

If we read this passage carefully, we can see that the religious leaders of Israel were very devout. But despite their devotion, they were destroyed because they offered the wrong sacrifices and disobeyed the law of God.

We can see that they neither followed the law of God when they offered sacrifices nor heeded the word of God. These leaders were so devoted that they made countless offerings before God. The Bible says that the blood flowed like a river inside the tabernacle.

However, when God looked at what they did, He said that it was like the sin of Gomorrah. He saw that they were making offerings before Him, but in fact, they were sinning. He said it was better not to bring offerings at all. He did not want to receive them.

As they offered the sacrifices before golden calves, God

could not forgive their sins. He could not stand it anymore. He told them they should offer sacrifices according to the way He commanded. If not, it would be better for them not to offer sacrifices at all.

Their sacrifices were not offered to God in the correct way, and as a result, the priests sinned against God. You should know that to serve God and do His work without washing away your sins is a grave sin before Him.

HERETICS ARE LIKE SCHOOL TEACHERS

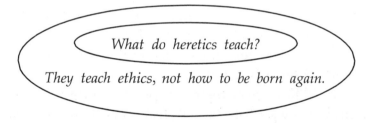

What do heretics teach?

They teach ethics, not how to be born again.

Heretics look outwardly holy. When they occupy the pulpit, they look so impressive that many are deceived by their appearance. They sound so logical. And they always conclude their sermons by admonishing the people to be good. What kind of sermon is that? What is the difference between their sermons and the lessons of school teachers?

The church of God is the place where the born again come together to worship God. Only this kind of church is a true church. The true church of God does not try to teach how to behave before God. The preacher of the true church preaches the gospel of the water and the Spirit. No matter how infirm you are, God washed away all your sins.

Heretical preachers tell their followers, "Do this, and

do that," putting heavy burdens on them, but they themselves are not willing to lift a finger to move them.

A heretical preacher buys his child an expensive violin and sends the child abroad to study. How can a priest afford to do that? Where does he get the money? If he has that kind of money, should he not spend it to preach the gospel? Should a preacher drive an expensive car? Does he have to ride in a luxury car to be dignified? A preacher who drives an expensive car is a thief. When his followers cannot even afford to buy a compact car, how can it be right for him to have a deluxe model? We can tell a heretical preacher just by looking at his deeds.

Heretical preachers ask for large sums of money. Some churches pay their preachers over $10,000 a month. And this is only the official pay. They are provided with educational fees, fees for books, child-care fees, visitation fees to name just a few.

And still, some of them complain that they are not paid enough. They get $10,000 a month and ask for more money. Is $10,000 such a low salay? A preacher should be content with earning just enough to get by as he preaches the gospel of the water and the Spirit.

A true preacher takes consolation and peace from God. But a heretical preacher who has no peace asks for monetary compensation. Such preachers are in fact worshiping golden calves.

The church of God is sometimes called Zion. There is no church as beautiful as Zion. The church of God is the place where the gospel of the water and the Spirit is preached.

Isaiah 1:21 says, *"How the faithful city has become a harlot! It was full of justice; righteousness lodged in it, but now murderers.* " Isaiah describes the church of God, saying, *"It was full of justice."*

God is just and fair. Because we are incomplete, because we are the descendants of Adam and born to sin, Jesus came to this world to wash away our sins with the water and the Spirit. This is how fair God is.

In the Old Testament, when people knew that they were insufficient, they came to God and offered sacrifices. "I did wrong in such and such a way. I was at fault." Then they were forgiven for their daily sins, and they were also able to obtain forgiveness for their year's sins once on the Day of Atonement.

Similarly, in the New Testament, Jesus Christ came to this world and was baptized and crucified to wash away the sins of humankind once and for all.

But at the New Year's Service, many people cry and repent, "Dear God, please forgive me for the sins I committed last year. And please bless me in the new year." Those people are heretics.

What then, is the truth of being born again of water and the Spirit? Jesus came to the world about 2000 years ago, washed away the sins of humankind once and for all and thus saved us from sin forever. He saved us from all the sins of the world with the water and the blood. But if we asked for forgiveness every day, what would He say?

"How the faithful city has become a harlot! It was full of justice, but now murderers." Anyone who calls himself a sinner is a heretic.

HERETICAL PRIESTS CANNOT PREACH THE GOSPEL OF BEING BORN AGAIN OF WATER AND THE SPIRIT

Does God hear the prayers of sinners?

No. He can't hear them because their sins separate them from God.

Our God calls those who believe in Him and ask Him for forgiveness murderers. Since they ask for forgiveness and also say they are sinners, do they expect Jesus to return and die for their sins a second time? The baptism and the Cross of Jesus are the reality of salvation.

In 1 Peter 3:21, it says that the baptism of Jesus is the antitype of our salvation. Jesus Christ died once to save humankind from sin. He washed away humankind's sins once for all and was resurrected three days later. He now sits at the right hand of God.

Jesus Christ was baptized once and died once on the Cross to save us from sin forever. He was baptized by John the Baptist when He was 30. He died once to save us from all the sins of the world. Doesn't this mean that judgement was given for all time?

If heretics say they are still sinners, they are asking Him to come down a second time and be crucified again. In fact, He would have to keep doing so every time they ask for forgiveness.

Those who believe in the gospel of the water and the Spirit in their hearts are saved from sin forever, become righteous, go to Heaven to receive God's blessing and eternal life. Whoever meets the righteous can be saved through water and the Spirit and become one of the blessed people of God. Anyone who asks righteous salvation before God shall be blessed.

Let us read Isaiah 1:18-20. *"'Come now, and let us reason together,' says the Lord, 'though your sins are like scarlet, they shall be as white as snow; though they are red like crimson, they shall be as wool. If you are willing and obedient, you shall eat the good of the land; but if you refuse and rebel, you shall be devoured by the sword;' for the mouth of the Lord has spoken."*

God is telling us that if we are obedient to the gospel of the water and the Spirit, we shall eat the good of the land, but if we refuse and rebel, we shall be devoured by the sword.

Our God said, "Come now, and let us reason together. Let us talk. Are you insufficient? Are you unrighteous? Do you love yourself too much? Can't you live by the commandments? Can't you do what the law dictates? You know but cannot practice? Then, come to Me. Though your sins are like scarlet, they shall be as white as snow; though they are red like crimson, they shall be as wool." This means that God saved sinners justly and made them righteous.

There was no sin when God created Adam and Eve. But Satan soon came on the scene. He tempted them to disobey God and made all humankind sinners by making them sin. Satan caused humanity's fall. In the beginning, Adam and Eve were not sinners before God. They lived with God in the garden of Eden. But they became sinners. So now, God is calling us. Come and let us reason together. Let us reason together!

"How much sin have you committed in this world? And

how much sin will you commit before you die?"

"Oh, God. It is impossible not to sin. We can't become sanctified no matter how hard we try."

"Well, then how much sin have you committed until now?"

"Well, Lord, I cannot remember everything, but there are a few that stick in my mind. You remember that time? You know what I am talking about . . . and there's that other time, You know . . . "

Then God says, "So go on and tell Me. Do you think that's all? Do you know how many besides those? However, all the sins that you remember, all the sins that you have forgotten, and even all the sins you shall commit in the future, I washed all of them away forever. But not just yours, but your children's and their children's, down to all your descendants' sins. I am the righteous God. I washed away your sins once for all."

God, who washed away all the sins of humankind from Adam's sin to the sins of the last person on earth, is the Alpha and the Omega, the Beginning and the End.

"I am the Savior and Almighty God."

"I am Jehovah, the Merciful God."

"I will have mercy on those who well deserve mercy, and I will have compassion on those who well deserve compassion."

If we ask for His mercy and are frank with Him, we can have God's compassion. Our Father wants to bless all of us. He wants all of us to become righteous. In His love and compassion, He wants to make all of us His righteous children.

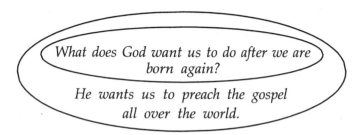

What does God want us to do after we are born again?

He wants us to preach the gospel all over the world.

He wants us to be white as snow. Jesus washed away the sins of humankind once and for all through His baptism and His blood. If a church cannot solve the problems of sin and life for all believers, it cannot be called the true church of God.

People come to priests and ask, "I have sin. What shall I do? I repent and have repented so many times, but my sins did not go away. I cannot go on any more. I don't think I can carry on with my religious life." If a priest cannot give such a person the right answer to his problems, he is a heretic. He may say, "It is up to you. Go pray in the mountains. Try a 40-day fast."

Heretical priests or religious leaders are so full of impurities that they don't even know the gospel of the water and the Spirit. They don't know whether their souls will end up in hell or Heaven.

Those leaders are not right before God. They are pseudo Christians and heretics. They look as if they believe in Jesus from the outside, but their hearts are still full of sin. They have not been washed of their sins. They cannot preach the gospel of the water and the Spirit that can wash away all sins. Let us not be deceived by them.

Titus 3:10-11 says of heretics, *"Reject a divisive man after the first and second admonition, knowing that such a person is warped and sinning, being self-condemned."* Because they believe in Jesus but are not born again, they condemn themselves as sinners. They ignore and trample down the gospel of the water and the Spirit, saying they are sinners who cannot but go to hell.

They are the heretics in Christianity. Anyone who believes in Jesus and has sin is a heretic. Heretics differ from God. God is holy. But they are not holy. Those who believe in the gospel of the water and the Spirit are cleansed of all their sins. Therefore, whoever believes in Jesus but has sin is a heretic. We have to stay away from those who say that they believe in God but are still sinners.

Let us preach the gospel to those who have not heard it yet and those who want to believe but cannot because they do not know it. Let us help them be born again. Let us repel those who stand in the way of the gospel of the water and the Spirit.

We must preach the gospel of being born again of water and the Spirit all over the world. Amen! ⊠

Sermon 3

The True Spiritual
Circumcision

Aaron shall lay both his hands on the head of the live goat, confess over it all the iniquities of the children of Israel, and all their transgressions, concerning all their sins, putting them on the head of the goat, and shall send it away into the wilderness by hand of a suitable man. The goat shall bear on itself all their iniquities to and uninhabited land; and he shall release the goat in the wilderness (Leviticus 16:21-22).

The True Spiritual Circumcision

<Exodus 12:43-49>

"And the Lord said to Moses and Aaron, 'This is the ordinance of the Passover: No outsider shall eat it. But every man's servant who is bought for money, when you have circumcised him, then he may eat it. A sojourner and a hired servant shall not eat it. In one house it shall be eaten; you shall not carry any of the flesh outside the house, nor shall you break one of its bones. All the congregation of Israel shall keep it. And when a stranger sojourns with you and wants to keep the Passover to the Lord, let all his males be circumcised, and then let him come near and keep it; and he shall be as a native of the land. For no uncircumcised person shall eat it. One law shall be for the native-born and for the stranger who sojourns among you."

What was the indispensable condition for the Israelites to become children of God in the Old Testament?

They had to be circumcised.

The words of God in both the Old Testament and the New Testament are important and precious to those of us who believe in God. We cannot be remiss about even one phrase of those words because the words of God are the words of life.

Today's passage tells us that anyone who wants to keep the Passover has to be circumcised beforehand. We should think about the reason God tells us this. Unless one is circumcised, he cannot keep the Passover.

If we are to believe in Jesus, we should understand God's purpose for giving us this edict. Circumcision is the cutting off of a man's foreskin. Why did God tell Abraham and his descendants to be circumcised? The reason is that He had promised that only the ones who "cut off" their sins would become His people.

That is why He tells the people of Israel in the Old Testament to be circumcised. To become the people of God, the people of Israel had to be circumcised. It was His ordinance, basis of consecration, and He became the God of those who severed their sins with faith through circumcision. Additionally, in the New Testament, He becomes the God of those who cut off sin with faith.

THE PASSOVER

What was the Passover?

It was the day for the Israelites to remember and thank God for the Exodus from Egypt.

The most important holiday for the people of Israel was the Passover. It was the day to remember and thank God for the Exodus from Egypt, where the Israelites had lived as slaves for approximately 400 years. God had brought 10 great plagues to move Pharaoh's hardened heart. It was by this means that He led the people of Israel out of Egypt and into the land of Canaan.

The people of Israel had been saved from the death of the firstborn, the last plague, through the blood of the sacrificial lamb and circumcision. Therefore, God told them to keep the Passover throughout their generations as a reminder of His mercy.

WHAT DID THE ISRAELITES HAVE TO DO IN ORDER TO KEEP THE PASSOVER?

What did the Israelites have to do in order to keep the Passover?

They had to be circumcised.

We have to understand that in order to keep the Passover spiritually, we have to be circumcised in our hearts. Even the people of Israel had to be circumcised to observe the Passover.

It is written in Exodus 12:43-49. *"This is the ordinance of the Passover: No outsider shall eat it. But every man's servant who is bought for money, when you have circumcised him, then he may eat it. A sojourner and a hired servant shall not eat it. In one house it shall be eaten; you shall not carry any of the flesh outside the house, nor shall you break one of its bones. All the congregation of Israel shall keep it. And when a stranger sojourns with you and wants to keep the Passover to the Lord, let all his males be circumcised, and then let him come near and keep it; and he shall be as a native of the land. For no uncircumcised person shall eat it. One law shall be for the native-born and for the stranger who sojourns among you."* Thus He told the Israelites to keep the Passover after they had been circumcised.

Who were the ones allowed to eat the meat of the lamb of the Passover and keep the Passover? Only those who were circumcised could keep the Passover.

The lamb of the Passover, as we all know, is Jesus Christ who took away the sins of the world.

Then, what is circumcision in the Old Testament and the New Testament? Circumcision means the cutting off of the foreskin. Jesus Christ was also circumcised eight days after He was born into this world. God had ordered that all who participated in the ritual of the Passover had to be circumcised, and made it clear that anyone who had not been circumcised could never participate in the Passover.

Therefore, everyone had to be circumcised just as God ordained. If you believe in Jesus, you have to understand the meaning of circumcision in the New Testament.

WHAT WAS THE RITUAL OF CIRCUMCISION THAT GOD ORDERED ABRAHAM TO PERFORM?

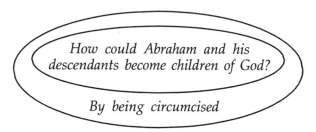

How could Abraham and his descendants become children of God?

By being circumcised

In Genesis, God appeared to Abraham and made His covenant with him and his descendants. In chapter 15, God promised that Abraham's descendants would multiply like the stars in the sky and that He would give them the land of Canaan as their inheritance.

And in chapter 17, He told Abraham that if he and his descendants entered His covenant and were circumcised, He would become their God and they would become His people. It was God's covenant with Abraham and his descendants. God promised that when they believed His covenant and were circumcised, it would mean they had become His people, and He would indeed have become their God.

Genesis 17:7-8 says, *"And I will establish My covenant between Me and you and your descendants after you in their generations, for an everlasting covenant, to be God to you and your descendants after you. Also I give to you and your descendants after you the land in which you are a stranger, all the land of Canaan, as an everlasting possession; and I will be their God."*

The circumcision was the mark of God's covenant with

Abraham and his descendants.

WHAT IS MEANT BY WAY OF SPIRITUAL CIRCUMCISION?

What is the spiritual circumcision?

It is to cut off all the sins in our hearts by believing in the baptism of Jesus.

Because Abraham believed in the word of God, God made him righteous and made him His child. It was circumcision that was the mark of the covenant between God and Abraham.

"This is My covenant which you shall keep, between Me and you and your descendants after you: Every male child among you shall be circumcised" (Genesis 17:10).

Physical circumcision means the cutting off of the foreskin: spiritually, it also signifies passing all our sins on to Jesus through our faith in His baptism. We are spiritually circumcised when we cut away all our sins by accepting the salvation of Jesus' baptism. Circumcision in the New Testament is to cut away all sins through the baptism of Jesus.

Therefore circumcision in the Old Testament is the baptism of Jesus in the New Testament, and both are the covenants of God, which make us His people. Therefore circumcision in the Old Testament and the baptism of Jesus in the New Testament are one and the same.

Just as the descendants of Abraham became the people of God when they cut off their foreskins, we become children of God when we cut off all sin from our hearts. We do this by believing that there is no sin in the world because Jesus took away all sin when He was baptized by John the Baptist.

The baptism of Jesus makes all sinners righteous by cutting off their sins. Just as a piece of skin was removed in the process of circumcision, so were the sins of humankind cut off from all people's hearts when Jesus was baptized by John the Baptist at the Jordan. Those who believe this can be spiritually circumcised and become the people of God, the righteous.

THE FALSE FAITH THAT MAKES PEOPLE CUT THEMSELVES OFF FROM GOD

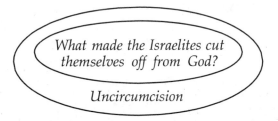

What made the Israelites cut themselves off from God?

Uncircumcision

God told Abraham that any uncircumcised man should be cut off from His people. Then, what is circumcision? And what is spiritual circumcision? If circumcision of the flesh is to cut off a bit of skin from a part of the body, then spiritual circumcision is to cut off all sin from our hearts and pass it on to Jesus through His baptism.

The baptism of Jesus is the spiritual circumcision of humankind, by which the sins of the world were cut off from us and passed on to Jesus. The reason Jesus was baptized by John the Baptist was to save all humankind through the spiritual circumcision, which took away all sin.

All the sins of humankind were passed on to Jesus. God, in becoming the God of Abraham, the God of Isaac, the God of Jacob, and the God of all their descendants, had made a covenant with Abraham and his descendants and had them cut off their foreskins. Thus He became God, the Savior to all those who cut off their sins through circumcision.

What is the circumcision that cuts off sin? It is the covenant of God with Abraham and all those who are born again by believing in the baptism of Jesus and His death on the Cross as their salvation. In this way, He gave us the right to become His people. Thus He is the God of those who have been circumcised.

God spoke to Abraham. *"He who is eight days old among you shall be circumcised, every male child in your generations, he who is born in our house or bought with money from any stranger who is not your descendant. He who is born in your house and he who is bought with your money must be circumcised, and My covenant shall be in your flesh for an everlasting covenant. And the uncircumcised male child, who is not circumcised in the flesh of his foreskin, that person shall be cut off from his people; he has broken My covenant"* (Genesis 17:12-14).

Anyone who tries to come into Jesus without spiritual circumcision shall be cut off from His people. Spiritual circumcision is the baptism of Jesus in the New Testament, through which all the sins of the world were passed on to Him.

Anyone who believes in Jesus should also believe in the circumcision of the Old Testament and the baptism of Jesus in the New Testament, so that they may receive the Spirit, be saved from all sin, and become a child of God. To us who believe in Jesus, circumcision in the Old Testament and the baptism of Jesus in the New Testament are the same.

If we fail to understand the true meaning of circumcision or cannot accept in our hearts the salvation through spiritual circumcision that allows us to be born again, our faith will be in vain. We may think we are faithful to God, but it is as if we had built our house of faith on sand.

God tells all those who believe in Him to be circumcised, to believe in redemption through the baptism of Jesus, the spiritual circumcision. Without circumcision, we cannot become His people. Without circumcision, we are to be excluded from the ranks of His people. Therefore God ordained that anyone, whether he was bought with money or was a stranger, should be circumcised before partaking of the feast of the Passover.

Even the native-born of Israel were to be cut off from His people if they hadn't been circumcised. The covenant of God with the people of Israel should also be applied to all those who believe in Jesus.

In Exodus chapter 12, the people of Israel who ate the meat of the Passover and the bitter herbs had to have already been circumcised. The right to eat the meat of the Passover was given only to those who had been circumcised.

It is important for us to know that when the people of Israel ate the meat of the Passover and put the blood of the lamb on the doorposts and the lintels of their houses, they had already been circumcised.

By the ordinance of God, if a person had not been circumcised, he would have been cut off from His people and lost the right to become one of God's children. This means the sin of unbelief in the spiritual circumcision leads people to ruin. Only those who have been spiritually circumcised through the baptism of Jesus can be saved.

"There is also an antitype which now saves us, namely baptism" (1 Peter 3:21). Do you truly believe that all your sins were passed on to Jesus through His baptism at the Jordan? If you really understand and believe the truth, the baptism of Jesus and His blood, you will realize that you have been spiritually circumcised and become a righteous person. And you will also have faith in the spiritual truth that the blood of Jesus on the Cross would be meaningless without His baptism.

If you were to believe in the Cross of Jesus without being circumcised spiritually through faith in the baptism of Jesus, you would find yourself cast out from God's mercy. You would find that you still have sin in your heart.

We have to believe in the truth that God's redemption started with the baptism of Jesus Christ and was accomplished by His blood on the Cross. To do so, we have to take into our hearts the words of truth, the baptism of Jesus and His blood, as our salvation.

With this faith, we can be delivered from the power of darkness and become the children of light. This faith spiritually separates those who have been truly born again from the ranks of ordinary believers.

Our Lord, Jesus, tells us to abide in Him. He has already washed away the sins of the world with His baptism and

His blood. Therefore, to bear the mark of being the people of God, we have to believe in the baptism of Jesus. If we fail to do so, we shall be cut off from Him.

The salvation of redemption is none other than the baptism of Jesus in the New Testament and circumcision in the Old Testament. Salvation becomes complete only when we have faith in both the baptism of Jesus (the spiritual circumcision) and His blood on the Cross (the blood of the Lamb of the Passover).

The circumcision of the flesh in the Old Testament is connected to the baptism of Jesus Christ in the New Testament. Isaiah 34:16 tells us that all the words in the Bible have their mates. *"Search from the book of the Lord, and read: not one of these shall fail; not one shall lack her mate. For My mouth has commanded it, and His Spirit has gathered them."*

Each word in the Old Testament is connected to the New Testament. Not one word of God lacks its counterpart.

WHAT ABOUT THOSE WHO FOOLISHLY BELIEVE IN AN INCORRECT MANNER?

Who will go to hell among all the believers in the world?

Those who don't believe in the spiritual circumcision

Today there are many who believe only in the blood of the Lamb of the Passover. They ask, "What do you mean, circumcision? It only applied to the Jews in the age of the Old Testament. We don't have to cut off our foreskin in the time of the New Testament."

Of course this is true. I am not suggesting that we should be physically circumcised. The apostle Paul explained spiritual circumcision very clearyly, and it is the circumcision of the heart to which I am referring now.

I am not telling you to be physically circumcised. The circumcision of the flesh has no meaning for us, but we have to come to Jesus and be spiritually circumcised by believing in the baptism of Jesus in order to be saved from all our sins.

In order for someone to be born again, they have to be spiritually circumcised. Anyone who believes in Jesus has to be spiritually circumcised. It is the only way to cut away all our sins, the only way to become righteous. Only after our spiritual circumcision are we completely without sin. Therefore we have to accept in our hearts spiritual circumcision by believing in the baptism of Jesus.

The apostle Paul also believed in the importance of spiritual circumcision. He said, *"Circumcision is that of the heart"* *(Romans 2:29).* Every one of us has to be spiritually circumcised to be free of sin.

Have your sins really been passed on to Jesus after being cut away from you? Even in the New Testament, the ones who believe in Jesus have to be circumcised in their hearts by believing in the baptism of Jesus.

The apostle Paul made this clear in his Epistles. God saved all humankind from the sins of the world, made them His people. The people of Israel become God's people by removing their foreskins and we become His children when we pass all our sins on to Jesus by believing in His baptism.

God accepts us as His people when He sees our faith in the baptism of Jesus and His blood on the Cross. This faith makes us spiritually circumcised and leads to our salvation.

SALVATION EXIST FOR SINNERS THROUGH THE BAPTISM OF JESUS AND HIS BLOOD

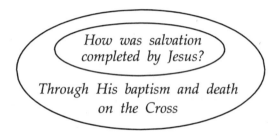

How was salvation completed by Jesus?

Through His baptism and death on the Cross

The salvation Jesus Christ completed through the water of His baptism and His blood on the Cross is for sinners. The blood of the Lamb was the judgment, and the baptism of Jesus was the spiritual circumcision which transferred all our sins to Him.

Christian churches today should not make light of this notion of spiritual circumcision. Even though circumcision in the Old Testament means little to us these days, the baptism of Jesus should never be ignored.

I told you that all your sins were taken away by the baptism of Jesus, and the baptism of Jesus saved you from all your sins. Do you believe it? If you ignore the baptism of Jesus, you will never know the gospel of being born again, the gospel of complete redemption through the baptism of Jesus.

How can we ignore the baptism of Jesus, the spiritual circumcision of which God tells us? If we read the Bible, we can see that circumcision and the blood of the lamb of the Passover are closely related. This is the secret of spiritual circumcision, the baptism of Jesus.

The gospel preached by the apostle John was none other than the gospel of the baptism of Jesus and His blood on the Cross. He said in 1 John 5:6, *"This is He who came by water and blood—Jesus Christ; not only by water, but by water and blood."*

He said that Jesus came by water, blood and the Spirit. Not only by water, and not only by blood, but by water, blood and the Spirit altogether. These three elements, the baptism of Jesus, the blood of Jesus on the Cross and His resurrection from the dead, are one, the proof of our salvation.

WHY DOES THE BIBLE SPEAK OF THE BAPTISM OF JESUS AND HIS BLOOD?

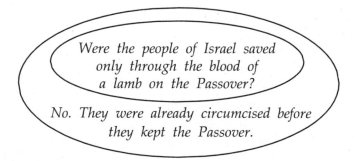

Were the people of Israel saved only through the blood of a lamb on the Passover?

No. They were already circumcised before they kept the Passover.

The baptism of Jesus and His blood is what allows us to be born again of water and the Spirit. Exodus chapter

12 says, "Take for yourself a lamb, and take some of the blood and put it on the two doorposts and on the lintel of your houses. When I see the blood, I will pass over you."

Knowing this, is it possible that we can be saved from all our sins by believing only in the blood of the lamb of the Passover? Then why is the baptism of Jesus talked about so much in the New Testament? The apostles said, *"Buried with Him in baptism" (Colossians 2:12). "For as many of you as were baptized into Christ have put on Christ" (Galatians 3:27). "... which now saves us, namely baptism" (1 Peter 3:21).*

The apostles Peter and Paul and all the other disciples of Jesus Christ talked about the baptism of Jesus. It is the baptism of Jesus at the Jordan to which they were referring, and it is the faith in the baptism of Jesus and His blood on the Cross that is the truth of being born again of water and the Spirit.

To tell you the truth, I believed in Jesus, but only in His blood, for over 10 years, without even acknowledging the baptism of Jesus. But this knowledge by itself did not take away the sins in my heart. I believed in Jesus with all my heart, but my heart was still full of sin.

After 10 years, I discovered the meaning of spiritual circumcision (the baptism of Jesus) and then was born again. Only then did I realize the truth: Circumcision in the Old Testament symbolizes the baptism of Jesus in the New Testament. I believed it and I still do.

"In the New Testament, is it the correct faith to believe in both the blood of Jesus and His baptism? Is my belief correct according to the Bible?" After I was born again, I wondered about these things.

Although I believed in the message of the baptism of Jesus and His blood, questions remained in my mind. "Is it right to believe in the truth that all my sins were passed on to Jesus when He was baptized or is it right to believe that Jesus saved us only through His death on the Cross. Isn't it enough just to believe that Jesus is my God and Savior?" I pondered this while reading Exodus chapter 12.

Many people today read Exodus chapter 12 and do not think twice about declaring that Jesus Christ died on the Cross as their Savior. They think it is correct to believe in the blood of Christ and they testify to the truth of their convictions. They may believe unflinchingly and say that the Lord is Christ and the Son of God but they are still sinners. They think that if they believe that Jesus Christ is the Savior, they will be saved even if they still have sin in their hearts.

This kind of faith is not true faith. This faith alone can not help them to be born again. Only the baptism of Jesus and His blood makes us righteous.

Then, what does Exodus chapter 12 actually mean? I looked into the Bible, thinking, "Isn't there any problem believing only in the blood of Jesus while ignoring His baptism?" Even before I finished reading Exodus, I discovered the truth that salvation is not only of the blood of Christ but also of His baptism. Through the Bible, I was assured that we are circumcised in our hearts through the baptism of Jesus as well as His blood on the Cross.

Why are most Christians still sinners?

Because they don't believe in the baptism of Jesus.

I realized in Exodus 12:47-49 that before one was allowed to eat the meat of the Passover, he had to be circumcised. It is for the reason that God says in verse 49, *"One law shall be for the native-born and for the stranger who sojourns among you."*

Therefore, anyone who was not circumcised could not eat the meat of the Passover. That is the truth I found. Similarly, when we believe in Jesus as our Savior, we first have to accept the fact that all our sins were passed on to Jesus through His baptism at the Jordan and then accept the fact that Jesus Christ died on the Cross for these sins.

When I realized that Jesus had died on the Cross to be judged for the sins He took away through His baptism, I also realized the meaning of the spiritual circumcision which saved us from all the sins and transgressions of the world.

At that moment, I realized that all my sins were gone. My heart became white as snow and I finally took into my heart the gospel of the water, the blood and the Spirit.

I realized that there are two things which save us, circumcision and the blood of the lamb in the Old Testament and the passing on of all sins to Him through the baptism of Jesus and His blood on the Cross in the New Testament. Circumcision in the Old Testament and the baptism of Jesus in the New Testament are really one and the same.

Jesus Christ was judged not because He committed any sins Himself, but because He took on all the sins of the world through His baptism. Those who believe that John the Baptist, as the representative of humankind, baptized Jesus and passed all the sins of the world on to Jesus also believe in both the baptism of Jesus and His blood on the

Cross.

Why do so many people deny His baptism even though it is repeatedly described in the Bible? By doing so they are still sinners even if they believe in Jesus. They may believe in Jesus but are still cut off from God. They are pitiful sinners who will go to hell even though they may believe in Jesus.

How can they still be sinners if they believe in Jesus? Why do they live as sinners? Why are they going down the pathway to destruction? It is so pitiful. They will continue to remain sinners because they do not believe the fact that all the sins of the world were passed on to Jesus Christ, who brought eternal salvation to all people through His spiritual baptism.

People think they are redeemed by believing in the blood of Jesus, but that kind of faith never makes them complete. Why? Because they failed to pass their sins on to Jesus!

We can only be saved by believing in the water (Christ's baptism) and His blood in the way that God ordained: the salvation of spiritual circumcision. Then, and only then, can we become true children of God.

We have to ask ourselves. "If we believe only in the blood of Jesus as the spiritual circumcision, can our sins be completely washed away?" We have to look deep in our hearts to find the answer.

In the Old Testament, people were saved through circumcision and the blood of the Passover lamb just as we won salvation through the baptism of Jesus and His blood on the Cross. In this way we were saved from God's judgment and from this sinful world. Those who believe become children of God and God becomes their Father.

A person is saved and becomes one of God's own by believing in these two things: circumcision and the blood of the lamb of the Passover, i.e., the baptism of Jesus and His blood. This is the truth according to Jesus. This is the true meaning of being born again of water, blood and the Spirit.

WHAT IS THE REDEMPTION OF THE WATER AND THE SPIRIT MEMTIONED IN THE BIBLE?

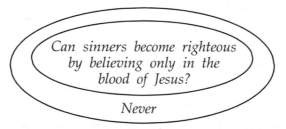

Can sinners become righteous by believing only in the blood of Jesus?

Never

Jesus abandoned His throne in Heaven and descended to this world. He was baptized by John the Baptist at the age of 30 to take away all the sins of the world.

The blood of Jesus on the Cross was His condemnation for the sins of all sinners in the world. Jesus Christ came as the Savior to this world and saved all sinners from their sins through the water and the blood.

Are we born again of the blood alone? No. We are saved from sin by the baptism of Jesus and His blood. I would like to ask a question to those who believe only in the blood of Jesus. "Can sinners become righteous by believing only in the blood of Christ, or is it through both the baptism of Jesus and His blood on the Cross? Is it by the belief that we pass all our sins on to Jesus through His baptism and blood or only through His blood? Which is the truth, I ask you?"

To be truly born again of water and the Spirit, we have to fulfill the following. We must believe that Jesus came to this world in the flesh, that He took on to Himself all the sins of the world at the Jordan with His baptism and was judged for all our sins on the Cross. By believing in Jesus Christ, our true Savior, in this way, we can truly be born again.

I ask you again. What is faith as defined in the Bible? Is it faith in the blood of Jesus, or in both the baptism of Jesus and His blood?

Faith in the blood of Jesus is as follows. Jesus was judged and condemned for all the sins of the world. Because He was crushed and wounded for our sins, we were saved from a terrible judgment. But that is not the complete truth. Before we accept this doctrine, we have to clear up one point. Why did Jesus have to be crucified on the Cross?

The Bible clearly says that the wages of sin is death. Jesus never committed any sin in this world. He came in the flesh of a man through the body of Mary, but He had come in the express image of His people as the Son of Holy God and the Savior of sinners. That was why He had to be baptized by John the Baptist before He died on the Cross. When He was baptized, He took all our sins upon Himself. Thus, without baptism, He could not have been sentenced to shed blood on the Cross.

THE SACRIFICIAL SYSTEM IN THE OLD TESTAMENT

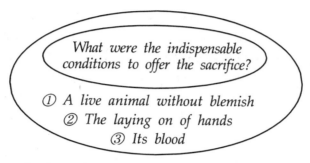

What were the indispensable conditions to offer the sacrifice?

① *A live animal without blemish*
② *The laying on of hands*
③ *Its blood*

Let us look at this truth through the sacrificial system of the Holy Tabernacle. In the Old Testament, either a sinner or the high priest laid his hands on the sacrificial lamb or goat to pass his own sin or the sins of Israel on to its head. The offerings were then killed and offered before the altar. The Old Testament was the precursor to the New Testament, and Jesus Christ was the sacrificial Lamb God had promised to send.

When did all of you pass all your sins on to Jesus? I want you to think about and answer this question. In the Old Testament, the Israelites couldn't kill sacrificial animals without the laying on of hands (the laying on of hands means to pass sin on to the sin offering). Before the sin offerings were brought in front of the altar, the laying on of hands had to take place in order to pass sins on to the sacrificial animals.

"Then he shall put his hand on the head of the burnt offering" *(Leviticus 1:4)*. It is written in Leviticus that all offerings required the laying on of hands. By laying their hands on the head of the offering, the people of Israel were able to pass their sins on to it, and by offering its blood and flesh

in faith before God, they could be saved from their sins. The Israelites were also saved by faith in the time of the Old Testament.

When a burnt offering was given before God, a sinner had to lay his hands on its head so as to pass on the sins of the sinner. The offering was then killed on behalf of the sinner. Its blood was sprinkled on the four horns of the altar and the remainder was poured on the ground at the base of the altar. This was how sinners were redeemed.

In the New Testament sinners can be redeemed of all their sins through their faith in the water and the blood of Jesus. 1 John 5:1-10 says that a sinner has been redeemed when he believes in the baptism of Jesus and the blood of the lamb (the Cross).

Therefore any sinner can be redeemed as long as he believes in both of the baptism of Jesus and His blood on the Cross. The baptism of Jesus and His blood, together with the Holy Spirit, are indispensable to being born again of water and the Spirit.

Dearly beloved, can you be redeemed only by believing in the blood of Jesus Christ? Those who think they can be born again by believing only in the blood of the Cross still have sin in their hearts. But we can be saved from all our sins by believing in the baptism of Jesus as the spiritual circumcision of the New Testament, which is the latter-day equivalent to the circumcision described in the Old Testament.

All denominations have their own doctrines. We know that they are all doomed to go to hell unless they abandon their false beliefs. The Presbyterian Church places emphasis on the doctrine of predestination; the Methodist Church stresses arminianism, i.e., humanism; the Baptist Church, baptism; and the Holiness Church, holy life; all these have diverged from the word of truth.

But what does the word of truth in the Bible say about being born again? The Bible says the truth is found in the baptism of Jesus and His blood. Anyone who believes and follows the word of God and has faith in being born again of water and the Spirit will find redemption.

WHAT IS THE SECRET OF THE BAPTISM OF JESUS?

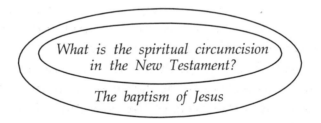

What is the spiritual circumcision in the New Testament?

The baptism of Jesus

The baptism of Jesus was the spiritual circumcision. In the Old Testament, God said that anyone who was not circumcised should be cut off from His people.

We have to know and believe that the spiritual circumcision in the New Testament is indeed the baptism of Jesus. Because Jesus was baptized by John the Baptist at the beginning of His public ministry, we can be spiritually circumcised by believing in His baptism. We should carefully ponder the reasons why Jesus had to be baptized by John the Baptist.

"Then Jesus came from Galilee to John at the Jordan to be baptized by him. And John tried to prevent Him, saying, 'I need

to be baptized by You, and are You coming to me?' But Jesus
answered and said to him, 'Permit it to be so now, for thus it
is fitting for us to fulfill all righteousness.' Then he allowed Him"
(Matthew 3:13-15).

Jesus was baptized by John the Baptist at the Jordan,
"the river of death." John the Baptist laid his hands on
the head of Jesus and He was fully immersed. This is the
correct way to be baptized (Baptism: to be immersed in
water). In order for Jesus to take away all the sins of the
world, He had to be baptized in the same way, with the
laying on of hands referred to in the Old Testament.

The baptism of Jesus is the spiritual circumcision to
those who believe in Jesus. *"For thus it is fitting for us to*
fulfill all righteousness" (Matthew 3:15). It was fitting that
Jesus took away all the sins of the world and became our
God and Savior. Thus, it was fitting, as it was written, that
He died on the Cross with all our sins on His head.

The baptism of Jesus has the power to make all sinners
born again. It is the secret of the gospel of the water and
the Spirit.

The first thing that Jesus did in His public ministry to
save sinners from all their sins was to be baptized by John
the Baptist. Baptism means "to be washed, to be buried,
to pass to."

By being baptized in the manner demanded by God,
Jesus took all the sins of the world on to Himself. *"Behold!*
The Lamb of God who takes away the sin of the world!" (John
1:29). The baptism of Jesus means that all the people of
the world who believe in Him are spiritually circumcised.

Later, He went to the Cross as the Lamb of God who
took away all the sins of the world and accepted judgement
for all sinners. Thus, He saved all humankind from sin.

Therefore all those who believe in the baptism of Jesus Christ, circumcision of the Old Testament, and His blood on the Cross as their salvation are saved from all their sins. Jesus Christ saved all sinners with His baptism and His blood. This is the truth of the spiritual circumcision.

IS SALVATION BY BLOOD ONLY?
NO, IT IS NOT

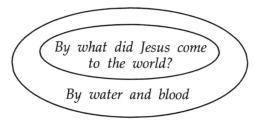

By what did Jesus come to the world?

By water and blood

1 John 5:4-8 says, *"For whatever is born of God overcomes the world. And this is the victory that has overcome the world—our faith. Who is he who overcomes the world, but he who believes that Jesus is the Son of God? This is He who came by water and blood—Jesus Christ; not only by water, but by water and blood. And it is the Spirit who bears witness, because the Spirit is truth. For there are three who bear witness in heaven: the Father, the Word, and the Holy Spirit; and these three are one. And there are three that bear witness on earth: the Spirit, the water, and the blood; and these three agree as one."*

Dear Christians, what is your testimony of Him as your Savior? It is none other than the faith in the Son of God who came by water and blood.

What is the victory that overcomes the world? It is none other than the power of faith in the water and the blood. It is Jesus Christ who came by water and blood. And it is the Spirit that bears witness, for the Spirit is the truth.

There are three things that bear witness on earth: the water, the blood, and the Spirit. And these three agree as one. Jesus came to this world in the flesh, He was baptized and died on the Cross to save us from eternal damnation. The proof that God, our Creator, became the Savior of all sinners is in the gospel of the water and the Spirit which saves us all.

It is our proof that Jesus, who came to this world as the Spirit in the flesh, was baptized at the Jordan to take on to Himself all our sins, and bled on the Cross in accepting the judgment for our sins. Thus, He saved all who believe in Him. This is the original gospel of the water and the Spirit.

WHAT IS THE WATER AND THE BLOOD WHICH BEARS WITNESS TO GOD'S SALVATION?

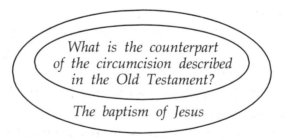

What is the counterpart of the circumcision described in the Old Testament?

The baptism of Jesus

The water refers to the baptism of Jesus Christ. In the Old Testament, the baptism of Jesus meant circumcision. The counterpart of circumcision in the Old Testament is the baptism of Jesus in the New Testament. The proof that all the sins of the world were passed on to Jesus is in the baptism of Jesus.

Anyone who believes in this truth is able to stand before God and say with a good conscience, "You are my Savior, My Lord because I believe in Your baptism and Your blood, the gospel of the water and the Spirit. Therefore, I have no sin. I am a child of God and You are my Savior." We are able to profess this with true faith. The reason we are able to say this is because of our faith in the baptism of Jesus and His blood.

What is the word that allows us to be born again? It is the baptism of Jesus and His blood on the Cross, which is the testimony of salvation in our hearts. This is the gospel of being born again of water and the Spirit.

Dear Christians, I ask you again, "Can a sinner be saved solely through belief in the blood of Christ? No. Salvation requires not just belief in His death on the Cross. It is only through belief in both the water and the blood — the gospel of the water and the Spirit — that sinners can be born again. Let me now refer you to the Bible, which talks about the water or in other words the baptism of Jesus.

1 Peter 3:21-22 says, *"There is also an antitype which now saves us, namely baptism (not the removal of the filth of the flesh, but the answer of a good conscience toward God), through the resurrection of Jesus Christ, who has gone into heaven and is at the right hand of God, angels and authorities and powers having been made subject to Him."*

The apostle Peter testified that the baptism of Jesus was the antitype which saves us, and it was also the proof of salvation from sin. The baptism of Jesus is the equivalent of circumcision in the Old Testament. Just as the people of Israel believed in the word of God and cut off their foreskin to become children of God in Old Testament times, the baptism of Jesus saves us from all our sins in the time of the New Testament.

Therefore circumcision in the Old Testament and the baptism of Jesus in the New Testament are one and the same. Do you all now believe that the baptism of Jesus is indeed the same as circumcision? As it is written in 1 Peter 3:21, there is also an antitype which now saves us, namely baptism. Can you argue with the written word of God?

How is it that we, who live in this world, can be free of sin? It is only because Jesus Christ was baptized to fulfill all righteousness that salvation from sin is available to us. Matthew 3:15 says, *"For thus it is fitting for us to fulfill all righteousness."*

Because all the sins of the world were passed on to Jesus, all who believe in Him are now without sin. We can all become righteous by accepting the truth that all our sins were passed on to Jesus through His baptism. Jesus Christ took all our sins on to Himself and died on the Cross to save us from all judgment.

Dear friends, the two things that save all sinners from their sins are the water and the blood. His taking on our sins and His dying for us on the Cross are the two main things that Jesus Christ did for us during the 3 years of His public ministry in this world.

John 1:29 says, *"Behold! The Lamb of God who takes away the sin of the world!"* Jesus Christ was baptized to take away the sin of the world and died on the Cross to atone for our transgressions. Jesus is the Son of God, and as the Creator, He fulfilled the covenant of circumcision that God made in the Old Testament by taking away the sins of the world.

Anyone who believes in his heart the gospel of the baptism of Jesus, the water and the blood shall be born again of water and the Spirit. And the Lord shall become the Savior to all those who believe. Thank the Lord, Hallelujah! Jesus fulfilled our salvation as God had promised, and He saved us from all the sins of the world.

Not the Removal of the Filth of the Flesh

> Does the flesh become sanctified with time?
>
> No. The flesh continues to accumulate sin until the day we die.

1 Peter 3:21 says, *"There is also an antitype which now saves us, namely baptism (not the removal of the filth of the flesh, but the answer of a good conscience toward God), through the resurrection of Jesus Christ."*

When someone comes to believe in Jesus Christ as his Savior, it doesn't mean he stops committing sins of the flesh. We may continue to sin, but by believing in the baptism of Jesus, we can pass all our worldly sins on to Jesus, who paid for them with His blood on the Cross. By believing in these two things as indispensable elements of our salvation, we are saved from our sins.

Being born again means welcoming Jesus into our hearts as the Savior of all humankind. The forgiveness of sin is also achieved in our hearts. When we believe in the baptism of Jesus and His blood on the Cross, our hearts are born again, but we continue to commit sins and transgressions with our flesh. But, all our sins of the flesh have already been forgiven.

The baptism of Jesus is testimony to all those who have been saved. We are without sin when we believe in the forgiveness of sin through Christ's baptism. We are born again when we take into our hearts the truth of salvation through the baptism of Jesus and become righteous through the gospel of the water and the Spirit.

This is the faith of Abraham in the Old Testament, the faith of becoming righteous about which the apostle Paul spoke, and the antitype of salvation to which the apostle Peter testified.

Just as Abraham heard and believed in the word of God and became righteous, we are saved when we believe in the baptism of Jesus and His death on the Cross.

John 1:12 says, *"But as many as received Him, to them He gave the right to become children of God, even to those who believe in His name."* Do you accept Jesus Christ, the One who saved us from all our sins through His baptism and blood, as your Savior? We must receive the salvation given to us through the water and the blood of the Son of God.

Is salvation just by the blood of Jesus Christ? No. It is by the water and the blood of Jesus. In the Bible, it is clearly stated that salvation is not by the blood of Jesus alone. It is by the baptism of Jesus and His blood.

The baptism of Jesus is the spiritual circumcision of the New Testament. It is the truth of salvation that cut off all our sins from us. The fact that He was judged for the sins of the world means that He was judged for us, you and me.

By receiving the gospel of the forgiveness of sins, the baptism of Jesus and His blood, we are freed from judgment for all our sins. With our faith, we are saved from all the sins we commit in this world. When we take the baptism of Jesus and His blood as our salvation, all the sins in our hearts are washed away. Do you believe and understand this to be true? I sincerely hope that you will all believe in the gospel of the water and the Spirit. Believe and earn everlasting life.

The apostle Paul said, *"Circumcision is that of the heart"* *(Romans 2:29)*. How are we circumcised in our hearts? We can be spiritually circumcised when we believe in the coming of Christ Jesus to this world in the flesh, in His baptism to take away all the sins of the world, in His death on the Cross for our sins, and in His resurrection from the dead.

The apostle Paul said that circumcision is that of the heart. Circumcision of the heart means believing in the baptism of Jesus and His blood. If you want to be circumcised in your heart, you have to take into your heart the gospel of the baptism of Jesus and His blood. Then, only then, can you truly become children of God.

WAS JOHN THE BAPTIST SENT BY GOD?

Who was John the Baptist?

He was the representative of mankind and the last high priest according to the lineage of Aaron.

Here, we need to ask who was John the Baptist who baptized Jesus Christ. John the Baptist was the representative of all humankind. Matthew 11:11-14 says, *"Assuredly, I say to you, among those born of women there has not risen one greater than John the Baptist; but he who is least in the kingdom of heaven is greater than he. And from the days of John the Baptist until now the kingdom of heaven suffers violence, and the violent take it by force. For all the prophets and the law prophesied until John. And if you are willing to receive it, he is Elijah who is to come."*

Dear Christians, Jesus says that there is no one greater than John the Baptist among those born of women. With the birth of John the Baptist, the Age of the First Covenant of God, the age of the Old Testament was over. It was over because Jesus Christ who was to fulfill the covenant of God had come at last.

Who was it then, who was to fulfill the covenant of God? Jesus Christ and John the Baptist. John the Baptist passed all the sins of the world on to Jesus. Who was the last high priest of the Old Testament? Who was the descendant of Aaron? Jesus Christ Himself testified that it was none other than John the Baptist. John the Baptist was the representative of humankind, the greatest among those born of women.

Let us ponder over the facts we have. Moses, Abraham, Isaac, and Jacob were all born of women. But among the people in both the Old Testament and the New Testament, who is the greatest among all born of women? It is John the Baptist.

John the Baptist, as the last prophet of the Old Testament and a descendant of Aaron, baptized the Lamb of God in the New Testament in the same way that Aaron laid his hands on the sacrificial offerings on the Day of Atonement in the Old Testament. He baptized Jesus Christ and passed all the sins of the world on to Jesus. He was a servant of God. He fulfilled the spiritual circumcision in the hearts of all humankind by baptizing Jesus Christ.

Together with the baptism of Jesus, we must believe in His blood as testimony to our salvation. Jesus Christ took away all the sins of the world through His baptism and was judged for them. And the only thing for us to do is simply to believe it. It is God's Will that we believe in what Jesus did.

Once you take into your heart the gospel of being born again of water and the Spirit, you can become a descendant of Abraham and a child of God. There are only a few who are in Christ while there are many who have not yet accepted Him in their hearts.

The day is almost over and darkness is falling. Believe in the baptism of Jesus and allow Him to enter your heart. Your faith in the baptism of Jesus and His blood will make you blessed with spiritual salvation.

Keep in mind always that spiritual anointment comes when you believe in the gospel of salvation, the gospel of the baptism of Jesus and His blood. I want you to know that you can prepare the spiritual lamp (Church) and oil (the Spirit) like the wise virgins (Matthew 25:4) by believing the gospel of the baptism of Jesus and His blood. Those who believe in Jesus go to church with the Spirit in their hearts.

FOR WHOM WAS JESUS BAPTIZED?

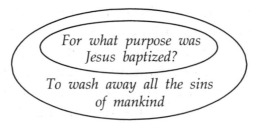

For what purpose was
Jesus baptized?

To wash away all the sins
of mankind

*"'I need to be baptized by You, and are You coming to me?'
Jesus answered and said to him, 'Permit it to be so now, for
thus it is fitting for us to fulfill all righteousness'" (Matthew
3:14-15).*

Jesus was baptized to wash away all the sins of
humankind. Jesus Christ is the Son of God and our Savior.
He is the Creator who made us. Jesus Christ came by the
will of God, the Father, to make us His people.

About whom did all the prophets speak in the Old
Testament? They spoke of Jesus Christ. All the prophets
of the Old Testament talked of Jesus' coming to this world
to take away all our sins and free us from sin forever.

Jesus came down to this world as was prophesied in
the Old Testament and took away all the sins of humankind
from Adam and Eve to the last person on earth.

Now, take into your heart the salvation through the
baptism of Jesus and His blood. Are you still unsure that
this is the truth? Do you still have sin in your heart? *"For
thus it is fitting for us to fulfill all righteousness."* Jesus was
baptized by John the Baptist to fulfill all righteousness.

The word "baptism" itself means "to be washed." Jesus
was baptized by John the Baptist in the way of the laying
on of hands described in the Old Testament.

After He had taken on all the sins of humankind, He

immersed Himself in the Jordan. The river signifies death and judgment for sinners. Christ's immersion in the water symbolizes His death on the Cross. His emergence from the water stands for resurrection. Jesus was resurrected on the third day after dying on the Cross.

Jesus is our God and Savior. The fact that Jesus came to this world to be baptized, bled to death on the Cross, was resurrected on the third day, and now sits at the right hand of God is clear proof that He saved all humankind from death. Do you believe sincerely in this truth?

The baptism of Jesus is the spiritual circumcision of the New Testament. *"Circumcision is that of the heart."* Circumcision of the heart is completed when we believe in the baptism of Jesus, the truth of the passing on of all our sins to Jesus. Circumcision of the heart is the acknowledgement of the baptism of Jesus through which we passed all our sins on to Jesus.

Have you been circumcised in your heart? If you believe in circumcision of the heart, your sins will be washed away once and for all. For this purpose Jesus fulfilled all righteousness and assured the salvation of all sinners.

Dear Christians, take this proof of salvation into your hearts and minds. This is the truth. Once you take into your heart the salvation of Jesus, you will be freed from all your sins. *"But as many as received Him, to them He gave the right to become children of God, even to those who believe in His name"* (John 1:12).

Can you see now why Jesus had to come to this world to be baptized? Do you believe it now? Jesus was baptized to take away the sins of all mankind. It was the baptism of circumcision. The baptism of Jesus gives us the spiritual circumcision. That is why the apostle Paul tells us to be circumcised in our hearts. Jesus so clearly saved us with His baptism and blood that we have no choice but to believe it in our hearts. We should say "Yes. Amen" to the word of God in our hearts. Is it not the truth? Do you believe in it?

DO YOU ACCEPT THIS TRUTH IN YOUR HEART?

What do we have to do before we worship Jesus?

We have to take into our hearts the truth of the water and the blood.

Almost 2000 years have passed since Jesus came to this world. In this day and age of God's grace, we must take into our hearts the truth, the water and the blood of Jesus. There is nothing else for us to do.

"Circumcision is that of the heart." We have to be circumcised through the faith in our hearts. We can only be saved through faith. In the Old Testament, the Israelites were saved through circumcision and the blood of the Passover which was put on the doorposts and the lintels of their houses.

Those who believe in the baptism of Jesus and His blood as their salvation are not afraid of the judgment of God because it will pass over them. But the judgement of God will fall on all who do not take the truth into their hearts. There are many who believe in Jesus in vain and are thus still slaves to their sins.

How have they arrived at this state? Why do they still suffer from sin? It is only because they do not know the truth of the baptism of Jesus and His blood. They believe only in the blood of Jesus, omitting or overlooking His baptism.

Is salvation obtainable through simple belief in the blood of Jesus only? Does the Bible tell us that this is so? What do the Old Testament and the New Testament say about this? According to the Bible, it is not only by the blood of the Lamb of God, but also by the baptism of Jesus that salvation is achieved (1 John 5:3-6).

Do you believe in the blood of Jesus alone? Those who do must still have sin in their hearts. They must overcome their incorrect faith and return to the true gospel.

Those who do not believe must acknowledge now that they have been misled, not knowing that Jesus took away all sin at the Jordan through His baptism. They must admit that they have been wrong in neglecting to accept the baptism of Jesus. They must take it into their hearts that Jesus took away all the sins of the world through His baptism. Salvation is available only when we believe in both the baptism of Jesus and His Cross. In other words, only through the gospel of the water and the Spirit are we able to earn everlasting life.

Dear Christians, have you lived until now depending only on belief in the blood of Jesus? If this is the case, surely you have sin in your heart. If you sin, then you have sin in your heart. If you think you are free of sin when you live up to the law of God, it is only a feeling that comes out of your emotions. This conviction is not in accordance with the word of God.

IT IS NOT YET TOO LATE

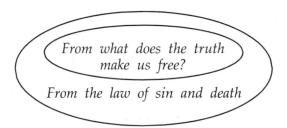

From what does the truth
make us free?

From the law of sin and death

It is not yet too late. All you must do is to believe in the baptism of Jesus and His blood, and you will be circumcised in your heart and become free of all sin. Becoming free of all sin means that you are saved by believing in the gospel of the baptism of Jesus and His blood.

Are you willing to believe in the baptism of Jesus and His blood for salvation from your sins? Once you believe in this, you will learn what salvation is like. You will receive peace of mind. Then, and only then, will you become righteous. Not through your works, but through your faith in the word of God. If any one of you still believes in and depends only on the blood of Jesus for salvation, I would like to urge you to believe in both the baptism of Jesus and His blood.

Dear Christians, the complete salvation of humankind from sin was fulfilled through the gospel of the baptism of Jesus and His blood. The Spirit is God. God came down to this world in the flesh of a human being.

God said through the prophets that we should call His name Jesus, for He was to save His people from their sins. God said, *"'A virgin shall be with child, and bear a Son, and they shall call His name Immanuel,' which is translated, 'God with us'"* (Matthew 1:23).

God came to this world to save sinners. He was baptized to take away all the sins of the world and thus saved all sinners. This is the truth and the salvation of the water and the blood. I am here to tell you this. Have we been saved only by the blood of Jesus? Of course not. We have been saved by the baptism of Jesus and His blood on the Cross.

There are so many false prophets and heretics today who do not believe in the baptism of Jesus. Jesus said, *"And you shall know the truth, and the truth shall make you free"* (John 8:32).

We must know the truth. We must know why Jesus talked about His baptism, and why we should believe in it. We should know why God told the people of Israel to be circumcised in the Old Testament and why He talked about the blood of the lamb of the Passover.

When we know only part of the story, we can never recognize the truth. Jesus said, *"Most assuredly, I say to you, unless one is born of water and the Spirit, he cannot enter the kingdom of God"* (John 3:5).

TO BE BAPTIZED INTO CHRIST

How can we unite with the death of Christ?

By passing all our sins on to Jesus through His baptism

The Bible testifies to the secret of salvation. Is it by the blood of Jesus only? No. It is by His blood and His baptism together. The apostle Paul talked about this often in Romans chapter 6 and again in many other Epistles.

Let us read Romans 6:3-8. *"Or do you not know that as many of us as were baptized into Christ Jesus were baptized into His death? Therefore we were buried with Him through baptism into death, that just as Christ was raised from the dead by the glory of the Father, even so we also should walk in newness of life. For if we have been united together in the likeness of His death, certainly we also shall be in the likeness of His resurrection, knowing this, that our old man was crucified with Him, that the body of sin might be done away with, that we should no longer be slaves of sin. For he who has died has been freed from sin. Now if we died with Christ, we believe that we shall also live with Him."*

Let us look at verse 5. It reads, *"For if we have been united together in the likeness of His death, certainly we also shall be in the likeness of His resurrection."*

His death was our death because all our sins were passed on to Him through His baptism. So the baptism of Jesus links His blood on the Cross with us.

Our faith in the baptism of Jesus and His blood allows us to unite with Jesus. *"The wages of sin is death" (Romans 6:23).* Therefore the death of Jesus on the Cross was our death. He was baptized to take all our sins on to Himself. To believe in this truth is to unite ourselves with Jesus Christ, our Savior.

WE SHOULD NOT BELIEVE IN JESUS SIMPLY AS A PART OF A RELIGIOUS WAY OF LIFE

*What is meant by
"He is faithful and just?"*

*It means that Jesus washed away our
sins once for all and saves anyone
who believes in the truth.*

Many people believe in Jesus as a religious way of life, so they go to church and cry their eyes out praying and repenting. They confess their sins and ask for forgiveness every day. They pray, "Jesus, I know and believe that You died on the Cross for me. Yes, I believe."

Clearly, they misunderstand the following passage. *"If we confess our sins, He is faithful and just to forgive us our sins and to cleanse us from all unrighteousness" (1 John 1:9).* They claim that they should be forgiven for their sins every day through the confession of sin. But the sin in the above passage does not mean trivial everyday transgressions. What the passage means is that we are forgiven for our sins once and for all when we confess that we have not yet been saved.

"So then faith comes by hearing, and hearing by the word of God" (Romans 10:17). "And you shall know the truth, and the truth shall make you free" (John 8:32).

Dear Christians, the truth is clear. If you believe that Jesus died on the Cross without taking away all our sins through His baptism at the Jordan, your faith is in vain.

If any Christian wants to be saved from all his sins, he must believe that his sins were passed on to Jesus through His baptism at the Jordan once and for all and that He took the judgment for all our sins on the Cross. In other words, we should believe in both the baptism of Jesus and His blood.

"For there is no other name under heaven given among men by which we must be saved" (Acts 4:12). Jesus Christ took on all our sins through His baptism and became our Savior. Jesus came by water and blood to save us from eternal damnation. *"For with the heart one believes to righteousness, and with the mouth confession is made to salvation" (Romans 10:10).* Are you a sinner or a righteous person?

Galatians 3:27 says, *"For as many of you as were baptized into Christ have put on Christ."* This verse tells us the truth that Jesus was crucified after taking on all the sins of the world through His baptism. He was resurrected from the dead after 3 days and now sits at the right hand of God. He became the Lord of Salvation for all those who believe in Him.

If Jesus had not been baptized, if He had not bled on the Cross for us, He would not have become our Savior. We can be saved only when we believe in the gospel of the water and the Spirit.

Even the Son of Moses

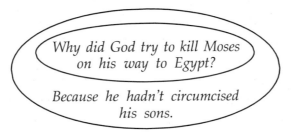

*Why did God try to kill Moses
on his way to Egypt?*

*Because he hadn't circumcised
his sons.*

Dearly beloved, you are listening to the secret of the redemption of all your sins through the water and the blood of Jesus. It is a wonderful blessing to be able to listen to these words of God.

Is it just the blood of Jesus Christ? In the time of the Old Testament, people became the descendants of Abraham through circumcision and the blood of the lamb of the Passover. Now we become people of God by believing in the baptism of Jesus and His blood. God has shown us the proof of this in the Old Testament through Moses.

To save the people of Israel, God spoke to Moses and told him to bring His people out of Egypt. So Moses, with the permission of his father-in-law Jethro, left the land of Midian and headed for Egypt with his wife and sons. When he set his family on a donkey, the Lord met him at his encampment and sought to kill him.

But his wise wife Zipporah knew the reason for this. She picked up a sharp stone and cut off the foreskin of her son and cast it at Moses' feet and said, *"Surely you are a husband of blood to me!"* So God let him go.

This was His way of saying that He would surely kill anyone, even the son of Moses, if he was not circumcised. To the people of Israel, circumcision was the sign of the covenant of God. They knew that God would surely cut off any one from His people, even the son of the leader, if he remained uncircumcised. Therefore, so as to avoid cutting off his son, God had alerted Moses in this way.

The Bible says that the reason Zipporah removed her son's foreskin and cast it at Moses' feet saying *"You are a husband of blood!"* was to accede to God's demand for circumcision (Exodus 4:26).

Anyone who was not circumcised among the Israelites had to be cut off from his people. Only those who were circumcised were allowed to eat the meat of the lamb of the Passover and join in the service as the people of God.

The apostle Paul was a Hebrew. He was circumcised 8 days after his birth, studied under the Great rabbi, Gamaliel, and understood exactly why Jesus Christ was baptized at the Jordan and why He had to be crucified. So the apostle Paul wrote about the baptism of Jesus in all his Epistles.

The apostle Paul also talked often about the blood of Jesus as the completion of our salvation. The blood was only the final stage of His redemption while the true spiritual circumcision was the baptism of Jesus. It is no use stressing the blood of Jesus without His baptism.

The apostle Paul talked often about the Cross of Jesus directly. Why was this so? Because it is the final proof of our salvation. If Jesus had taken all the sins of the world on to Himself but failed to bleed on the Cross to receive the judgment for us, we would not have been completely saved. That is why the apostle Paul talked about the Cross so often. The Cross is the final step in our salvation.

If the truth of salvation had been handed down to this generation without distortion, there would by now have been many more people without sin. But unfortunately, the truth has been lost over time and many people only know about the Cross without realizing the true meaning of His baptism.

Because they have faith only in the empty shell of the gospel, they will remain sinners no matter how many years they fervently believe in Jesus. They will still be sinners after 10 years, even after 50 years of religious life.

MY TESTIMONY

Does God consider sinners righteous?

No. He is just. The righteous are those who are free of sin, having passed all their sins on to Jesus through His baptism.

I began to believe in Jesus when I was 20 years old. Before that time, I had no idea how much sin I had committed in my life because I didn't know the law of God. I had lived in my own way without ever knowing God until that time.

Then I became sick. I was so sick that I thought I was going to die. So, I decided that I should at least be redeemed of all my sins before my death. Because I had heard that Jesus died for sinners like me, I decided to believe in Him. In the beginning, I was so full of joy and gratitude.

But the feeling began to fade after a while. After a few

years, I could not but commit new sins every day. I became a sinner over and over again. After 10 years, I was still a sinner, actually a worse sinner than before. I believed in Jesus for 10 years, and the fact that I was a sinner never changed. I was both a believer and a sinner.

Even though I sang, " ♪ *Weeping will not save me! Tho' my face were bathed in tears, that could not allay my fears, could not wash the sin of years! Weeping will not save me! ♪* " I cried every time I sinned.

"Dear God, please forgive me for this one sin. Forgive me this once, and I will never sin again." After I sinned, I used to pray for three days. I locked myself in a corner room and would pray while fasting for three days. Because my conscience was so heavy, I cried and asked for God's forgiveness. After three days, I would feel better and think I could be readmitted to His presence.

"Again, I have washed away my sins. Hallelujah!" So I came out and lived diligently for a while. But I soon sinned again and my desperation grew. I used to repeat this gloomy process again and again. It felt so great to believe in Jesus in the beginning, but the longer I believed, the higher my sins piled up like the dust in an unused room.

After 10 years, I had became a worse sinner than I started out to be. "Why did I believe in Jesus so early in my life? It would have been much easier to believe in Jesus if I had waited until I was 80, just before I died. Then, I wouldn't be conscious of sin and would have no need to repent every day." I thought that I should live in accordance with God's Will, but it was impossible. I felt like I was going out of my mind!

I began to search and search anew for God. I spent a lot of time studying theology but after a few years, my heart became even more barren. Before I started reading books on religious theories, I used to say I would live like Saint Damien, never sleeping comfortably in a warm bed. I had vowed that I would never indulge myself, instead devoting myself completely to the needy.

As I read about the life of this Saint, I vowed to live just like him. I tried to make an ascetic life for myself. I used to kneel on hard cement floors and pray for hours at a time. Then, I would feel as if my prayers had more meaning and I felt better about myself afterwards.

But after 10 years, I couldn't stand it any more. So I prayed to God. "Dear God in Heaven, please save me. I believe in You with all my heart. I know that I wouldn't change my devotion to You even if someone put a knife to my throat. But even though I believe in You with all my heart, why do I still feel empty inside? Why am I so frustrated? Why am I becoming a worse sinner than ever? I never thought about sin much before. I came to believe in You and now I wonder why I have become so much worse after having faith in You for years. What is the matter with me?"

It was at this point that I came to know the reason. I had believed in God without being saved from my sins. I didn't know the truth at that time, and it was enough to drive me crazy.

With sin in my heart, how could I tell others about the redemption of God's grace? How could I tell others to believe in Jesus? I prayed again and again. "Dear God, I will soon graduate from the seminary and be ordained as a minister. But if I become a minister laden with sin, how will I be able to tell other sinners about redemption? I am a sinner myself and when I read the Epistles of the apostle Paul I found out that if anyone does not have the Spirit of Christ, he is not a child of God. But no matter how eagerly I search, the Spirit is not in me. I felt that it was there in the beginning, but it has disappeared. What happened? Please tell me why, Lord."

In fact, the reason was that I had deceived myself into thinking I had been redeemed through simple belief in Jesus. I agonized over this for a long time.

God promised to show Himself to those who eagerly seek Him. He met me in His truth at last. I was still a sinner for 10 years after I began to believe in Jesus, but when I learned the secret of the baptism of Jesus and His blood, when I discovered the meaning of the circumcision in the Old Testament and the spiritual circumcision in the New Testament, when I realized and believed in the secret of salvation through the baptism of Christ, all my sufferings were over. My soul became as white as snow.

It will be the same for you. If you believe in the gospel of the baptism of Jesus and His blood, you will also become sinless. You may still be incomplete, but you will be righteous. When you take this truth into your hearts and make it known to others, they will also be saved and praise God, shouting out "Hallelujah!"

I want to congratulate all the brothers and sisters who have been redeemed. I praise Jesus for saving us from all our sins. Hallelujah! We have been happily redeemed of all our sins.

It is such a great blessing that we are unable to express all our happiness with mere words. Let us sing a song together. " ♪ *His name has become a secret, for we have not yet proclaimed the secrets to every creature. He was thrown out like the stones the builders rejected, but His name became most precious jewels in my heart ♪"*

THE BAPTISM OF JESUS AND HIS BLOOD IS MORE THAN ENOUGH TO SAVE ALL SINNERS FROM THEIR SINS

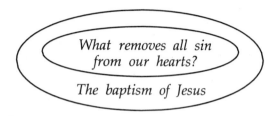

What removes all sin
from our hearts?

The baptism of Jesus

Jesus Christ washed away all the sins of the world through His baptism and blood. He spiritually circumcised us and made us His people. He is the God of the born again.

There is always judgment for sin. But Jesus was baptized and judged on the Cross to save us. With His blood, He saved us all and He was resurrected after three days. It was the Father God who raised Jesus from the dead.

The Life of Jesus is our life and the mark of our existence as the children of God. His baptism took away all our sins and the precious blood of Jesus on the Cross is proof that He bore the judgment on our behalf.

Dear friends, do you have this proof of the baptism of Jesus and His blood in your hearts? I ask you again. Does our salvation come only through the blood of Jesus? No. It comes through the baptism of Jesus and His blood together.

WHO IS A HERETIC?

Who is a heretic?

The one who condemns himself by failing to believe in the baptism of Jesus

Dear friends, are you still a sinner despite confessing your faith in Jesus every day of your life? If you are a sinner even though you believe in Jesus, then you are a heretic. Heresy is disbelieving in God's truth. Titus 3:10 talks about heresy, *"Reject a divisive man after the first ·and second admonition, knowing that such a person is warped and sinning, being self-condemned."*

A self-condemning person says, "Dear God! I am a sinner. I believe in You, but I am still a sinner. No matter what anybody says, I am a sinner and I know it to be the truth."

God says to him, "Are you still a sinner and not yet a child of Mine? Then, you are a heretic, and you shall be thrown into the fires of hell."

If you believe in Jesus without believing in the gospel of the baptism of Jesus in your heart, if you condemn yourself as a sinner and confess to God that your spirit is with sin, then you are a heretic before God.

WHO ARE THE TRUE BELIEVERS?

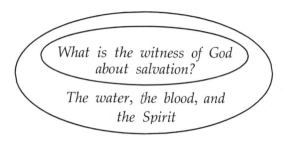

What is the witness of God about salvation?

The water, the blood, and the Spirit

All those who believe in the gospel of the baptism of Jesus and His blood, all those who have become the people of God, and all those who have had their sins washed away are the righteous. How can you still be a sinner while you believe in Jesus? A sinner cannot enter into the kingdom of God.

Those who became righteous by believing in Jesus have the witness of God in their hearts. The testimony is the baptism of Jesus and His blood. This work of salvation is what Jesus Christ did in this world.

Therefore, anyone who refuses to believe in the gospel of the baptism through which Jesus took away all our sins will be cut off from God.

Dear brothers and sisters in faith, do you accept in your hearts the gospel that the salvation of sinners is not just of the blood of Jesus alone, but also of the water which is the baptism of Jesus?

Whoever believes in the work that Jesus did in this world, and whoever accepts the water, the blood, and the Spirit, will be saved from all sin. This is the truth and the wisdom of the gospel of the water, the blood, and the Spirit.

Jesus completely cleansed us of all sin through His baptism so that all humankind could be saved through

Him. Now, if you truly believe in Jesus, there is no way for you to be a sinner.

Jesus resurrected us from the dead. He saved all the souls that had drifted away and become far from God owing to the deceptions of the devil. Jesus wants to find all the lost souls. God works through Jesus with the gospel of the water, the blood, and the Spirit. He has called us and we can be now redeemed and saved by Him.

Do you believe in this most profound truth? I am telling you that salvation is not just by the blood, but by both the baptism of Jesus and His blood on the Cross. Those who say that they have been saved only by the blood must recognize that they have sin in their hearts.

We all used to think that it was enough for our salvation to believe in the blood of Jesus. We thought so before, but now we should realize that it is not enough. We have been saved and born again by believing in Jesus Christ, who came by water, blood, and the Spirit.

Every sinner can be born again through faith in the baptism of Jesus and His blood (1 John 5:5-10). Let us praise God. Hallelujah! ⊠

SERMON 4

How to Make a True and
Correct Confession of Sin

For God so loved the world that He gave His only begotten Son, that whoever believes in Him should not perish but have everlasting life. For God did not send His Son into the world to condemn the world, but that the world through Him might be saved (John3:16-17).

How to Make a True and Correct Confession of Sin

<1 John 1:9>
"If we confess our sins, He is faithful and just to forgive us our sins and to cleanse us from all unrighteousness."

THE GOSPEL OF THE BLOOD IS A HALF GOSPEL

Can we enter the kingdom of heaven only with the gospel of the blood?

Never. We have to believe in the complete gospel (the gospel of the water and the Spirit).

1 John 1:9 applies only to the righteous. If a sinner who was not yet redeemed tried to atone for his daily sins according to the words of this passage and confessed his wrongdoing, his sins would not be expiated. Do you see what I'm saying here? This passage does not apply to sinners who are not born again.

There are many in this world who are not yet born again, but they take this passage from 1 John chapter 1 and pray and repent for their sins, hoping for forgiveness.

But can one who is not born again be redeemed completely of his sins through prayers of confession? This is an important point we have to consider and clarify before going any further.

Before you read 1 John, you have to decide whether the apostle John was a righteous man or a sinner. Let me ask you the following question. Was the apostle John a righteous man who was born again by believing in the gospel of the water and the Spirit, or was he a sinner?

If you say the apostle John was a sinner, you are biblically incorrect in your belief. If the apostle John was a righteous man who was born again when he believed in Jesus, it becomes clear that his faith was different from yours. You have to have the same faith as the apostle John.

Let me ask you another question. Was the apostle John writing those letters to the righteous or sinners? The apostle John was writing the letters to the righteous.

Therefore, if sinners who are not born again cited the words of 1 John 1:8-9 and applied them to themselves, it would be wrong. If you are to become righteous, confess your sins before God and believe the gospel of the water and the Spirit. Then the Lord will wash away all your sins with the gospel that has already cleansed the sins of the world.

The apostle John's faith is like this. In 1 John chapter 5 he says that he has faith in "the water, the blood, and the Spirit." Do you believe in Jesus Christ who came by water, blood, and the Spirit? Do you believe only in Jesus who came by the Cross, or by His baptism, His blood, and the Spirit?

Can you enter the kingdom of Heaven by believing

in the gospel of the blood only? If your faith is only in the gospel of the blood on the Cross, you understand only half the gospel. If you believe only in the blood on the Cross, no doubt you find yourself praying for forgiveness every day. The chances are that you believe your sins can be washed away simply through prayers of repentance.

But can your sins be washed away when you believe only in the blood on the Cross, repent and pray for forgiveness of your daily sins? If you are one of these people, then your sins will remain in your heart, because no one can wash away his sins through faith in the blood on the Cross alone, or daily prayers of repentance. If you are one of these people, then you do not yet know the gospel of the water and the Spirit, and your faith is incomplete.

The apostle John was born again because he believed in the gospel of the water and the blood and the Spirit. But you believe only in the blood on the Cross. When you do not have a clear idea of the gospel yourself, how can you lead others to salvation? You are not born again yourself, but are trying to atone for your sins through prayers of repentance. This path will never lead anywhere.

No matter how hard someone prays and repents, his sins cannot be washed away from his heart. If you feel sometimes that your sins have been washed away, it is only your imagination and the power of your emotions. If you pray and repent, you might be able to feel refreshed for a day or so. But you can never become free of your sins in this way.

Sinners pray and repent, hoping to be saved from their sins. That is why they are still sinners even after believing in Jesus for a long time. They do not know the gospel of the water and the Spirit. If you believe in Jesus but have not yet been born again, you might be one of these people. If you are trying to atone for your sins by praying and repenting every day, that is a clear testimony that you are not yet born again. You have to decide whether to believe in the gospel of the water and the Spirit as the Apostle John did, or to put your faith in your own thoughts and emotions. One is the clear truth, and the other is untruth.

The true gospel according to the Bible is that Jesus was baptized and took away the sins of the world once and for all and received the judgment for all sinners on the Cross. If someone believes in the baptism of Jesus and His death on the Cross, he shall be saved at once from all his sins. On the other hand, if someone tries to wash away his transgressions with prayers of repentance, he will never become free of his sins. Do you think you can remember all your daily sins? Does God take care of sins for which you have not repented? Are prayers of repentance a clear solution to the problem of daily sins? The only answer to these questions is no.

True Repentance and the Purpose of Confession

What are the limits of confession and good works?

Although we have to confess our sins throughout our lives, we can never be saved simply by confessing to our transgressions and doing good deeds.

Repentance in the Bible means turning back from the wrong faith to the true faith, and for the righteous, it means acknowledging one's wrong doing and coming back into the light of the gospel.

If you are a sinner now, you should make a confession like the following: "Dear God, I have sinned and I deserve to be sent to hell. But I long to be saved from my sins. Please save me from all my sins. I am not yet born again, and I know am bound for hell." This is a correct confession.

Then what kind of confession should a born again make? "Dear God, I have committed the sin of following my flesh. I believe that Jesus was baptized by John the Baptist and saved me from all my sins, even the sins I have just committed, whereas I should have had to die for my sins. I thank the Lord that He has saved me with the water and the blood." The confessions of the born again and those not born again are different.

We should all have the same faith as the apostle John. If you try to hide your sins behind the confession that is for the righteous, then you will never be saved from death, which is the wages of sin.

All sinners who are not born again should stop hiding behind prayers of confession and start believing in the true gospel of the water and the blood and the Spirit. They should learn the faith of the apostle John and thereby earn salvation.

Sinners do not realize how terrible the judgement for their sins will be. The most terrible sin before God is not to believe in the gospel of being born again of water and the Spirit.

All those who believe in Jesus but are not yet born again should confess before God, "Lord, I am a sinner to be thrown into the burning fires of hell," while refraining from saying, "Lord, please wash away my sins." When a sinner takes into his heart the gospel that Jesus saved him through His baptism at the Jordan and His blood on the Cross, he can be freed from all his sins. This is a the kind of confession a sinner should make in order to be saved from all his sins before God.

A sinner has only to confess that he has not yet been born again and believe in the gospel of the water and the Spirit. Then he will be saved at once. By the gospel of the water and the Spirit, the salvation of all sinners was completed. *"Nor is there salvation in any other, for there is no other name under heaven given among men by which we must be saved" (Acts 4:12).* God saved all sinners from their sins by having His Son, Jesus, baptized by John the Baptist and die on the Cross.

The Lord washed away all the sins that people commit with their flesh and their hearts from their birth to their death. We have to believe in the true gospel to be saved. It is the only way we can be freed from all our sins and become truly sanctified. We can become righteous once and for all when we believe in the true gospel of the water and the Spirit.

Jesus was baptized, took away the sins of the world, paid for them on the Cross with His life, was resurrected after three days and now sits at the right hand of God. This is the ultimate truth.

We should all make this confession. "Lord, I cannot help but sin till the day I die. I was born a sinner from the womb of my mother, and owing to all the sins I have committed, I should be thrown into the burning fires of hell. For this reason, I want to believe in Jesus, who came by water, blood, and the Spirit and became my Savior."

Just as it is written in Matthew chapter 3, Jesus took away the sins of the world, including all the sins we commit until the day we die, when He was baptized at the Jordan river. *"You shall know the truth and the truth shall make you free" (John 8:32).*

If Jesus saved us only from original sin and told us to solve the problem of our own sins by ourselves, we would be in constant agony. But Jesus freed us from all our sins with His baptism and blood. What do we have to be worried about? When we believe in the baptism of Jesus and His blood on the Cross, and thank the Lord, the Spirit dwells in our hearts.

Do you believe in Jesus? Do you believe the Spirit dwells in you? All your sins were passed on to Jesus when He took away the sin of the world with His baptism. He was later judged for our sins on the Cross, freeing us from eternal damnation. This is the true gospel.

THE CONFESSION OF THE RIGHTEOUS

What is true confession of the righteous?

To confess that they sin every day but to have faith in the fact that Jesus washed away their daily sins about 2000 years ago.

1 John 1:9 says, *"If we confess our sins, He is faithful and just to forgive us our sins and to cleanse us from all*

unrighteousness." This means that someone who decides to believe in the gospel of the water and the Spirit must confess his sins, saying, "Lord. I cannot help but sin all my life but I know I can't be saved from all my sins through prayers for forgiveness. I believe the wages of sin is death and nothing except the baptism of Jesus and His crucifixion could wash away all my sins. I confess I sinned today but I believe Jesus already washed away the sin that I committed today at the Jordan 2000 years ago." If such a person prays in this way, the problem of sins on his conscience will be solved at once.

Those who are already born again have only to confess their sins. They only confirm that Jesus has already washed away whatever sins they commit. Because Jesus was baptized and died for sinners 2000 years ago, no matter how weak they are, all their sins were completely washed away.

The text we have read today is a very good one for the righteous. But if a sinner takes this verse and uses it in the wrong way, he will end up in hell. Nonetheless, it is one of the most frequently misused passages in the Bible. It has for a long time caused great misunderstanding among Christians.

There is a saying that an inept doctor may kill his patients. When an inept doctor tries to do more than he is capable of, he may end up killing his patient.

It is a rule of life that someone has to be well trained and become experienced to perform his duties well. It is the same with the world of faith. Those who teach the word of God have to convey the truth as it is written both accurately and clearly, and those who learn from them should have faith in what they are taught.

If preachers teach their followers wrong doctrines, or if believers learn the Bible incorrectly, it will only result in judgment and hell for both of them. Only the born again can teach the Bible correctly. Even good medicine can kill patients if it is prescribed incorrectly, and it is the same with teaching and learning the word of God. It is as essential as fire in our lives. But just as it would bring on disaster if fire were put in the hands of children, the word of God can bring terrible disaster in the wrong hands.

We have to discern the difference between confession of the righteous and that of sinners. 1 John 1:9 is for the righteous. When a righteous person confesses his sins before the Lord with faith, he is freed of them because Jesus already washed away all sin about 2000 years ago.

It is wrong for sinners to believe their sins are washed away every time they pray for forgiveness. When one is not born again, can his sins be washed away just by confessing?

God is just. He sent His only begotten Son to this world and had Him take away the sins of the world through His baptism and save all those who believe in the water of His baptism and His blood on the Cross. Therefore, when a righteous person confesses his sins, God tells him that Jesus already took away all sin about 2000 years ago. Such a person thus confirms that he has no sin in his heart, even though his flesh still sins. ✉

SERMON 5

The Fallacy which lies in the Theory of Predestination and Divine Election

For the wrath of God is revealed from haven against all ungodliness and unrighteousness of men, who suppress the truth in unrighteousness (Romans 1:18).

The Fallacy which lies in the Theory of Predestination and Divine Election

<Romans 8:28-30>

"And we know that all things work together for good to those who love God, to those who are called according to His purpose. For whom He foreknew, He also predestined to be conformed to the image of His Son, that He might be the firstborn among many brethren. Moreover whom He predestined, these He also called; whom He called, these He also justified; and whom He justified, these He also glorified."

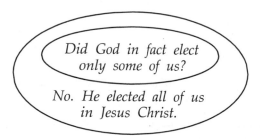

Did God in fact elect only some of us?

No. He elected all of us in Jesus Christ.

The theological theory of predestination and divine election, which is one of the basic theologies which make up Christian doctrine, has led many who want to believe in Jesus to misunderstand the word of God. This misguided theory has caused much confusion.

What untrue theologies say about predestination is that God elected the people He loves while condemning those He dislikes. This means that some who were elected are born again of water and the Spirit and accepted into Heaven while the others who were not elected are destined to burn in hell.

If God in fact elects only some of us, we cannot help but agonize over the question, "Was I elected for salvation?" If we were not elected, it would be useless for us to believe in Jesus. Thus this theory has made many people more concerned with whether they were elected by God than with faith itself.

If we believe this how can we be free of doubts and believe only in God? How do we confirm that God really elected us? He would be God only to those elected, even though He says, *"Is He the God of the Jews only? Is He not also the God of the Gentiles? Yes, of the Gentiles also" (Romans 3:29).*

Because many people misunderstand the meaning of predestination and divine election, they fear they will be destroyed even though they believe in Jesus.

Ephesians 1:3-5 says, *"Blessed be the God and Father of our Lord Jesus Christ, who has blessed us with every spiritual blessing in the heavenly places in Christ, just as He chose us in Him before the foundation of the world, that we should be holy and without blame before Him in love, having predestined us to adoption as sons by Jesus Christ to Himself, according to the good pleasure of His will."*

Therefore we should review the concept of theological predestination and divine election. We should first understand what the Bible says about predestination and divine election and strengthen our belief in salvation through the water and the Spirit.

What does Romans tell us? Some theologians developed the unfounded theory of "unconditional election." Is theology God, then? Theology itself is not God.

Even before the creation of the world, God chose all of humankind in Jesus Christ and made up His mind to save all of us by making us righteous. Jesus loves us unconditionally. Don't make Him a discriminating God. Unbelievers have faith in their own thoughts but believers put the basis of their faith in the written word of God.

DIVINE ELECTION IN THE OLD TESTAMENT

Is the theory of unconditional election true?

No. Our Lord is not such a narrow-minded God. God chose all sinners in Jesus, not just a select few.

In Genesis 25:21-26, we read about the two sons of Isaac, Esau and Jacob. God chose Jacob while the two sons of Isaac were still in their mother's womb.

Those who misunderstand the word of God take this as the basis of the theory of unconditional election. This is like mixing a god of fate into Christianity.

If we believe that God chooses us on the basis of "unconditional election" and not in Jesus Christ, then it is the same as if we worship a god of fate and idols. God is not a god of fate. If we were to believe in a god of fate, we would be denying God's plan for us and falling into Satan's trap.

If people are not obedient to God's will, then they are nothing more than the beasts which are destined to perish. Since we believers are not beasts, we should become true believers who read and believe the truth written in the Bible. Not to think first of the written truth in the Bible is to deliver oneself over to Satan.

To have true faith, we should first think about the written truth in the Bible and follow the faith of those reborn in Christ.

Calvinism insists on limited redemption. This implies that the love of God and the redemption of the Lord do not apply to some. Can this be true?

The Bible says, *"God desires all men to be saved"* (1 Timothy 2:4). If the blessing of redemption only applied to some, many believers would give up believing in Jesus. After all, who would want to believe in such a narrow-minded God?

We have to have confidence that our God is not narrow-minded. He is the God of Truth, Love, and Justice. We have to believe in Jesus and the gospel of being born again of water and the Spirit and thus be saved from all our sins. Jesus is the Savior of all who are born again of water and the Spirit.

According to Calvinism, if there were ten people, some of them would be saved by God while the others would be left to be burn in the fires of hell. This is untrue.

It doesn't make any sense to say that God loves some and discards others. Imagine that God is here with us today. If He decided to elect those who are sitting on the right side while making up His mind to send all those who are sitting on the left side to hell, would we treat Him as God?

Wouldn't those who were discarded raise their voices in protest? All creatures would cry out, "How can God be so unfair?" Unconditional election is untrue because God elected all of humankind in Jesus Christ.

Therefore anybody who is called by God in the name of Christ is elected. Then, who does God call to Him? He calls sinners, not the righteous. God does not call those who regard themselves as the righteous.

God's blessing of redemption is for sinners and those who are damned to hell. Election means God's calls sinners in order to make them His righteous sons.

GOD IS JUST

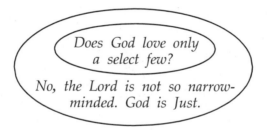

Does God love only a select few?

No, the Lord is not so narrow-minded. God is Just.

God is Just. He is not the God who loves only unconditionally elected ones. He called sinners in the name of Christ. Without salvation through the redemption of Jesus Christ and His forgiveness of sins, how could we know God's love and salvation? Never make Him an unjust God.

Try to find what is missing when you read Ephesians 1:3-5. *"Blessed be the God and Father of our Lord Jesus Christ, who has blessed us with every spiritual blessing in the heavenly places in Christ, just as He chose us before the foundation of*

*the world, that we should be holy and without blame before Him
in love, having predestined us to adoption as sons by Jesus Christ
to Himself, according to the good pleasure of His will."* What
is missing? The missing word is *"in Jesus Christ."*

Unconditional election in Calvinism does not corre-
spond with the words of the Bible. The Bible says, *"He chose
us in Jesus Christ before the foundation of the world."*

God chose all of humankind in Christ to be born again
of water and the Spirit. Those who cannot help but be born
sinners can be redeemed of sin and become His children.
He included all of humankind in the list of those to be
saved and elected them in Jesus Christ.

Because many theologians who insist on unconditional
election say that only some are chosen, many people are
trapped in the chaos of belief in completely irrational
doctrines. These false theologians say that God chooses
some and discards the others through unconditional
election, while the truth of His word is that God chose
all sinners in Jesus. Many people fall victim to untrue
doctrine owing to their superstitious beliefs.

Recognize that if we recognize that God decided to save
all of humankind in Jesus and that the remission of sin
applies to everyone who believes in Jesus. By doing so,
we can be saved from all our sins, become children of God,
become righteous people, have everlasting life, and have
confidence that God is Just.

DIVINE ELECTION IN THE STORY OF JACOB AND ESAU

Whom did God elect?
Only the chosen ones?

No. God elected all humankind in Christ.
So, whoever believes in Christ and
has no sin through the baptism of
Jesus is elected.

In Genesis 25:19-28, Esau and Jacob were struggling together within their mother Rebekah's womb. God said in Genesis 25:23, *"And the Lord said to her: 'Two nations are in your womb, two peoples shall be separated from your body; one people shall be stronger than the other, and the older shall serve the younger.'"*

Sinners turned these words into the theory of theological predestination and divine election, leaving many who believe in Jesus confused as to whether they were chosen or not! When they consider themselves chosen, they think that they are saved and lose interest in being born again of water and the Spirit.

The concept of unconditional election has turned many people who believed in Jesus away from redemption and condemned them to hell. It has also made God appear unjust.

Because so many theologians teach untrue doctrine which sprang from their own thoughts, many who believe in Jesus become insecure and wonder if they were chosen, or whether their redemption was predestined.

Of Jacob and Esau, whom did God elect? He chose

Jacob in Jesus Christ. In Romans 9:10-11, it is said that God called Jacob instead of his brother even though they were conceived by one man, as yet unborn, and had done nothing either good or bad.

God's purpose was to elect Jacob, not because of his works but because of His election. The Bible also tells us that Jesus came to call sinners, not just those who have lived upright lives.

All people, as descendants of Adam, are born sinners. David said he was a sinner from the time he was in his mother's womb and that he was born in iniquity. *"I was brought forth in iniquity, and in sin my mother conceived me"* (Psalms 51:5).

All people are born as sinners because of the sins of their ancestors. So everyone who is born in this world unwittingly becomes a sinner, acts as a sinner, and bears the fruits of sin.

A child who has not yet committed any sin is already a sinner because he was born with the seed of sin. He has evil thoughts, adultery, fornication and murder in his heart. He was born with his ancestor's sins. All people are sinners even before they are born.

The reason God made us infirm is as follows. Humankind is God's creation, but the Lord had plans to make us His children by saving us from sin. That is why He allowed Adam to sin.

When we became sinners as a result, God sent Jesus to this world, allowing His only begotten Son to take away all the sins of humankind through His baptism.

God's intention was to redeem humankind through the baptism of Jesus and His blood on the Cross and to give them the power to become His children by believing in

Jesus. He allowed Adam to sin on the promise of washing away all sin in Christ.

Sinners who believe in false doctrine say, "Look at Jacob and Esau. He chose one and discarded the other unconditionally." God didn't elect us unconditionally, but elected us in Jesus Christ. We only have to look up the written words in the Bible. Romans 9:10-12 says, *"And not only this, but when Rebekah also had conceived by one man, even by our father Isaac (for the children not yet being born, nor having done any good or evil, that the purpose of God according to election might stand, not of works but of Him who calls), it was said to her, 'The older shall serve the younger.'"*

God chose Jacob in Jesus. Jacob was a model of sinners who are unworthy and bereft of their own righteousness. Ephesians 1:4 says God chose us in Him.

Who did God call? He called Jacob because he knew that he was sinful and unrighteous before God and he relied on God. He called Jacob in the name of His own Son Jesus and redeemed him with the gospel of the water and the blood to make him His child. So, God called Jacob and blessed him with redemption.

He called sinners to make them righteous through redemption in Jesus. That is God's plan.

THE FALSE DOCTRINE OF UNCONDITIONAL ELECTION

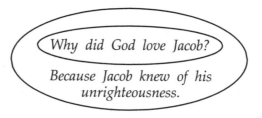

Why did God love Jacob?

Because Jacob knew of his unrighteousness.

I recently read a book based on a story of unconditional election. A young man had a dream. An old woman appeared in the dream and told the young man to come to a certain place, and he went. Then the old woman told him that he was chosen by God.

He asked the old woman how could God have elected him when he doesn't even believe in God? She told him that God unconditionally chose him despite his faithlessness.

This is untrue. How could God arbitrarily condemn some people to hell and choose others for salvation? God elected everyone in Jesus.

Theological election theory that excludes Jesus is false. It is untrue. But many theologians insist that God chose only some of us. That is not true. God wants to save everyone in Jesus. Only those who don't believe in the redemption of the water and the Spirit in Jesus will not be saved.

God predestined all humankind for salvation through His Son, Jesus, and intended to make us His children even before He created the world. He planned to save humankind from all the sins of the world through the redemption of Jesus Christ. This is the truth as it is written in the Bible.

The righteous who are reborn in Christ are the chosen ones. But theologians insist that God chooses only some of us. They say, for example, that Buddhist monks are among those who God did not choose. But God also elected them in Jesus.

If God unconditionally elected some without Jesus, we would not need to preach the gospel. If God had planned to elect someone without Jesus, sinners would not need to believe in Jesus. How then could His words of Love, Truth and Deliverance be fulfilled?

Would there be any reason for the servants of God to preach the gospel in this world? Does it make any sense that God has already unconditionally elected the redeemed and the damned without Jesus?

The reason God chose Jacob in Jesus, the reason He loved Jacob and hated Esau is that He already knew before they were created that Jacob would believe in Jesus and Esau would not believe in Him.

There are many sinners in this world who believe in Jesus. Some of them are like Esau and the others are like Jacob.

Why did God love Jacob? Jacob was unrighteous and knew of his unworthiness. Therefore he admitted that he was a sinner before God and asked for His Grace. That is why God saved Jacob.

But Esau relied more on himself than the Lord and didn't hunger for the Grace of God. So God said He loved Jacob and hated Esau. This is the word of truth.

God predestined us all for salvation in Jesus. All sinners have to do is to believe in Jesus. Then God's Truth and Justice will be instilled in their hearts. We sinners can

do nothing but believe with all our hearts in being saved
through Jesus. All we have to do is believe in redemption
through Jesus.

THE FALSE GRADUAL SANCTIFICATION THEORY

Is it true that a sinner can gradually become righteous?

No. It is impossible. Once for all, God made sinners righteous and without blemish through the redemption of His baptism and His death on the Cross.

Satan deceives sinners with the gradual sanctification
theory so that they cannot be saved from their sins. Gradual
sanctification means that sinners gradually become holy
after they believe in Jesus.

The theory goes like this. Sinners cannot become
righteous once for all but are saved only from original sin
when they believe in Jesus. Actual sins are washed away
through daily prayers of repentance and people gradually
become sanctified.

The crux of this theory is gradual sanctification. It
sounds great that someone can believe in Jesus and
gradually become a holier Christian. This theory has
deceived many Christians over the years, making them feel
secure. That's the reason why there are so many
holier-than-thou Christians in Christianity.

They think that one day they will simply be changed

and sin no more. But they live out their lives as sinners and will be judged as sinners before God after they die.

Read the true word in the Bible. In Romans 8:30, *"Moreover whom He predestined, these He also called; whom He called, these He also justified; and whom He justified, these He also glorified."*

And in verse 29, *"For whom He foreknew, He also predestined to be conformed to the image of His Son, that He might be the firstborn among many brethren."* At first glance it seems there are steps to becoming righteous. But the Word tells us that righteousness was granted once for all.

"Whom He called, these He also justified." Jesus called sinners and made them righteous through His baptism at the Jordan and His death on the Cross.

Therefore one who believes in redemption in Jesus becomes a glorified child of God. It is the Grace of God to redeem sinners and glorify them in this name.

This is what God tells us. But some Christians tell us to look at Romans 8:30. "There are steps to becoming sanctified. Doesn't that mean we change gradually?" This is how they deceive. They tell people in the future tense that a sinner will become righteous with time.

But the Bible tells us not in the future tense, but in the past perfect tense that we have been made righteous once for all. There's a definite difference between the future concept and the past perfect one.

We should fully believe in the Bible. According to what is written, we can become children of God once and for all. This is totally different from the gradual sanctification theory.

The gradual sanctification theory says that only original sin is forgiven when we believe in Jesus. This suggests that we should lead a religious life and repent for our sins every day, so that when we stand before God we will become righteous.

Because many people believe in this theory, they still remain sinners even after they begin to believe in Jesus. That's why the gradual sanctification theory is untrue.

The Bible clearly tells us that we become righteous and children of God by faith. Just as babies come into the world, children of God also become sanctified as soon as they realize and believe in the redemption of Jesus. The false gradual sanctification theory sprang from lies.

THE COMPLETE DELIVERANCE FROM ALL SINS

What do we have to do to be completely sanctified?

We have to believe in the redemption of the water and the Spirit.

Romans 8:1-2 says, *"There is therefore now no condemnation to those who are in Christ Jesus, who do not walk according to the flesh, but according to the Spirit. For the law of the Spirit of life in Christ Jesus has made me free from the law of sin and death."* This tells us that God made all sinners righteous and delivered all who came to Jesus from the law of sin and death.

The Bible tells us about complete redemption in Hebrews 9:12. *"Not with the blood of goats and calves, but with His own blood He entered the Most Holy Place once and for all, having obtained eternal redemption."* This means that we who believe in Jesus are redeemed and admitted into Heaven.

We heard and believed the gospel of the redemption of the water and the Spirit in Christ Jesus and were forgiven for all our sins. But sinners who believe that they were only forgiven for original sin cannot truly be saved. In order to be sanctified for sins that they commit after they come to believe in Jesus, they feel that they should repent every day.

Their misguided faith leads them to hell. Their mistaken beliefs cause them to repent every day so as to free themselves from all their iniquities. That is not the true faith that saves us from hell.

If they had believed in Jesus and been redeemed once for all time, they would have become righteous and children of God. True redemption makes believers righteous and transforms them into children of God once and for all.

Even though believers are delivered from all the sins of the world, their flesh does not change until the day they die. But their hearts are soaked with the righteousness of God. We must never misunderstand this fact.

The Bible tells us that we are sanctified and become righteous when we believe in the gospel.

Let's look at Hebrews 10:9-14 to see the true gospel. *"Then He said, 'Behold, I have come to do Your will, O God.' He takes away the first that He may establish the second. By that will we have been sanctified through the offering of the body of Jesus Christ once for all. And every priest stands ministering daily and offering repeatedly the same sacrifices, which can never take away sins. But this Man, after He had offered one sacrifice for sins forever, sat down at the right hand of God, from that time waiting till His enemies are made His footstool. For by one offering He has perfected forever those who are being sanctified."*

"By that will we have been sanctified through the offering of the body of Jesus Christ once for all" Note that this is written in the present perfect tense and not in the future tense.

To be completely sanctified, all of us have to believe in the redemption of the water and the Spirit that Jesus gave us.

JESUS GRANTED ETERNAL REDEMPTION ONCE AND FOR ALL

Why is a man entitled to rejoice all the time? (1 Thessalonians 5:16)

Because Jesus took away all his sins, he cannot but become humble before Him and thankful for His Grace.

If we believe in the eternal redemption of Jesus, we become righteous all at once. The Bible says, *"Rejoice always, pray without ceasing, in everything give thanks"* (1 Thessalonians 5:16-18).

Rejoice always. How can we rejoice all the time? Those who receive eternal redemption once for all time can endlessly rejoice. Becausethey are free of sin, they are safe in the knowledge that Jesus took away all their sins at the Jordan. They become humble before Him and thankful for His Grace and can thus rejoice without ceasing.

"Blessed are those whose lawless deeds are forgiven, and whose sins are covered" (Romans 4:7). This doesn't mean that our sins are covered despite the fact they still exist in our heart. Our heart has been cleansed. Jesus completely washed away all his sins and saved us once for all time.

This eternal redemption is referred to in the New Testament. When Jesus was baptized, He said, *"Permit it to be so now, for thus it is fitting for us to fulfill all righteousness" (Matthew 3:15).*

Just as goats or sheep took away people's sins through the laying on of hands in the Old Testament, Jesus took on all the sins of the world and purified humankind in the most proper and fitting way.

"It is fitting for us to fulfill all righteousness," said Jesus. Jesus was baptized in the most proper way and took on to Himself all the sins of humankind, thus saving us.

In Matthew 3:15, it is written that Jesus took away all the sins of the world. God's Justice was complete. We should not try to understand this eternal redemption. We should take it as His word of deliverance. *"Blessed is he whose transgression is forgiven, whose sin is covered" (Psalms 32:1).*

All the sins of the heart and flesh, Jesus washed them away when He was baptized by John the Baptist at the Jordan river. He was judged for the sins we commit in this corrupt and depraved world. After He took away all our sins, He died on the Cross.

Anyone who believes in this redemption of sin can become righteous and without blemish once and for all. Because Jesus lives eternally, anyone who believes in redemption in Christ remains righteous.

We can now stand before God with confidence and say, "How are You, Lord? I believe in Your one begotten

Son, Jesus Christ and I am also Your son. Thank You, Father. Thank You for accepting me as Your child. This is not through my works, but only through my faith in being born again of water and the Spirit in Jesus. You saved me from all the sins of this world. I believe what You said, *"For thus it is fitting for us to fulfill all righteousness" (Matthew 3:15).* Through the baptism of Jesus and His Cross, I have become Your child. For that I am grateful to You."

Have you passed all your sins on to Jesus? Were all your sins taken away by Him? The Bible tells us that thanks to the baptism of Jesus and His death on the Cross, sinners can become sanctified just by believing in them.

THE RELATION BETWEEN THE BAPTISM OF JESUS AND REDEMPTION

What's the relation between the baptism of Jesus and redemption?

The baptism of Jesus is the antitype of redemption prophesied through the laying on of hands in the Old Testament.

Imagine a man who lives as a sinner even though he believes in Jesus and prays in church, "Dear God, please forgive me for the sins I committed last week. Forgive me for these past three days' sins. O Lord, forgive me for today's sins. I believe in Jesus."

Let's assume that this man is forgiven for his daily sins by that prayer. But afterwards, he goes back to his everyday life and sins again. Then, he will become a sinner again.

Jesus became the Lamb of God and took away the sins of all sinners through His baptism and redeemed them by being crucified on the Cross. In order to be redeemed, sinners should believe the following to be redeemed.

All sin was taken away by Jesus when He was baptized by John the Baptist, thus fulfilling God's righteousness. All the sins of the world were washed away. Whoever believes in this truth is delivered. As it is written in Matthew 3:13-17, "for thus" was Jesus baptized by John the Baptist and made the Savior of all believers.

The gospel of truth tells us that Jesus took away the sins of the world once and for all. But the false theology tells us that we are redeemed every day. Which should we believe? Are we redeemed once and for all, or are we redeemed every day?

It is obvious that Jesus delivered us once and for all. The true belief is faith in the redemption of the water and the Spirit once and for all. Those who believe that we must be redeemed every day will never be delivered.

They should know that real redemption comes from believing that Jesus delivered us once and for all through His baptism and death on the Cross. All we have to do is give thanks to God and believe in this true gospel.

But those who are misguided in their faith say that we are only delivered of original sin, that we should be redeemed every day from actual sins, and that we can "gradually" become righteous. That is wrong.

The baptism of Jesus and His death on the Cross accomplished the forgiveness of sin once and for all. This is the truth. Our sins had to be passed on to Jesus through John the Baptist and Jesus had to die on the Cross in order for us to be saved.

Saying "forgive me" after we sin does not fit the Justice of God. The law of God says that the wages of sin is death. We should know that God is Just and Holy.

Those who pray to God, "I am sorry, please forgive me" after they sin do not know the Justice of God. They pray for forgiveness, but only to assuage their own conscience. Is it right that one sins everyday and consoles one's conscience by repeatedly repenting for his transgressions? The only way to be delivered is by believing in the baptism of Jesus and His blood on the Cross. We should believe it in our hearts. It is the only way we can avoid the judgment of God.

Let's think more about deliverance from sin. Hebrews 9:22 says, *"And according to the Law almost all things are purged with blood, and without shedding of blood there is no remission."*

According to the just Law of God, sins should be purged with blood, and without the shedding of blood there is no remission. This is the just Law of God. Without paying the wages of sin, there can never be remission.

The law of God is just. Jesus was baptized by John the Baptist and bled on the Cross to deliver us sinners. He took away all our trespasses through His baptism and bled on the Cross to pay for all our sins. He paid the wages of sin for us.

Is redemption granted once and for all, or every day?

Once and for all. Jesus took away the sins of all sinners through His baptism.

In Matthew 3:15, when Jesus was baptized in the most
fitting way, He washed away all sin through His baptism
and died on the Cross to deliver us from all the sins of
the world.

To ask for forgiveness every day would be the same
as asking Him to take away our sins and die all over again.
We should truly understand the just law of God. Jesus does
not have to die over and over again to deliver us from
our sins.

God considers it most insolent for those who believe
in Jesus to ask again and again for the forgiveness of actual
sins. "These insolent fools! They are asking My Son, Jesus,
to be baptized for a second time and die again on the Cross!
They believe in the redemption in Jesus and still call
themselves sinners! I will judge them with My just Law
and send all of them down into the burning pits of hell.
Are you willing to kill your own begotten son twice? You
are asking Me to kill My Son again because of your actual
sins. I have already killed My own Son to save you once
from all the sins of the world. So don't raise my ire by
asking me to forgive your actual sins again and again, just
believe in the gospel of the redemption of the water and
the Spirit."

Jesus tells those who remain sinners that they should
go to a church where true gospel is preached, abandon
false belief and receive redemption by overcoming untruth
with faith.

Now is the time for you to be saved by believing in
your heart. Do you believe?

THE RESULT OF FAITH NOT IN TRUTH, BUT IN WORKS

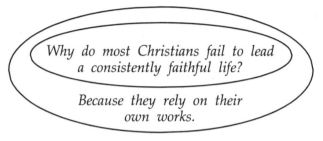

*Why do most Christians fail to lead
a consistently faithful life?*

*Because they rely on their
own works.*

Even sinners who believe in Jesus but are not delivered may shine brightly for 3-5 years. They are enthusiastic in the beginning, but their faith diminishes with time. If you believe in Jesus through your works, your enthusiasm will soon disappear, too.

The blind cannot see. So they rely on their other senses and accumulate knowledge in this way. When they feel tears welling up, they mistake it for a sign of remission. True remission is not a feeling.

The spiritually blind seek to regain their first love by vainly attending revival meetings, but they cannot recover the feeling. Remission of sin is similarly impossible to achieve. If they had believed accurately from the beginning, remission and His Grace would shine more brightly as days go by.

But untrue remission only shines in the beginning and loses its luster from then on. The glow of enthusiasm soon disappears because the spiritually blind failed to listen to the true gospel from the beginning.

Hypocritical scribes and Pharisees carry Bibles under their arms, memorize the Lord's Prayer and the Apostle's Creed, and pray all the time. They get promoted in the church and emotionally charged up but their sins accumulate and they are finally dismissed by God. Outside they are covered with the white plaster of religious fervor, but inside their minds are rotting with sin. This is the result of faith not in truth but in a religion based on works.

WE BECOME RIGHTEOUS BY FAITH

Has redemption of all sin in this world already been fulfilled?

Yes. It was fulfilled through the baptism of Jesus and His death on the Cross.

Let us now read Hebrews 10:16-18. *"This is the covenant that I will make with them after those days, says the Lord: I will put My laws into their hearts, and in their minds I will write them,' then He adds, 'Their sins and their lawless deeds I will remember no more. Now where there is remission of these, there is no longer an offering for sin.'"*

Now that we are redeemed through the water of Jesus' baptism and His blood on the Cross, we no longer need to atone for sin. It might sound strange when you first hear it, but it is in accordance with the words of the Bible. Are those the words of humankind? The Bible is the bench mark and the plumb line for measuring everything.

"After those days, I will put My laws into their hearts, and in their minds I will write them." How do you feel after being redeemed? Now that your heart is free of sin, you feel refreshed. You have become a righteous person and can

live in the light.

And the Lord says in Hebrews 10:17 *"Their sins and their lawless deeds I will remember no more."* He tells us that He will not remember the sins and lawless deeds of the redeemed. Why? Because Jesus was baptized in the most fitting way, *"for thus."* After taking away all sin, Jesus was judged on behalf of those who believe in Him.

Now that He has paid for all our sins, we may remember them but we need not feel guilty about them. We no longer have to die for our sins because Jesus washed away all sin and bled on the Cross for us.

Hebrews 10:18 says, *"Now where there is remission of these, there is no longer an offering for sin."* This means that He blotted out all the sins of the world. It also means that those who are reborn in Jesus no longer need to make any offering for sin.

"O God, please forgive me. The reason I believe in Jesus and yet still live in misery is that I have not yet been redeemed. I am a Christian, but my mind is completely rotten with sin." We don't need to pray like that.

Sinners commit sin without recognizing it as such. They do not know what sin is because they do not know God's Law of Truth. They only know that they should not sin in their conscience but they don't know what it is to sin before God. God pointed out to us that it is a sin not to believe in Jesus.

In John 16:9 He says what it is to sin before God. *"Of sin, because they do not believe in Me."* It is a sin before God not to believe in Him. John 16:10 says what righteousness is. *"Of righteousness, because I go to My Father and you see Me no more."* In other words, Jesus has already delivered this world from all sin, and thus He does not have to deliver us again with a second baptism and death on the Cross.

He called those who believe in redemption to sanctify and make them righteous. Redemption in this world was completed through His baptism and death on the Cross. No other redemption is needed to deliver sinners.

"For there is no other name under heaven given among men by which we must be saved" (Acts 4:12). Jesus came down to this world, was baptized by John the Baptist, and bled on the Cross to deliver all sinners. Believe this in your heart and be saved. Jesus sanctified you with the water and the Spirit.

Jesus swept away all sins from our flesh through the water and the Spirit. We are saved with faith. If we believe in the truth, if we believe in the gospel through Jesus Christ, we become righteous once and for all. The baptism of Jesus and His death on the Cross; these two elements constitute the fundamental truth.

VERSES THAT SINNERS USE AS THEIR SHELTER

> *Can we really be redeemed by confessing our sins, or have we already been redeemed?*
>
> *God granted redemption from sin once and for all.*

1 John 1:9 says, *"If we confess our sins, He is faithful and just to forgive us our sins and to cleanse us from all unrighteousness."*

It would be nice if we only needed to confess our sins

to be forgiven. With this in mind, some theologians came up with a great idea for a new doctrine. They insist that every time someone confesses his sins he can be forgiven. Isn't that convenient? But Jesus never said that we would be forgiven every time we confessed ourselves to God.

Can we really be forgiven by simply confessing our sins, or have we already been redeemed? Which do you believe? People who advocate this false doctrine believe that they are forgiven every time they confess their sins, but in fact, sin remains in their hearts because they do not know the true words of redemption. It makes no sense that sinners who believe in Jesus are forgiven whenever they pray for the forgiveness of actual sins.

For this reason, we ought to heed His Words on redemption and discriminate between truth and falsehood, regardless of what we may have been told.

Sinners misunderstand 1 John 1:9. They mistakenly think it concerns the forgiveness of daily sins. Let's read the teachings carefully. *"If we confess our sins, He is faithful and just to forgive us our sins and to cleanse us from all unrighteousness."* Do you think that we are only saved from original sin and that we must confess our actual sins for Him to be Faithful and Just and forgive them? These are only misguided thoughts which owe to the weakness of our flesh.

We realize that this is not true when we believe in the baptism and blood of Jesus. All sin was already washed away with His baptism and blood on the Cross a long, long time ago.

To believe according to the Spirit and to believe according to misguided thoughts are two quite different things. Those who believe according to their own thoughts feel the need to wash away their sins every day, but those who believe in the redemption of the water and the blood know that they were delivered once and for all through the baptism and blood of Jesus Christ.

Those who believe that they should confess every day to be redeemed anew are in fact committing the sin of not believing in redemption through the baptism and blood of Jesus.

Have you been redeemed once and for all through the baptism and blood of Jesus? Those who are not redeemed try to win salvation by confessing their sins every day. This still leaves the problem of what to do about the actual sins they will commit in the future.

They may try to confess in advance for their future sins. But in so doing they show a lack of belief in Jesus. These people are blind to the gospel of redemption. Jesus delivered us from sin once and for all with His baptism and blood, taking the judgment upon Himself. We are delivered simply by believing in Him.

If you think you must confess even your future sins to be saved, you are no different from unbelievers who know nothing of being born again of water and the Spirit. Sinners cannot be redeemed through confession.

Therefore if you confess honestly, "I am a sinner who is not yet redeemed," and then if you listen and believe in the gospel of His baptism and death on the Cross, God will deliver you from all your sins.

But if you don't believe in the gospel of redemption and only hide under repentant prayer, you will face terrible judgment when Jesus comes again to this world as the Just Judge.

Those who do not believe in the gospel of redemption

of the water and the Spirit will be judged. If they hide behind their confessions, they will face the judgment. So, don't wait for Judgment day. Believe now in the blessed gospel of the water and the Spirit.

THE PROPER CONFESSION AND THE TRUE FAITH

What is the proper confession for a sinner?

To confess that he still has sin and will go to hell unless he believes in the true gospel

God redeemed us once and for all. Here's a real-life example to illustrate what I'm trying to say. Let's suppose that a North Korean spy comes down to the South. He sees how prosperous we are, realizes that he has been deceived, and decides to give himself up.

After he going to the nearest police station, he could confess like this, saying, "I am a spy from the North," or "I came to the South to assassinate so and so, and blow up this and that, and I have already blown up this, but now I am giving myself up. Therefore I am not really a spy any more."

Is this a proper confession? If he really wanted to confess, all he would have to say is "I am a spy." This simple statement implies everything: that he is a bad person and has to be judged. With that simple statement, regardless of the mission he was assigned, he would be pardoned.

Just like that, if a sinner confesses before God, "I am a sinner not yet redeemed. I am destined to be thrown into hell and to be judged. Please save me" and believes in Jesus, he will be redeemed. Jesus was baptized and shed blood for us, and all we have to do is believe in salvation through Him to be saved.

Revelation 2:17 says, *"I will give him a white stone, and on the stone a new name written which no one knows except him who receives it."* The Bible says that only he who receives the true gospel will know the name of Jesus. Only one who is redeemed once and for all knows the secret of becoming righteous.

Those who do not know it will still be a sinner despite repentant daily prayers. To confess doesn't mean to pray for forgiveness every day. Even if someone had been a Christian for 10 years, he would still be a sinner if he asked for God's forgiveness every day. He would not yet be a child of God.

To be saved they would have to confess that they are sinners and believe in the redemption of Jesus. This is the true faith.

TO SIMPLY LIST ONE'S SINS IS NOT WHAT 1 JOHN 1:9 TELLS US ABOUT CONFESSION

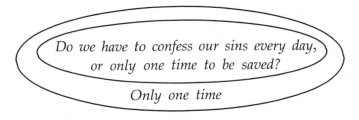

Do we have to confess our sins every day, or only one time to be saved?

Only one time

Can a thief and a murderer confess their deeds and be redeemed? Sinners are not redeemed just by confessing their sins. They can only be redeemed through the blessed gospel of being born again of water and the Spirit in Jesus. Some misguided Christians make confessions like this.

"Dear God, I quarreled with someone again today. I sinned. I deceived someone. I stole something."

If they went on like that God would say, "Be quiet, you sinner! So what?"

"Please keep listening to me. God, You told us to confess our sins. I beg for Your mercy."

This kind of praying is not what God wants to hear. He wants to hear the prayers of those who believe in the redemption of the water and the Spirit: Those who admit their sins and believe in the gospel of truly being born again.

Augustine said that he repented having suckled on his mother's breast. He thought that kind of confession would lead him to the kingdom of Heaven. We can only laugh at this. Just confessing one's sins won't do.

God says, "Be quiet and just tell Me if you have sinned. If you have, then stop talking about it. You have believed wrongly until now, so go to a church where the truth is taught. Believe in the gospel of redemption in the proper way and be redeemed. If not, I will come and judge you."

Repentant prayers for forgiveness and any other attempts to be saved through confession indicate misguided and untrue belief.

It is written in 1 John 1:9 that when we admit all our sins, the gospel of the water and the blood will deliver us from all sin.

"DEPART FROM ME"

What does it mean to practice lawlessness?

It means to believe in Jesus with sin in one's heart.

Christian sinners have misguided faith, practicing lawlessness before Jesus. *"Many will say to Me in that day, 'Lord, Lord, have we not prophesied in Your name, cast out demons in Your name, and done many wonders in Your name?' And then I will declare to them, 'I never knew you; depart from Me, you who practice lawlessness!'"* (Matthew 7:22-23)

Imagine that one who believes in untruth dies, comes to stand before God, and says, "How have You been, Lord? You seemed so beautiful when I was thinking about You down there, but You look even more beautiful up here. Thank you, Lord. You saved me. I believe that You look upon me as sinless even though I have sin in my heart. I came here since You promised to take me to Heaven. Now I will go over there where the flowers are in full bloom. Good-bye and I hope to see You around."

He starts toward the garden, but Jesus stops him. "Wait! Let's see if this man has sin in his heart. Are you a sinner?"

"Of course I have sin. But haven't I believed in You?"

"Do you have sin even though you believe in Me?"

"Sure, I have sin."

"What? You have sin? Bring me the Book of Life. And bring the Book of Works, too. Look up his name. See which book his name is in."

To be sure, his name is in the Book of Works.

"Now, confess the sins you have committed on earth."

The man tries not to, but God forces him to open his mouth and confess his sins.

"Yes, I committed such and such sins . . . "

He is all confused and cannot keep his mouth shut.

"All right, that's enough! He has done enough to be admitted to hell. He is more than qualified! Send him to that burning place."

He is not sent to the place where flowers are in full bloom, but to the place which is filled with fire and brimstone. He grinds his teeth while being taken to hell.

"I believed in You, prophesied in Your name, preached in Your name, sold my house to serve You, helped orphans, endured so much in Your name, prayed at dawn, treated the sick . . . I deserve to go to Heaven."

He grinds his teeth so much that he wears them down to nothing. When he arrives in hell, he sees all the Christians who didn't know the true meaning of redemption in Jesus. Those who misunderstand the gospel of redemption are discarded by Him.

SINS OF FALSE BELIEVERS ARE RECORDED IN THE BOOK OF WORKS

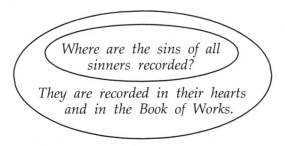

Where are the sins of all sinners recorded?

They are recorded in their hearts and in the Book of Works.

Whether we believe in Jesus or not, God destroys those who have sin in their hearts. If He finds even a speck of sin in someone's heart, that person is condemned to hell on Judgment day. God urges sinners who have not yet been redeemed to confess that they have not been delivered if they wish to achieve redemption.

The sins of a sinner are recorded in his heart. Those who are born again of water and the Spirit may remember their sin, but it is erased from their hearts. They are the righteous.

But those who are not reborn have sin in their hearts. Therefore they are sinners before God. Whenever they kneel to pray, their sins separate them from God and prevent Him from hearing their prayers. They are praying for this and that, but their sins remain. They end up confessing their sins, repenting for transgressions committed 10 years ago, 11 years ago, even 20 years ago.

Do they really have to repent again and again in their prayers? Why do they do it? They do not want to do so, but whenever they begin to pray, they remember that they are guilty before God. So they feel they have to atone for their sins before praying in earnest.

God wrote their sins with a pen of iron on the tablets of their hearts so that their sins could never be erased. As a result, they feel they have to confess their sins every time they come before God. So those who believe in only half of the complete gospel of Jesus have to live in misery as sinners and end up in hell.

In Jeremiah 17:1, it is written, *"The sin of Judah is written with a pen of iron; with the point of a diamond it is engraved on the tablet of their heart, and on the horns of your altars."*

Judah is the name of the royal tribe of the people of

Israel. The Bible holds up Judah to represent all humankind, so Judah means all people.

The sin of Judah is written with a pen of iron and engraved with the point of a diamond which can cut through steel. Diamond is the strongest material in the world. With a pen of iron with the point of diamond our sins are recorded.

Once they are engraved, they cannot be erased. They won't be erased unless we believe in the truth of the water and the Spirit.

It is of no use to be redeemed in their thoughts, to believe in Christian doctrines, to memorize theology, and to devote themselves to church if sin remains in their hearts.

As their sins can never be erased without the baptism of Jesus, sinners keep remembering them, saying, "Lord, I am a sinner," whenever they pray. They still have sin in their hearts however much they may try to have fellowship with God, taking on a lot of responsibility in church, and studying theology and doctrine.

So they go into the mountains, try in vain to speak in tongues and seek visions of burning flames, but it is all useless. If sin remains in your heart, you will never be at peace.

Our sin, as written in Jeremiah 17:1, is engraved on the horns of our altars. In Heaven, there is the Book of Life and the Book of Works. The sins of sinners are recorded in the Book of Works and thus people can never escape their trespasses. God records them in the Book of Works and the tablets of our consciences and shows them to us through His Law.

We should wipe these records clean by believing in the baptism of Jesus and the blood He shed for us and be saved.

Then we will be ready for everlasting life, and our names will be written in the Book of Life.

Is Your Name in the Book of Life?

> *Whose names are listed in the Book of Life?*
>
> *The names of those who have no sin in their heart are listed there.*

It is important to have your name listed in the Book of Life. If your name is not listed therein, what is the use of believing in Jesus? To be truly redeemed, you have to believe in being born again of water and the Spirit.

Jesus came down to this world, was baptized when He was 30 years old to wash away all the sins of the world, and died on the Cross to deliver us. As recorded in Matthew 3:15, Jesus was "for thus" baptized and crucified on the Cross. We have to believe this to have our names recorded in the Book of Life.

When people die and stand before God, God says, "See if this person's name is in the Book of Life."

"It is, Lord."

"Yes, you have suffered and shed tears on earth for Me, now I shall make it so that you will never have to do so again."

God bestows on such a person a crown of righteousness as a reward.

"Thank you, Lord. I am forever grateful."

"Angels, put a crown on this person."

"Lord, it is more than enough that You have saved me.
The crown would be just too much for me. Thank you.
I am so grateful that You saved me. I am more than satisfied
just to live in Your presence."

"Angels, kneel down and take this 10,000th son of Mine
on your back."

The angels answer, "Yes, Sir."

"Please get on my back."

"It's so comfortable. Am I doing this right? Let's get
going."

The angel takes careful steps.

"Would you like to go for a walk?"

"Wow, it is so beautiful here. How big is this place?"

"I have been going all over the place for several billion
years, but I have yet to find its end."

"Is that true? I must be getting heavy for you. You can
put me down now."

"We never run out of energy up here."

"Thank you, but I want to stand on the ground of the
kingdom of Heaven. Now where are all the righteous who
arrived before me?"

"They are over there."

"Let's go over."

Hallelujah! They hug each other and smile and live
happily ever after.

Now imagine that a man who believes in Jesus but is
still a sinner dies and stands before God. He also says that
he believes in Jesus and admits that he is a sinner.

God says, "See if this man's name is written in the Book
of Life."

"It is not in the Book, Lord."

"Then look in the Book of Works."

"His name and his sins are in here."

"Then send this man to the place where he will never have to worry about the cost of fuel, and let him live there forever."

"Oh, Lord, it is so unfair..."

He says it is unfair. Why should he be sent to hell even though he believed in Jesus so fervently?

The reason is that he was deceived by Satan and he only listened to half the truth of the gospel. If we misunderstand the true meaning of the redemption of Jesus, we will end up in hell, too.

This man believed in Jesus, yet he was deceived by Satan and thought he was a sinner. If he had heard the true gospel, he would have realized that his belief was wrong. But he failed to believe due to his egotistical attachment to his own mistaken beliefs.

If you want to go to the kingdom of Heaven, you must believe in being born again of water and the Spirit. As it is written in Matthew 3:15, "for thus" Jesus took away all the sins of the world. You must believe in the salvation of the water and the blood.

Whose names are recorded in the Book of Works?

The names of those who have sin in their heart are recorded there.

If you choose to believe anything, like a good-natured person who never refuses another's request, you may end up in hell. There are many good-natured people in hell, but in Heaven, there are true fighters who fought for what they believe in.

Those who are in Heaven knew that they were sinners who were destined to go to hell and gratefully believed that their sins were washed away through the baptism and the blood of Jesus.

It is said that there are mounds of ears and mouths in Heaven. Because many people believe in the redemption of Jesus with only their mouths or ears, God throws the rest of their bodies into the burning fires of sulphur.

Imagine that one who believes in Jesus but still has sin in his heart stands before God and says, "Lord, people called me righteous because I believed in Jesus, even though I still had sin in my heart. I believed that You would also look on me as sinless. That is what I learned and what I believed. I only believed as many people do. It was the most widely accepted belief where I come from."

The Lord replies. "I cannot forgive those who have sin in their hearts. I washed away all your sins with the blessing of being born again of water and the Spirit. But you refused to believe in it. Angels! Throw this insolent man into the fires of hell."

Anyone who believes in Jesus but still thinks he has sin in his heart will end up in hell. Listen to the true gospel of redemption and be delivered from all sin. Otherwise, you will burn in hell.

To say that you are sinless when you have sin in your heart is to deceive God. We can see how much difference there is between sinners and the righteous in the end. You will realize why I implore you to be redeemed.

You will see the difference between those who believe in complete redemption (the baptism of Jesus and His death on the Cross) and those who do not when you stand on the crossroads to Heaven and hell. It will make a big difference. Some will enter into the kingdom of Heaven but others will go to hell.

Do you believe in Jesus but still remain a sinner? Then you should realize that you ought to be born again of water and the Spirit. God sends those who have sin in their hearts to hell. Only those who believe in the complete forgiveness of sin can enter the kingdom of Heaven.

Do it right now. If you put it off, it may be too late. Be ready in advance. Before you end up in hell, believe in the redemption of the water and the Spirit and become sanctified.

Glory be to our Lord Jesus! We thank Him for His graciousness in making us sinners righteous. Hallelujah!

JESUS: THE ADVOCATE FOR THE RIGHTEOUS

Can our sins be blotted out by repentant prayer?

No, it is thoroughly impossible. That is one of the ways Satan deceives us.

Let's read 1 John 2:1-2. *"My little children, these things I write to you, so that you may not sin. And if anyone sins, we have an Advocate with the Father, Jesus Christ the righteous. And He Himself is the propitiation for our sins, and not for ours only but also for the whole world."*

Can you see what is written here? Is there anyone who

believes but still has sin in his heart? If you have sin in
your heart but tell God that you do not, you are deceiving
Him. And you are deceiving yourself, too.

But if you truly understand Jesus and believe what He
did to wash away all sins at the Jordan, you will be
completely free of sin. You can then say, "Lord, I was born
again with water and the Spirit in You. I have no sin. I
can stand before You without shame."

Then the Lord will reply. "Yes, you are right. As
Abraham believed in Me and believed himself to be
righteous, you are also righteous because I washed away
all your sins."

But consider a man who still has sin in his heart even
though he believes in Jesus. He says, "Because I believe
in Jesus, I will go to Heaven even if I have a little sin in
my heart."

He wants so much to be admitted to Heaven that he
tries to resist while standing before the judgment seat, but
he will still end up in hell. Why? He didn't know the blessed
gospel of being born again of water and the Spirit.

Everyone should confess that he is a sinner during his
days on earth. "I am a sinner. I will go to hell. Please save
me." A sinner is not redeemed with repentant prayers.
Rather, he has to admit that he is a sinner and accept the
redemption of the water and the Spirit to be delivered. He
can only become righteous through the redemption of the
water and the Spirit.

It is false gospel to insist that only original sin is
forgiven in Jesus and we should repent our actual sins to
obtain salvation. This leads us straight to hell. So many
believers doom themselves to hell by believing this false
gospel and this tendency is even more prevalent these days.

Would you know it if you had fallen into false gospel? Can you still be a debtor even after paying all your debts? Think about it. If you still consider yourself a sinner while believing in Jesus, can it be said that you believe in Him properly? Are you a believer and sinner, or are you a believer and a righteous man?

You can choose for yourself. You can either believe that all your sins are forgiven, or you can believe that you should repent every day for your transgressions. Your choice will determine whether you go to Heaven or hell. You have to heed the evangelist who tells you the true gospel.

Those who believe in false gospel still pray for the forgiveness of sins at every dawn prayer meeting, every Wednesday service, every Friday all-night prayer in a bid to wash away their sins.

"Lord, I have sinned. I have sinned this week," they say. Then they remember the sins of years ago and pray again for His forgiveness. That is defying the blessed gospel of being born again of water and the Spirit.

Our sins must be paid for with blood. Hebrews 9:22 says, *"Without shedding of blood there is no remission."* If you think you have sin, then are you asking Him to bleed for you again? Those who don't believe in the complete redemption are guilty of turning the redemption of Jesus into a lie. They are in fact insisting that Jesus did not deliver us once and for all and that He is a liar.

To be redeemed in Jesus, you have to believe in the truth of the redemption of the water and the Spirit. Can you really be forgiven for sins with hundreds, thousands, millions of prayers? The true gospel redeems us once and for all. Become righteous, go to the kingdom of Heaven, and live a righteous life for all time.

♪I live a new life in Jesus. The past is over and I have become a new creature. The wasted past has gone away. O, Jesus is my true life. I live a new life in Jesus. ♪

You live a new life in Jesus. Regardless of whether you do not look as handsome as you would like to, whether you are too short, or a little too fat around the middle, those who are blessed with the gospel of being born again of water and the Spirit live a happy life. What does it matter that your nose isn't the ideal shape, or that you are a little short? Because we are not perfect, we are saved by believing in being born again of water and the Spirit in Jesus. But those who are conceited will end up in hell.

Thank you, Lord. I always give thanks to the Lord. Because we believe in being born again of water and the Spirit, we will be welcomed in Heaven.

THE UNTRUTH LEADS US TO HELL

Who will receive a crown of righteousness in the end?

He who overcomes the untruth

The untruth tells us that we have to repent every day to be forgiven, but the gospel of the water and the Spirit tells us that we are already completely forgiven and all we have to do is believe it.

Which is the truth? Do we have to repent every day? Or is it right to believe that Jesus delivered us when He was baptized in the most fitting manner to take away all our sins? The truth is that Jesus took away our sins once and for all and in this proper way offered us salvation.

We have to triumph over the untruth in the spiritual war. Many people follow the untruth. *"And to the angel of the church in Pergamos write, 'These things says He who has the sharp two-edged sword: I know your works, and where you dwell, where Satan's throne is'"* (Revelation 2:12-13).

"To him who overcomes I will give some of the hidden manna to eat. And I will give him a white stone, and on the stone a new name written which no one knows except him who receives it" (Revelation 2:17).

Where numerous evil spirits dwell and untruth stands pretending to be truth, Satan appears as if he were a bright angel. God cannot help anyone who hears and knows the truth of salvation of the water and the Spirit but doesn't believe it. Such a person will surely end up in hell.

Everyone has to decide for himself whether to believe in the salvation of Jesus. Nobody kneels before you, begging you to believe and be delivered.

If you want to be saved from sin, then believe in the salvation of the water and the Spirit. If you feel thankful for His love in salvation and His grace in saving us, then believe it. If you are a sinner destined to go to hell, then believe in the water and the Spirit, the baptism of Jesus and His death on the Cross. Then you will become righteous.

If you think you are not a sinner, you do not have to be redeemed by believing in Jesus. Only sinners are delivered from all sins by believing in the gospel of being born again of water and the Spirit. Jesus is the Savior of sinners and Consoler of the troubled. He is the Creator.

He is the Master of Love.

I sincerely urge you to believe in the gospel of being born again of water and the Spirit. Believe in it. You can be sure that Jesus will be Savior, Friend, Shepherd and God to you. Sinners should believe in Jesus. If you don't want to end up in hell, you must believe it. God does not beg us to believe the gospel of salvation.

Do you want to be admitted to Heaven? Then believe in the gospel of being born again of water and the Spirit. Jesus says, "I am the way, the truth, and the life. Believe in Me." Are you saying that you want to be thrown into hell? Then do not believe. He says He has already prepared a place in hell for you.

God does not beg. A merchant welcomes people indiscriminately in a bid to sell his wares, but God gives the kingdom of Heaven for free only to those who are redeemed. God is Just.

People say that the end of the world is near. Yes, I also think so. And it is foolish not to believe in the true gospel of being born again of water and the Spirit.

Believe in the salvation of the blessed gospel of being born again of water and the Spirit. Let's go together to the kingdom of Heaven. Won't you go with me to the dwelling place of Jesus?

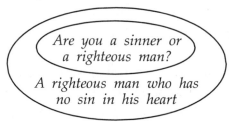

Let us read from Romans 8:1-2. *"There is therefore now no condemnation to those who are in Christ Jesus, who do not*

walk according to the flesh, but according to the Spirit. For the law of the Spirit of life in Christ Jesus has made me free from the law of sin and death."

Jesus took away all our sins through His baptism and His death on the Cross. He saved all sinners who had to be judged for their sins.

God's salvation consists of two things. One is the Law and the other is His Love. The Law teaches us that we are sinners. According to the Law, the wages of sin is death. We can't be saved by the Law. It only teaches us our sinful nature and fate. It lets us know that we are sinners.

To pay the wages of sin, Jesus came down to this world, took away all our sins and paid for them with his life to save us from judgment. It is the love of God that saved us from all sin.

We must triumph over the untruth. God gives the blessing of being born again of water and the Spirit to those who overcome the untruth.

We are saved by believing in Jesus. By believing in His words, we achieve righteousness and understand the truth. Believe in the truth of being born again of water and the Spirit in your hearts, and you will be saved. ✉

SERMON 6

The Changed Priesthood

Therefore it was necessary that the copies of the things in the heavens should be purified with these, but the heavenly things themselves with better sacrifices than these (Hebrews 9:23).

The Changed Priesthood

<Hebrews 7:1-28>

"For this Melchizedek, king of Salem, priest of the Most High God, who met Abraham returning from the slaughter of the kings and blessed him, to whom also Abraham gave a tenth part of all, first being translated 'king of righteousness,' and then also king of Salem, meaning 'king of peace,' without father, without mother, without genealogy, having neither beginning of days nor end of life, but made like the Son of God, remains a priest continually. Now consider how great this man was, to whom even the patriarch Abraham gave a tenth of the spoils. And indeed those who are of the sons of Levi, who receive the priesthood, have a commandment to receive tithes from the people according to the law, that is, from their brethren, though they have come from the loins of Abraham; but he whose genealogy is not derived from them received tithes from Abraham and blessed him who had the promises. Now beyond all contradiction the lesser is blessed by the better. Here mortal men receive tithes, but there he receives them, of whom it is witnessed that he lives. Even Levi, who receives tithes, paid tithes through Abraham, so to speak, for he was still in the loins of his father when Melchizedek met him. Therefore, if perfection were through the Levitical priesthood (for under it the people received the law), what further need was there that another priest should rise according to the order of Melchizedek, and not be called according to the order of Aaron? For the priesthood being changed, of necessity there is also a change of the law. For He of whom these things are spoken belongs to another tribe, from which no man has officiated at the altar. For it is evident that our Lord arose from Judah, of which tribe Moses spoke nothing concerning priesthood. And it is yet far more evident if, in the likeness of Melchizedek, there arises another priest who has come, not according to the law of a fleshly commandment, but according to the power of an endless life. For He testifies: 'You are a priest forever according to the order of Melchizedek.' For on the one hand there is an annulling of the former commandment because of its weakness and unprofitableness, for the law made nothing perfect; on the other hand, there is the bringing in of a better hope, through which we draw near to God. And inasmuch as He was not made priest without an oath (for they have become priests without an oath, but He with an oath by Him who said to Him: "The Lord has sworn and will not relent, 'You are a priest forever according to the order of Melchizedek'"), by so much more Jesus has become a surety of a better covenant. And there were many priests, because they were prevented by death from continuing. But He, because He continues forever, has an unchangeable priesthood. Therefore He is also able to save to the uttermost those who come to God through Him, since He ever lives to make intercession of them. For such a High Priest was fitting for us, who is holy, harmless, undefiled, separate from sinners, and has become higher than the heavens; who does not need daily, as those high priests, to offer up sacrifices, first for His own sins and then for the people's, for this He did once for all when He offered up Himself. For the law appoints as high priests men who have weakness, but the word of the oath, which came after the law, appoints the Son who has been perfected forever."

JESUS MINISTERED THE HEAVENLY PRIESTHOOD

Who is superior, the high priest Melchizedek or the earthly high priest of the order of Aaron?

The high priest Melchizedek

In the Old Testament, there was a high priest named Melchizedek. In the time of Abraham, Chedorlaomer and the kings allied with him, took away with them all the goods of Sodom and Gomorrah. Abraham armed his trained servants, who were born in his household, and led them into the war against Chedorlaomer and his allies.

There, he defeated Chedorlaomer, the king of Elam, and the kings allied with him and brought back his nephew Lot and his possessions. After Abraham returned from defeating his enemies, Melchizedek, King of Salem and the priest of God Most High, brought out bread and wine and blessed Abraham. And Abraham gave him a tenth of everything (Genesis chapter 14).

In the Bible, the greatness of the high priest Melchizedek and the high priests in his order is illustrated in detail. The high priest Melchizedek was "king of peace," "king of righteousness," without father, without mother, without genealogy. Having neither beginning of days nor end of life, but made like the Son of God, he remains a priest continually.

The Bible tells us to consider carefully the greatness of Jesus Christ, who was the high priest of the order of Melchizedek, by comparing the priesthood of Jesus of the New Testament and that of the high priest Aaron of the Old Testament.

The descendants of Levi became priests and collected a tithe from the people, that is, their brethren, even though they were descended from Abraham. But when Abraham gave tithe to the high priest Melchizedek, Levi was still in the loins of his father.

Were the priests of the Old Testament greater than Jesus? It is explained in the Bible. Is Jesus greater than the earthly high priests? Who should be blessed by whom? The writer of Hebrews talked about this from the beginning. *"Now beyond all contradiction the lesser is blessed by the better."* Abraham was blessed through the high priest Melchizedek.

How are we to live in our faith? Should we rely on the commandments of God through the sacrificial system of the holy tabernacle of the Old Testament, or should we rely on Jesus Christ who came to us as the heavenly high priest through His sacrifice of the water and the Spirit?

Depending on which interpretation we choose, we are either blessed or damned. Do we live according to the word of God and offer sacrifices every day, or do we choose to believe in the salvation Jesus has given us by offering

Himself once for all with water and blood? We have to choose one out of these two.

In the days of the Old Testament, the people of Israel looked up to the descendants of Aaron and Levi. In the days of the New Testament, if we are asked who is greater, Jesus or the priests of the order of Aaron, then, without question, we can answer that Jesus is greater. But while people know this fact clearly, few follow it in their faith.

The Bible gives us a definite answer to this question. It tells us that Jesus, who was of a different tribe from which no one had ever served at the altar, took over the heavenly priesthood. *"For the priesthood being changed, of necessity there is also a change of the law."*

God gave the people of Israel commandments and 613 detailed articles of the Law through Moses. Moses told the people to live according to the Law and commandments, and the people agreed to do so.

Why did God set aside the first covenant and establish the second?

Because man was too weak to live according to the first covenant.

In the Bible, the people of Israel took an oath to live by the commandments of God in the Pentateuch: Genesis, Exodus, Leviticus, Numbers, and Deuteronomy. God proclaimed each commandment to them and they said "Yes" to every commandment without hesitation.

However, we can see that after Deuteronomy, from Joshua on, they have never lived according to the commandments of God. From Judges on to 1 Kings and

2 Kings, they began to discredit their leaders, and afterwards, they had decayed as much as to change the sacrificial system of the holy tabernacle.

And finally in Malachi, they brought animals not fit to be offered despite God's instruction to offer one without blemish. They asked the priests, "Please overlook it. Please accept this one." Instead of offering sacrifices according to the law of God, they changed it arbitrarily.

The people of Israel never kept the law of God completely even once in the time of the Old Testament. They forgot and simply ignored the salvation revealed in the system. Therefore God had to change the sacrificial system. In Jeremiah, God said, *"I will make a new covenant with the house of Israel and with the house of Judah."*

Let's us look at Jeremiah 31:31-34. *"Behold, the days are coming, says the Lord, when I will make a new covenant with the house of Israel and with the house of Judah—not according to the covenant that I made with their fathers in the day that I took them by the hand to bring them out of the land of Egypt, My covenant which they broke, though I was a husband to them, says the Lord. But this is the covenant that I will make with the house of Israel after those days, says the Lord: I will put My law in their minds, and write it on their hearts; and I will be their God, and they shall be My people. No more shall every man teach his neighbor, and every man his brother, saying, 'Know the Lord,' for they all shall know Me, from the least of them to the greatest of them, says the Lord. For I will forgive their iniquity, and their sin I will remember no more."*

God said that He would make a new covenant. He had already made a covenant with the people of Israel, but they failed to live by the word of God. Thus, He decided to make a new covenant of salvation with His people.

They had taken an oath before God, "We will worship only You and live by Your Words and commandments." God had told them, "You shall have no other gods before Me," and the people of Israel had said, "Sure, we would never worship any other god. You are the only God to us. There can never be any other god to us." But they failed to keep their oath.

The core of the Law consists of the Ten Commandments: "Do not have any other gods before Me. Do not make for yourself any carved or craven image, or any likeness of anything and bow down to them nor serve them. Remember the Sabbath day to keep it holy. Do not take the name of the Lord your God in vain. Honor your father and your mother. You shall not kill. You shall not commit adultery. You shall not steal. You shall not bear false witness against your neighbor. You shall not covet your neighbor's house" (Exodus chapter 20).

It is also subdivided into 613 detailed articles which were to be kept throughout their lives. "What not to do to daughters, and what not to do to sons, what to do to stepmothers. . . ." The law of God commanded them to do all good things and not to do any evil things. These are the Ten Commandments and 613 detailed articles.

However, among all of humankind, there has not been even one person who could keep all the articles of His Law. Therefore God had to determine another way for them to be saved from all their sins.

When did the priesthood change? After Jesus came to this world, the priesthood changed. Jesus took over the priesthood from all the priests of the order of Aaron. He set aside the sacrifice of the tabernacles that was the inherent right of the priests of the order of Levi. He alone ministered the heavenly high priesthood.

He came to this world, not as a descendant of Aaron, but as the descendant of Judah, the house of kings. He offered Himself as a sacrifice through His baptism and His blood on the Cross and saved all of humankind from their sins.

By offering Himself, He made it possible for us to resolve the problem of sin. He washed away all the sins of humankind through the sacrifice of His baptism and blood. He offered for all time one eternal sacrifice for all sin.

ALONGSIDE THE CHANGE IN THE PRIESTHOOD THERE WAS ALSO A CHANGE IN THE LAW

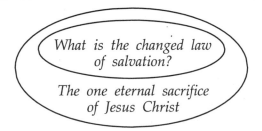

What is the changed law of salvation?

The one eternal sacrifice of Jesus Christ

Dear friends, the priesthood of the Old Testament was changed in the New Testament. In the days of the Old Testament, the high priest among the descendants of Aaron, of the house of Levi, offered the sacrifice to atone for the Israelites' sins over the past year. The high priest entered the Most Holy Place. He went before the mercy seat with the blood of the sacrificial animal. Only the high priest could go beyond the veil, which was the Most Holy Place.

But after the coming of Jesus, the priesthood of Aaron was passed on to Him. Jesus took over the eternal priesthood. He ministered the eternal priesthood by offering Himself, so that all of humankind could be saved from all their sins.

In the Old Testament, the high priest also had to atone for his sins by laying his hands on the head of the bull before he could minister for all his people. He passed on his sins by the laying on of hands, saying, "God, I have sinned." Then he killed the animal and sprinkled its blood on and in front of the mercy seat seven times.

If the high priest Aaron himself was not complete, you can imagine how infirm the people were. A son of Levi, the high priest Aaron himself was a sinner, so that he had to offer a bull to atone for his own sins and those of his family.

The Lord said in Jeremiah chapter 31, "I shall break the covenant. I have made the covenant with you, but you have not kept it. Therefore I shall set aside the covenant that could not sanctify you and give you a new covenant of salvation. I shall no longer save you through My commandments, but rather offer you salvation through the gospel of the water and the Spirit."

God gave us the new covenant. When the time came, Jesus came to this world in the likeness of man, offered Himself to take away the sins of the world and bled on the Cross to save us who believe in Him. He took away the sins of all of humankind through His baptism.

The law of God was set aside and replaced. The people of Israel could have been saved if they had lived according to the law of God, but they failed to do so. *"For by the law is the knowledge of sin" (Romans 3:20).*

God wanted the Israelites to realize that they were sinners and that the Law could not save them. He saved them through the law of salvation of the water and the Spirit, not through their works. In His infinite love, God gave us a new covenant by which we could be saved from all the sins of the world through the baptism and the blood of Jesus.

If you believe in Jesus without knowing the meaning of His baptism and blood, all your faith is in vain. When you do that, you are more troubled than when you did not believe in Jesus at all.

God said that He had to make a new covenant to save humankind from their sins. As a result, we are now saved not by the law of our works, but by the righteous law of salvation through the water and the blood.

This was His eternal promise and He fulfilled His promise for us who believe in Jesus. And He told us about the greatness of Jesus. He told us how great He is by comparing Him to the priests of the order of Aaron in the Old Testament.

We become special by believing in salvation through the water and the blood of Jesus. Please consider this carefully. No matter how learned and well spoken your pastor is, how can he be greater than Jesus? There is no way. We can only be saved through the gospel of the water and the blood, never by simply obeying the commandments of God. Because the priesthood was changed, the law of salvation was also changed.

THE SUPERIORITY OF THE LOVE OF GOD

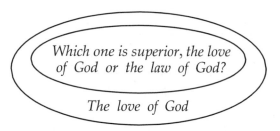

Which one is superior, the love of God or the law of God?

The love of God

We can only be saved when we believe in Jesus. Knowing how Jesus saved us, how great the love of God is for us. What then, is the difference between faith in the commandments and faith in the greatness of the love of God?

The legalists attach more importance on their own denominational doctrines and personal experiences than on God's word. However, true and complete spiritual faith in Jesus comes about by believing in the greatness of the salvation fulfilled through the water and the Spirit.

Even today, many people say that original sin is forgiven, but that they have to repent every day for their daily sins. Many people believe this and try to live their lives according to the commandments of the Old Testament. They are still unaware of the superiority of the salvation of Jesus that came by water and the Spirit.

In the Old Testament, the Israelites had to live by the law of God to be saved from their sins, but they couldn't be saved. Because the Lord knows our weaknesses and the fact that we are incomplete, He set aside His commandments. We can never be saved through our works alone. Jesus said that He would save us through His gospel of the water and the Spirit. He said, "I shall deliver all of you from your sins Myself." God prophesied thus in

Genesis.

"The Seed of woman shall bruise your head, and you shall bruise His heel" (Genesis 3:15). After Adam and Eve sinned and fell, they made garments of fig leaves in a bid to keep their sinfulness from God. But God called them and made garments of skin as a symbol of salvation. Genesis talks about two kinds of garments of salvation. One was made of fig leaves, and the other was made of skins. Which one do you think is better? Of course, garments of skins are better because the life of an animal was offered to protect man.

Garments of fig leaves soon wither away. As you know, a fig leaf looks like a hand with five fingers. So, to put on a garment of fig leaves means to hide one's sins behind good deeds. If you put on garments of fig leaves and sat down, the leaves would soon be torn to pieces. I used to make armor out of arrowroot leaves to play soldier when I was a child. But no matter how carefully I wore them, they would be torn apart by the end of the day. In the same way, humankind's fragile flesh makes sanctification impossible.

But the salvation of the water and the blood, the baptism of Jesus and His death on the Cross saved more than enough sinners to testify to the greatness of the love of God. That is how superior the love of God is to the law of God.

THOSE WHO STILL HAVE FAITH IN THE LAW OF GOD

Why do legalists make new garments with their works every day?

Because they don't know their works cannot make them righteous.

Those who make their garments with fig leaves are leading legalistic lives. These misguided believers have to change their garments on a regular basis. They have to make new garments every Sunday when they go to church. "Dear God, I sinned so much last week. But Lord, I believe that You saved me on the Cross. Lord, please wash away my sins with the blood of the Cross!" They sew up a new set of garments right then and there. "Oh, praise the Lord. Hallelujah!"

But they soon have to make another set of garments at home. Why? Because their old ones have worn out. "Dear Lord, I have sinned again over the last three days. Please forgive me." They make and wear new garments of repentance again and again.

In the beginning, the garments may last several days, but after a while, they need a new set every day. As they can never live by the law of God, they become ashamed of themselves. "Oh, this is so embarrassing. Lord, oh, Lord, I have sinned once agin!" And they have to make new garments of repentance. "Oh, Lord, it is so difficult to make garments of fig leaves today." They work so hard to sew up a new set.

Whenever such people call out to the Lord, it is to confess their sins. They bite their lips and call out to God, "Go~d!" and keep making up new garments every day. Then, what happens when they get tired of it?

Once or twice a year, they go up to the mountains and fast. They try and make stronger and more hard-wearing garments. "Lord, please wash away my sins. Please make me anew. I believe in You, Lord." They think it better to pray at night. So, they rest during the daytime and as soon as darkness falls, they hang on to trees with all their might, or go into dark caves and cry out to God. "Lord, I believe!" " ♪ I repent and fill my heart with a contrite mind ♪ " They pray loudly and shout, "I believe." In this way they make special garments which they hope to last a long time, but they never do.

How invigorating it is to come down after mountain prayers! Like a refreshing breeze, or like a spring rain sprinkling over trees and flowers, their souls are filled with peace and the grace of the Almighty. Feeling purer than the spirit of the mountain, they face the world wearing their special new garments.

But as soon as they get back to their house and church, and start living again, the garments get dirty and begin to wear out.

Their friends ask, "Where have you been?"

"Well, I have been away for a while."

"You look like you lost some weight!"

"Well, yes, but that's another story."

They never divulge that they fasted, they just go to church and pray. "I shall never lust after women. I shall never lie. I shall not covet my neighbor's house. I shall love all people."

But the moment they see a beautiful bosomy woman with slim legs, the holiness in their hearts changes instantly into pure lust. "Look how short that skirt is! Skirts are getting shorter and shorter! I've got to see those legs again! Oh! No! Oh, Lord! I have sinned again!"

Legalists seem pious, but you should know that they have to make new garments every day. Legalism is the faith in garments of fig leaves, the wrong faith. Many people try so hard to live piously according to the law of God. They bellow at the top of their lungs on the mountains so that their voice begins to sound quite pious.

Legalists cut an impressive figure when they lead prayer meetings at church. "Holy Father in Heaven! We have sinned this past week. Please forgive us . . ." They break into tears and the rest of the congregation follow suit. They think to themselves, "He must have spent a long time in the mountains praying and fasting. He sounds so pious and faithful." But because his faith is legalistic, even before the prayer ends, the legalist's heart begins to fill with arrogance and sin.

When people make up special new garments of fig leaves, they may last as long as two or three months. But sooner or later, the garments become rags and they have to make up a new set and carry on with their hypocritical lives. This is the life of legalists who try to live up to the law in order to be saved. They have to continuously make new garments out of fig leaves.

Legalism is the faith of fig leaves. Legalists tell you, "You have all sinned over the past week, haven't you? Then, repent."

They shout at you in a loud voice. "Repent! Pray!"

A legalist knows how to make his voice sound holy.

"Lord! I am sorry. I didn't live by the Law. I didn't keep Your commandments. Forgive me Lord, forgive me just once more."

They can never live by the Law even though they try valiantly to do so. In fact they are challenging the law of God and God Himself. They are arrogant before God.

THE LIKES OF CHUDAL BAE

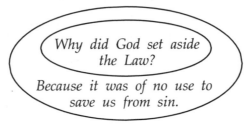

Why did God set aside the Law?

Because it was of no use to save us from sin.

There was once a young man named Chudal Bae. In 1950, during the Korean War, the communist soldiers came and ordered him to sweep the yard on the Sabbath day in a bid to rob him of his steadfast religious faith and make him a communist. But this religious young man refused to obey their orders. They insisted, but the young man refused again.

Finally, the soldiers tied him to a tree and pointed rifles at him. "Which do you want, to sweep the yard or to be killed?"

When forced to make a decision, he said, "I would rather die than work on the holy Sabbath day."

"You made your choice, and we will be glad to oblige you."

They then promptly shot him dead. Later, the church leaders appointed him a deacon posthumously to commemorate his unshakable religious faith.

Despite his strength of will, his religious faith was misguided. Why couldn't he have swept the yard and preached the gospel to those soldiers? Why did he have to be so stubborn and die for it? Would God praise him for not working on the Sabbath day? No.

We should lead a spiritual life. Not our deeds but our faith is important in the presence of God. The leaders of the church want to celebrate someone like Chudal Bae because they want to show off the superiority and orthodoxy of their own denomination. It is just like the hypocritical Pharisees who challenged Jesus.

There is nothing we can learn from legalists. We should learn about spiritual faith. We should ponder why Jesus had to be baptized and bleed on the Cross, and inquire into the nature of the gospel of the water and the Spirit.

We should try to find answers to those questions first, and then try to spread the gospel to all the people of the world, so that they may be born again. We should devote our lives to spiritual works.

If a preacher tells you, "Be like this young man Chudal Bae. Keep the Sabbath holy," he is only trying to get you to come to church on Sundays.

Here is another story which may prove enlightening. There was an woman who had to go through many trials to go to church on Sundays. Her parents-in-law were not Christians, and they tried hard to prevent her from going to church. They told her to work on Sunday. But she went out into the fields on Saturday nights and worked under the moonlight so that the family wouldn't have any excuse to prevent her from going to church on Sunday.

Of course, it is important to go to church, but is it

enough to come to worship every Sunday just to show how faithful we are? The true faithful were born again of water and the Spirit. True faith begins when someone is born again.

Can you be saved from your sins by living up to the law of God? No. I am not telling you to ignore the Law, but we all know that it is humanly impossible to keep all the articles of the Law.

James 2:10 says, *"For whoever shall keep the whole law, and yet stumble in one point, he is guilty of all."* Therefore think first how you can be born again of the gospel of water and the Spirit. Then, go to a church where you can hear the gospel. You can lead a faithful life after you are born again. Then, when the Lord calls, you can go before Him with joy.

Do not waste your time going to a false church, do not waste your money making misguided offerings. False priests cannot keep you from going to hell. First hear the gospel of the water and the Spirit and be born again.

Think about the reason Jesus came to this world. If we could enter the kingdom of Heaven by living according to the Law, He wouldn't have had to come to this world. After He came, the priesthood changed. Legalism became a thing of the past. Before we were saved, we thought we could be saved by living according to the Law. But this is no longer a sign of true faith.

Jesus saved us from all the sins of the world with His love, with the water of His baptism, with His blood and the Spirit. He fulfilled our salvation through His baptism at the Jordan, His blood on the Cross, and His resurrection.

God set aside the former regulations because they were weak and useless. *"For the law made nothing perfect; on the other hand, there is the bringing in of a better hope, through which we draw near to God. And inasmuch as He was not made priest without an oath" (Hebrews 7:19-20).* Jesus made an oath and saved us from all our sins with His baptism and blood. Martyrdom out of legalism is a fruitless death, and the only true faith is to believe in the gospel of the water and the Spirit.

We have to have fruitful faith. Which do you think is good for your soul? Would it be better to attend church regularly and live by the Law, or would it be better to attend the church of God where the gospel of being born again of water and the Spirit is preached, so that you may be born again? Which church and which preacher would be more beneficial to your soul? Think about it and choose the one that would be good for your soul.

God saves your soul through a preacher who has the words of the gospel of the water and the Spirit. Everyone must take responsibility for his own soul. A truly wise believer is one who commits his soul to the word of God.

JESUS BECAME PRIEST THROUGH AN OATH

Were the descendants of the order of Levi made priests through an oath?

No. Only Jesus was made Priest through an oath.

Hebrews 7:20-21 says, *"And inasmuch as He was not made priest without an oath (for they have become priests without an oath, but He with an oath by Him who said to Him; 'The Lord has sworn and will not relent, 'You are a priest forever according to the order of Melchizedek.')"*

And Psalms 110:4 says, *"The Lord has sworn and will not relent, 'You are a priest forever according to the order of Melchizedek.'"* The Lord made a vow. He made a covenant with us and showed it to us through the written Word. "I shall become the eternal High Priest in the order of Melchizedek. Melchizedek is king of righteousness, king of peace and the high priest forever. I shall become the eternal High Priest in the order of Melchizedek for your salvation."

Jesus came to this world and has became the surety of a better covenant (Hebrews 7:22). Instead of the blood of bulls and goats, He offered Himself up as the sacrifice by being baptized and bleeding on the Cross to wash away all our sins.

In the time of the Old Testament, when a high priest died, his son carried on the priesthood when he became 30. When he got old and his son reached the age of 30, he passed the priesthood on to his son.

There were so many descendants of high priest. So David set up a system by which they all took on the role in turns. As all the descendants of Aaron were appointed as priests, they had the right and obligation to minister the priesthood. Luke says, *"Zacharias, of the division of Abijah. ...So it was, that while he was serving as priest before God in the order of his division. . . ."*

Jesus came to this world and took over the ministering of the priesthood forever. He came as Priest of the good things to come. He fulfilled the salvation of being born again of water and the Spirit.

The descendants of Aaron were weak and incomplete

in their flesh. What happened when a high priest died? His son took over the high priesthood, but such sacrifices could never be enough to assure the salvation of humankind. Faith through humankind can never be a true and complete faith.

In the time of the New Testament, Jesus came to this world. But He didn't need to offer sacrifice continually because He lives forever. He took away our sins forever with His baptism. He offered Himself and was crucified to make all who believe in Him completely free of sin.

Now, He is alive and sits at the right hand of God to testify for us. "Dear Father, they may still be incomplete, but they believe in Me. Didn't I take away all their sins a long time ago?" Jesus is the eternal High Priest of our salvation.

The earthly priests were never complete. When they died, their sons took over the priesthood. Our Lord lives forever. He fulfilled eternal salvation for us by coming to this world, being baptized by John the Baptist, and then bleeding on the Cross for all our sins.

"Now where there is remission of these, there is no longer an offering for sin" (Hebrews 10:18). Jesus testifies to our salvation until the end of time. Have you been born again of water and the Spirit?

"For such a High Priest was fitting for us, who is holy, harmless, undefiled, separate from sinners, and has become higher than the heavens" (Hebrews 7:26). "For the law appoints as high priests men who have weaknesses, but the word of the oath, which came after the law, appoints the Son who has been perfected forever" (Hebrews 7:28).

What I would like to tell you is that Jesus Christ, without blemish, washed away our sins once and for all through the water of His baptism and His blood on the Cross. He saved us from all our sins not by the law of works, but by taking away all our sins and being judged forever.

Do you believe that He saved us from all our sins through eternal salvation? If you do, you are saved. But if you don't, you still have much to learn about the eternal salvation of Jesus.

True faith comes from the gospel of the water and the Spirit, strictly based on the Scripture. Jesus Christ, the eternal heavenly High Priest, became our eternal Savior through His baptism and blood on the Cross.

WE HAVE TO FULLY UNDERSTAND OUR FAITH

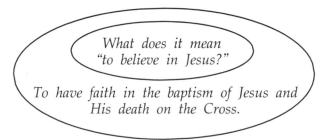

What does it mean "to believe in Jesus?"

To have faith in the baptism of Jesus and His death on the Cross.

We have to think about how we can believe in Jesus in the right way and set our faith straight. How can we believe in Jesus in the proper and correct way? We can do it by believing in the gospel of the baptism of Jesus and His blood on the Cross.

The correct faith is to believe in the work of Jesus, His baptism and blood, without adding our own mistaken notions. Do you believe this to be true? How is your spiritual condition? Do you rely too much upon your own works and efforts?

Not much time has passed since I started believing in Jesus, but I suffered for about 10 years because of legalism. Eventually I became tired of that kind of life. I don't even like to remind myself of that time. My wife is sitting here now. She knows how terrible it was for us.

On Sundays, I would say, "Honey, let's enjoy ourselves today."

"But today is Sunday!"

She didn't even wash clothes on Sunday. One Sunday, my pants were torn. But she told me to wait until Monday. As a matter of fact, I was even more insistent that we observe the Sabbath correctly. But it was so hard. We never rested on Sundays because it was so difficult to keep the Sabbath correctly. I still remember those days.

Dear friends, to truly believe in Jesus, we have to believe in the atonement of our sins through His baptism and blood on the Cross. True faith is to believe in the divinity and humanity of Jesus and all the things He did in this world. The true faithful believe in all His Words.

What does it mean by "to believe in Jesus?" It is to believe in the baptism of Jesus and His blood. There is a profound simplicity to this. All we have to do is to look into the Bible and believe in the gospel. We should all believe in the correct way.

"Thank You, Lord. I see now that it is not done through my efforts! For by the Law is the knowledge of sin (Romans 3:20). I understand it all now. I thought that because the Law was good, because it was the commandment of God, I should try and live by it. I tried so hard until now, but I see now that I was wrong to think that I could live according to the Law. I see now that I can never keep the commandments of God! Therefore, through the law of God, I now realize my heart is filled with evil thoughts and transgressions. I understand now that the Law is given to instill in us the knowledge of sin. Oh, thank You, Lord. I misunderstood Your Will and tried so hard to keep the Law. It was really arrogant of me to even try. I repent. I know now that Jesus was baptized and bled for my salvation! I believe!"

You have to believe frankly and purely. You should only believe in the written words in the Bible. It is the only way you can be completely born again.

What is it to believe in Jesus? Is it something we have to complete over a period of time? Is our faith a religion that you have to work for? People have made gods, and they have made religions to fit those gods. Religion is a process that people work through to reach a goal; to aspire to the goodness of man.

Then what is faith?　It means to believe in God and to look up to Him. We look up to the salvation of Jesus and thank Him for this blessing. This is true faith. This is the difference between faith and religion. Once you can distinguish between those two, you get 100 points for your understanding of faith.

Theologians who are not born again tell us that we should believe in Jesus and live piously. Can one be faithful just by being pious? Of course we have to be good. Who leads more pious lives than those of us who are born again?

But the point is that they are telling this to sinners. There are 12 kinds of sins inside of the average sinner. How can he live piously? Certainly, his mind may comprehend what has to be done, but his heart cannot carry it out. When a sinner steps outside the church, living piously becomes a mere theory, and his instinct leads him to sin.

Therefore we have to decide in our hearts whether we are going to live by the Law or be saved by believing in the baptism of Jesus and His blood on the Cross, by having faith in the eternal High Priest of the kingdom of Heaven.

Remember that Jesus is the true High Priest for those who believe. Let us all be saved by knowing and believing in true salvation through the baptism of Jesus and His blood on the Cross.

The Born Again are not Afraid of the End of the World

Why are the born again unafraid of the end of the world?

Because their faith in the gospel of the water and the Spirit makes them free of sin.

When you are truly born again, you don't have to be afraid of the world coming to an end. Many Christians in Korea claimed that the world would come to an end on the 28th of October, 1992. What a tumultuous and dreadful day it would be, they said. But all their claims turned out to be false. The truly born again live piously, spreading the gospel to the last moment. Whenever this world comes to an end, all we have to do is preach the gospel of the water and the Spirit.

When the Bridegroom comes, the brides who are truly born again of water and the Spirit can meet Him with great joy, saying, "Oh, You have finally come! My flesh is still so incomplete, but You loved me and saved me from all my sins. So I have no sin in my heart. Thank You, Lord. You are my Savior!"

Jesus is the spiritual bridegroom to all the righteous. The marriage takes place because the bridegroom loves the bride, not the other way around. I know it sometimes happens that way in this world, but in Heaven, it is the bridegroom who decides whether the marriage is to take place. It is the bridegroom Jesus who chooses to get married based on His love and offer of salvation, regardless of the brides. This is how marriage in Heaven is made.

The Bridegroom knows all about the brides. Because His beloved brides were such sinners, He took pity on them and saved them from all sin by being baptized and bleeding on the Cross.

Our Lord Jesus didn't come to this world as a descendant of Aaron. He didn't come to this world to offer an earthly sacrifice. There were plenty of Levites, the descendants of Aaron, to do the work.

In fact, the main character of the sacrifices of the Old Testament was none other than Jesus Himself. Therefore, when the real thing came to this world, what happened to its shadow? The shadow was set aside.

When Jesus came to this world, He never offered sacrifices like Aaron did. He offered Himself for humankind by being baptized and bleeding for the salvation of sinners. He fulfilled salvation on the Cross.

For those who believe in the baptism of Jesus and His blood on the Cross, salvation will come in no uncertain terms. Jesus didn't atone for our sins in an unclear way. He did it clearly. *"I am the way, the truth, and the life" (John 14:6).* Jesus came to this world and saved us with His baptism, His death, and His resurrection.

THE OLD TESTAMENT IS THE MODEL OF JESUS

What was the reason for establishing another covenant?

Because the first covenant was infirm and useless.

The Old Testament is the shadow of the New Testament. Although Jesus never offered sacrifices like the high priests of the Old Testament, He ministered a better priesthood, the eternal heavenly priesthood. Because people in this world are sinful from their birth, they become sinners, and they can never become righteous through the law of God. Therefore God established another covenant.

Our Father in Heaven sent His only begotten Son to this world and asked us in return to have faith in His baptism, His blood, and His resurrection. This is the second covenant of God. The second covenant requires us to believe in the gospel of the water and the Spirit.

The Lord is no longer asking for our good works. He doesn't tell us how to live to be saved. He only asks us to believe in salvation through His Son. He asks us to believe in His baptism and blood on the Cross above all. And we have to say yes.

In the Bible, the house of Judah maintained royalty. All the kings of Israel were born in the house of Judah until King Solomon. Even after the division of the kingdom, the house of Judah held the throne of the Southern Kingdom until its collapse in 586 B.C. In this way, the people of Judah stand for the Israelites. The tribe of Levi was one of priests. Each tribe of Israel had its own role. God promised the tribe of Judah that Jesus would emerge from its ranks.

Why did He make this covenant with the tribe of Judah? Making this covenant was the same as making a covenant with all the people of the world because the Israelites stand for the people of the world. Jesus fulfilled the new covenant, which was the salvation of humankind through His baptism, His death on the Cross, and His resurrection.

THE SINS OF HUMANKIND CANNOT BE WASHED AWAY BY REPENTANCE

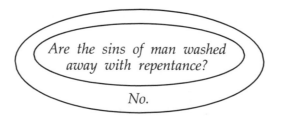

Are the sins of man washed away with repentance?

No.

In Jeremiah 17:1, it is written that the sin of each person is recorded in two places. *"The sin of Judah is written with a pen of iron; with the point of a diamond it is engraved on the tablet of their heart, and on the horns of your altars."*

Our sins are recorded in our hearts. That is how we know that we are sinners. Before one comes to believe in Jesus, he is not aware that he is a sinner. Why? Because the law of God is abscent in his heart. Therefore, once someone believes in Jesus, he realizes that he is a sinner before God.

Some only realize they are sinners 10 years after coming to believe in Jesus. "Oh, dear! I am a sinner! I thought I was saved, but somehow I am still a sinner!" The realization comes one day when we finally see ourselves as we truly are. They were so happy for ten years, but suddenly they see the truth. Do you know why? This realization comes because finally their true sins and transgressions are at last made clear through the law of God. Such a person has believed in Jesus for 10 years without being born again.

Since the sinner can't erase his sins from his heart, he remains a sinner before God. Some take 5 years, and others take 10 years to reach this realization. Some come to the realization after 30 years, some after 50 years, and some never realize the truth until the end. "Dear God, I used to be good before I had the commandments in my mind. I was confident that I was keeping the Law well, but now I realize that I have sinned every day. Just like the apostle Paul said, *"I was alive once without the law, but when the commandment came, sin revived and I died" (Romans 7:9).* I am a sinner even though I believe in Christ.

It is your own sins that prevent you from living by the word of God. Your sins are recorded in your heart. Because God records your sins there, when you bow your head to pray, all your sins emerge. "Surprise! I am the sin you committed."

"But I atoned for you 2 years ago. Why are you showing

yourself again all of a sudden? Why haven't you gone away?"

"Oh, don't be so nasty! I am recorded in your heart. No matter what you think, you are still a sinner."

"No! No!"

So, the sinner repents again for the sins committed 2 years ago. "Please forgive me, Lord. I am still tormented by the sins I committed before. I repented for my sins, but they are still with me. Please forgive me, for I have sinned."

But do those sins go away with repentance? Because the sins of people are recorded in their hearts, they can never be erased without the gospel of the water and the Spirit. Only through the gospel of the water and the Spirit can true atonement be attained. We can only be saved through our faith in the true gospel of Jesus.

I SHALL BE YOUR SAVIOR

How should we respond to the new covenant?

We have to believe in it in our hearts and preach it all over the world.

Our Lord in Heaven made a new covenant with us. "I shall become your Savior. I shall make you completely free of all the sins of the world through the water and the blood. I shall surely bless all those who believe in Me."

Do you believe in this new covenant with God? We can be saved from all our sins and be born again when we believe in the truth of His covenant and His salvation through the water and the blood.

We don't trust a doctor if he does not diagnose us correctly. A doctor first has to diagnose his patients correctly and then prescribe the proper medicine. There are all sorts of medicines, but the doctor has to know exactly which one to use. Once a doctor diagnoses his/her patients correctly, there are many medicines available to heal them. But with the wrong diagnosis, all those good medicines can only make the patient worse.

Likewise, when you believe in Jesus, you have to diagnose the condition of your spirit based on the word of God. When you examine your spirit with the word of God, you can see exactly what the condition of your spirit is. The Doctor of spirits can heal all his patients without exception. They can all be born again.

If you say, "I don't know whether I was redeemed," it means that you are not saved. If a pastor is truly a disciple of Jesus, he has to be able to solve the problem of sin for his followers. Then, he can go on to solve the problems of their faith and lead them spiritually. He has to be able to see the exact spiritual conditions of his followers.

Jesus came to this world to take away all the sin of the world. He came and was baptized and died on the Cross. When He atoned for all sin, did He leave your sins out? The word of the water and the Spirit blots out the sins of all believers.

The gospel is like dynamite. It blows up everything from tall buildings to mountains. The work of Jesus is exactly like this. He wipes out the sins of those who believe in Him with His gospel of the water and the Spirit. Let us now look at the gospel of the water and the Spirit as it is expressed in the Bible.

THE GOSPEL OF THE LAYING ON OF HANDS IN THE OLD TESTAMENT

What was the purpose of the laying on of hands in the Old Testament?

Its purpose was to pass sins on to the sin offering.

Let us look up the truth of the gospel of redemption in Leviticus 1:3-4. *"If his offering is a burnt sacrifice of the herd, let him offer a male without blemish; he shall offer it of his own free will at the door of the tabernacle of meeting before the Lord. Then he shall put his hand on the head of the burnt offering, and it will be accepted on his behalf to make atonement for him."*

This passage tells us that the burnt offering should be offered at the door of the tabernacle of meeting before the Lord by laying hands on the head of the offering, and the offering should be a live animal without blemish.

In the Old Testament era, a sinner put his hands on the offering to make atonement for his daily sins. He killed the sin offering before the Lord and the priest took some of the blood and put it on the horns of the altar of burnt offering. He then poured out the rest of the blood at the base of the altar and the sinner was forgiven for a day's sin.

For a year's sin, it is written in Leviticus 16:6-10, *"Aaron shall offer the bull as a sin offering, which is for himself, and make atonement for himself and for his house. He shall take the two goats and present them before the Lord at the door of the tabernacle of meeting. Then Aaron shall cast lots for the two goats: one lot for the Lord and the other lot for the scapegoat. And Aaron shall bring the goat on which the Lord's lot fell, and offer it as a sin offering. But the goat on which the lot fell to be the scapegoat shall be presented alive before the Lord, to make atonement upon it, and to let it go as the scapegoat into the wilderness."* As explained in the Bible, scapegoat means "to put out." So a year's sin was expiated on the tenth day of the seventh month.

In Leviticus 16:29-30, it is written, *"This shall be a statute forever for you: In the seventh month, on the tenth day of the month, you shall afflict your souls, and do no work at all, whether a native of your own country or a stranger who dwells among you. For on that day the priest shall make atonement for you, to cleanse you, that you may be clean from all your sins before the Lord."*

This was the day on which the Israelites atoned for a year's sin. How could this be done? First, the high priest Aaron had to be present at the sacrifice. Who represented the people of Israel? Aaron. God designated Aaron and his descendants as the high priests.

Aaron offered the bull to atone for himself and for his household. He killed the bull and sprinkled some of its blood on and in front of the mercy seat seven times. He had to atone for himself and his household first of all.

Atonement means to transfer one's sins to the sin offering and to let the sin offering die in one's place. The sinner should be the one to die, but can atone for his sins by passing them on to the offering and having it die in his place.

After his sins and those of his household were expiated, he offered one goat before God while sending another goat into the wilderness as a scapegoat in the presence of the people of Israel.

One goat was offered as the sin offering. Aaron laid his hands on the head of the sin offering and confessed, "O God, Your people Israel violated all of the Ten Commandments and the 613 articles of Your Law. The Israelites have become sinners. I now lay my hands on this goat to transfer all our yearly sins."

He cut the goat's throat and entered the Most Holy place within the tabernacle with its blood. He then sprinkled some of the blood on and in front of the mercy seat seven times.

Inside the Most Holy place sits the ark of the covenant. Its cover is called the mercy seat, and in it are two stone tablets of the covenant, the golden pot of manna, and Aaron's rod that had budded.

Aaron's rod signifies resurrection, the two stone tablets of the covenant His Justice, and the golden pot of manna His word of Life.

There is a cover on the ark of the covenant. The blood was sprinkled before the mercy seat seven times. As there were golden bells hung on the hem of the high priest's robe they rang out when he sprinkled the blood.

In Leviticus 16:14-15, it is written, *"He shall take some of the blood of the bull and sprinkle it with his finger on the mercy seat on the east side; and before the mercy seat he shall sprinkle some of the blood with his finger seven times. Then he shall kill the goat of the sin offering, which is for the people, bring its blood inside the veil, do with that blood as he did with the blood of the bull, and sprinkle it on the mercy seat and before the mercy seat."*

The bells rang out every time he sprinkled some of the goat's blood, and all the Israelites who gathered outside would hear the sound. Since atonement for their sins had to be done through the high priest, the sound of the bells meant their sins had been forgiven. It was the sound of blessing for all the people of Israel.

When the bells rang seven times, they said, "Now I am so relieved. I had been worried for the whole year's sin, and now I feel free." And the people went back to their lives, feeling free of guilt. The sound of the bells at that time was the same as the good news of being born again of water and the Spirit.

When we hear the gospel of redemption of the water and the Spirit and believe it with our hearts and admit it with our mouths, this is what the gospel of the water and the Spirit is all about. When the bell rang seven times, all the yearly sins of the Israelites were cleansed. Their sins were washed away before God.

After offering a goat for the Israelites, the high priest took the other goat and went to the people waiting outside the tabernacle. While they looked on, the high priest Aaron laid his hands on the other goat's head.

In Leviticus 16:21-22, *"Aaron shall lay both his hands on the head of the live goat, confess over it all the iniquities of the children of Israel, and all their transgressions, concerning all their sins, putting them on the head of the goat, and shall send it away into the wilderness by the hand of a suitable man. The goat shall bear on itself all their iniquities to an uninhabited land; and he shall release the goat in the wilderness."*

The high priest, Aaron, laid his hands on the head of

the other goat (the scapegoat) and confessed all the yearly sins of the Israelites before God. "O God, the Israelites sinned before You. We violated the Ten Commandment and all 613 articles of Your Law. O God, I pass all the yearly sins of the Israelites on to the head of this goat."

According to Jeremiah 17:1, sins are recorded in two places. One is in the Book of Works, and the other is on the tablets of their hearts.

So if people are to atone for their sins, their sins have to be erased from the Book of Works and from the tablets of their hearts. On the Day of Atonement, one goat was for the sins written in the Book of Judgment and the other was for those engraved on the tablets of their hearts.

What did God show the Israelites through the sacrificial system in the Old Testament?

That the Savior would come and blot out their sins once and for all in the most proper way

By laying hands on the head of the goat, the high priest showed the people that their yearly sins were transferred to the goat. When the sins were put on the head of the goat, a suitable man led the goat into the wilderness.

Palestine is a land of desert. The goat that took away all the yearly sins of the Israelites was led by a man appointed for the task to the desert where there was neither water nor grass. People stood and watched the scapegoat go into the wilderness.

They said to themselves, "I should have died, but the

goat dies instead for my sins. The wages of sin is death, but the goat dies instead of me. Thank you, goat. Your death means that I can live." The goat was led far into the desert and the Israelites were forgiven for a year's sin.

When the sin in your heart is passed on to the sin offering, you are cleansed. It is that simple. Truth is always simple once we understand it.

The goat disappeared over the horizon. The man came back alone after releasing it. All the yearly sins of the Israelites were gone. The goat wandered in the desert without water or grass, and eventually died along with a year's worth of the Israelites' sins.

The wages of sin is death, and the Justice of God was accomplished. God sacrificed the goat so that the Israelites might live. All the transgressions of the Israelites during the year were washed clean.

As a day's sin and a year's sin were forgiven like that in Old Testament times, it was the covenant of God that our sins would be similarly forgiven once and for all. It was His covenant that He would send us the Messiah and deliver us from all our lifelong sins. The covenant was carried out through the baptism of Jesus.

TO BE BORN AGAIN OF WATER AND THE SPIRIT IN THE NEW TESTAMENT

> *Why was Jesus baptized by John the Baptist?*
>
> *To fulfill all righteousness by taking away all the sins of the world. The baptism of Jesus in the New Testament was the very laying on of hands of the Old Testament.*

Let us read Matthew 3:13-15. *"Then Jesus came from Galilee to John at the Jordan to be baptized by him. And John tried to prevent Him, saying, 'I need to be baptized by You, and are You coming to me?' But Jesus answered and said to him, 'Permit it to be so now, for thus it is fitting for us to fulfill all righteousness.' Then he allowed Him."*

Jesus went to the Jordan and was baptized by John the Baptist and in so doing, He fulfilled all righteousness. He was baptized by John. John was the greatest among those born of women.

Matthew 11:11-12 says *"Among those born of women there has not risen one greater than John the Baptist. And from the days of John the Baptist until now the kingdom of heaven suffers violence."*

John the Baptist was elected by God to be the representative of humankind and sent 6 months before Christ. He was a descendant of Aaron and the last high priest.

John the Baptist said when Jesus came to him, *"I need to be baptized by You, and You are coming to me?"*

"Permit it to be so now, for thus it is fitting for us to fulfill

all righteousness." His purpose was to free humankind from sin so that they could become children of God. Jesus said to John, "We have to complete the gospel of being born again of water and the Spirit. So baptize Me now."

John baptized Jesus. It was fitting for Jesus to be baptized to take away all the sins of the world. Because He was baptized in the most fitting manner, we were properly saved from all our sins. Jesus was baptized so that all our sins could be passed on to Him.

Jesus came to this world and was baptized when He was 30. It was His first ministry. Jesus fulfilled all righteousness by blotting out all the sins of the world, thus consecrating all people.

Jesus came to this world and was baptized in the most fitting manner to deliver us from all our sins. "For thus" all righteousness was fulfilled.

God said, *"This is My beloved Son, in whom I am well pleased" (Matthew 3:17).* Jesus Christ knew that He would take away all the sins of humankind and bleed to death on the Cross, but He obeyed His Father's Will, saying, *"Not as I will, but as You will" (Matthew 26:39).* The Father's Will was to wash away all the sins of humankind and thus offer salvation to the people of the world.

So Jesus, the obedient Son, obeyed His Father's Will and was baptized by the John the Baptist.

In John 1:29, *"The next day John saw Jesus coming toward him, and said, 'Behold! The Lamb of God who takes away the sin of the world!'"* Jesus took away all sin and bled on the Cross at Golgotha. *"Behold! The Lamb of God who takes away the sin of the world,"* witnessed John the Baptist.

Do you have sin or not? Are you a righteous man or a sinner? The truth is that Jesus took away the sin of the world and was crucified on the Cross for all of us.

When were the sins of all sinners in this world transferred to Jesus?

Jesus took on our sins when He was baptized by John the Baptist at the Jordan.

After we are born into this world, we sin even between the ages of 1 and 10. Jesus took away those sins. We also sin between the ages of 11 and 20. The sins we commit in our hearts and in our actions, He took them all.

We also sin between the ages of 21 and 45. He took them all as well. He took on all the sins of the world and was crucified on the Cross. We sin from day of our birth till the day we die. But He took them all away.

"Behold! The Lamb of God who takes away the sin of the world!" All sin, from those of the first man, Adam, to those of the last man born in this world—whenever that may be—He took them all. He did not pick and choose whose sins He would take.

He did not decide to love only some of us. He came in the flesh and took on all the sins of the world and was crucified on the Cross. He received the Judgment for all of us and blotted out the sins of this world forever.

No one was excluded from His salvation. *"All the sins of the world"* includes all our sins. Jesus took them all.

With His baptism and blood, He cleansed all the sins of the world. He took them all away through His baptism and was judged for our sins on the Cross. Before Jesus died on the Cross, He said, *"It is finished"* (John 19:30), meaning the salvation of humankind was complete.

Why was Jesus crucified on the Cross? Because the life of the flesh is in the blood, and the blood makes atonement for one's life (Leviticus 17:11). Why did Jesus have to be baptized? Because He wanted to take on all the sins of the world.

"After this, Jesus, knowing that all things were now accomplished, that the Scripture might be fulfilled, said, 'I thirst!'" *(John 19:28).* Jesus died, knowing that all the covenants of God in the Old Testament were accomplished with His baptism at the Jordan and His death on the Cross.

Jesus knew that redemption was fulfilled through Him and said, *"It is finished."* He died on the Cross. He sanctified us, rose again from the dead after 3 days and ascended to Heaven, where He now sits at the right hand of God.

The washing away of all sins through the baptism of Jesus and His death on the Cross is the blessed gospel of being born again of water and the Spirit. Believe it, and you will be forgiven for all your sins.

We can't atone for our sins by praying for repentance every day. Redemption was granted once and for all only through the baptism of Jesus and His death on the Cross. *"Now where there is remission of these, there is no longer an offering for sin"* *(Hebrews 10:18).*

Now all we have to do is believe in redemption through the baptism of Jesus and His crucifixion. Believe and you will be saved.

Romans 5:1-2 says, *"Therefore, having been justified by faith, we have peace with God through our Lord Jesus Christ, through whom also we have access by faith into this grace in which we stand, and rejoice in hope of the glory of God."*

There is no other way to be justified but to believe in

the blessed gospel of being born again of water and the Spirit.

THE PURPOSE OF THE LAW OF GOD

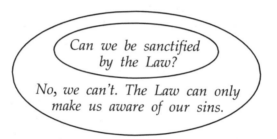

Can we be sanctified by the Law?

No, we can't. The Law can only make us aware of our sins.

In Hebrews 10:9, it is written, *"Then He said, 'Behold, I have come to do Your will, O God.' He takes away the first that He may establish the second."* We cannot be sanctified through the Law. It only make us sinners. God did not mean for us to obey the Law.

Romans 3:20 says, *"For by the law is the knowledge of sin."* God gave the Israelites the Law through Moses after 430 years had passed since Abraham had received the Covenant. He gave them the Law so that they might know what it meant to sin before God. In the absence of the law of God, humankind would have no knowledge of sin. God gave us His Law so that we might come to an understanding of sin.

So the only purpose of the Law is to let us know that we are all sinners before God. Through this knowledge, we are meant to come back to Jesus by believing in the blessed gospel of being born again of water and the Spirit. This is the purpose of the Law that God gave us.

THE LORD HAS COME TO DO GOD'S WILL

What do we have to do before God?

We have to believe in God's redemption through Jesus.

"'I have come to do Your will, O God.' He takes away the first that He may establish the second" (Hebrews 10:9). Because we cannot become sanctified by the Law, God did not deliver us with His Law, but with His complete redemption. God saved us with His love and justice.

"By that will we have been sanctified through the offering of the body of Jesus Christ once for all. And every priest stands ministering daily and offering repeatedly the same sacrifices, which can never take away sins. But this Man, after He had offered one sacrifice for sins forever, sat down at the right hand of God" (Hebrews 10:10-12).

He sat down at the right hand of God because His work of redemption was complete and there was nothing more for Him to do. He will neither be baptized nor sacrifice Himself again to save us.

Now that all the sins of the world have been washed away, all He has to do is to provide eternal life to those who believe in Him. He now seals those who believe in the salvation of the water and the Spirit with the Spirit.

Jesus came down to this world and took away all the sins of the world and died on the Cross, thus completing His work. Now that the Lord's work is finished, He sits at the right hand of God.

We must believe our Lord Jesus saved us from sin for

all eternity. He made us perfect forever with His baptism and blood.

THOSE WHO BECOME ENEMIES OF GOD

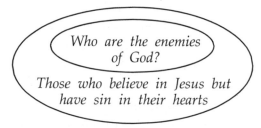

Who are the enemies of God?

Those who believe in Jesus but have sin in their hearts

In Hebrews 10:12-13, the Lord says, *"But this Man, after He had offered one sacrifice for sins forever, sat down at the right hand of God, from that time waiting till His enemies are made His footstool. For by one offering He has perfected forever those who are being sanctified."* He said He would wait until the last judgment to decide their fate.

His enemies still say, "God, please forgive my sins." Satan and his followers do not believe in the gospel of the water and the Spirit and continue to ask for His forgiveness.

Our Lord God will not judge them for now. But on the day of the Second Coming of Jesus, they will be judged and condemned to hell forever. God tolerates them until that day in hopes that they will repent and become righteous through redemption.

Our Lord Jesus took away all our sins and died for us who believe in Him. Jesus will someday appear a second time to deliver all those who believe in Him. "O please come to us soon, Lord." He will come a second time to take the sinless to live with Him forever in the kingdom of Heaven.

Those who insist that they are sinners when the Lord returns will find no place in Heaven. On the Last Day, they will be judged and thrown into the fires of hell. This punishment awaits those who refuse to believe in being born again of water and the Spirit.

Our Lord Jesus regards those who believe in untruth as His enemies. That is why we have to fight against this untruth. That is why we have to believe in the blessed gospel of being born again of water and the Spirit.

WE HAVE TO BELIEVE IN THE GOSPEL OF THE WATER AND THE SPIRIT

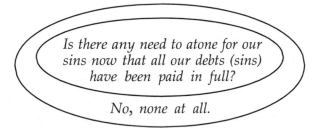

Is there any need to atone for our sins now that all our debts (sins) have been paid in full?

No, none at all.

Hebrews 10:15-16 says, *"But the Holy Spirit also witnesses to us; for after He had said before, 'This is the covenant that I will make with them after those days, says the Lord: I will put My laws into their hearts, and in their minds I will write them.'"*

After He blotted out all our sins, He said, *"this is the covenant that I will make with them."* What is this covenant? *"I will put My laws into their hearts, and in their minds I will write them."* We first tried to lead a legalistic life according to His Law, but we could not be truly saved by the Law.

Later we came to know that Jesus has already saved

those who believe in their hearts the blessed gospel of being born again of water and the Spirit. Whoever believes in the baptism and blood of Jesus is redeemed.

Jesus is the Lord of salvation. *"There is no other name under heaven given among men by which we must be saved" (Acts 4:12).* Jesus came to the world as our Savior. Because we cannot be saved through our works, Jesus saved us and recorded on the tablets of our hearts that He saved us with His Law of love and salvation.

"'Their sins and their lawless deeds I will remember no more.' Now where there is remission of these, there is no longer an offering for sin" (Hebrews 10:17-18).

Now He remembers our lawless deeds no more. Now that He has taken away all sins, we believers have no more sins for which to be forgiven. Our debts were paid in full and there is nothing left to repay. People are saved by faith in the ministry of Jesus, who saved us through His baptism and blood on the Cross.

Now all we have to do is believe in the water and the blood of Jesus. *"And you shall know the truth, and the truth shall make you free" (John 8:32).* Believe in the salvation in Jesus. To obtain redemption is easier than breathing. All you have to do is believe things as they are. Salvation is just believing in the word of God.

Believe that Jesus is our Savior (in the baptism of Jesus and His death on the Cross), and just have faith that salvation is yours. Deny your own thoughts and just believe in the salvation in Jesus. I pray that you really believe in Jesus and are ready to be led into eternal life with Him. ⊠

SERMON 7

The Baptism of Jesus is the Indispensable Process for Redemption

Previously saying, "Sacrifice and offering, burnt offerings, and offerings for sin You did not desire, nor had pleasure in them"(which are offered according to the law), then He said, "Behold, I have come to do Your will, O God." He takes away the first that He may establish the second (Hebrews 10:8-9).

The Baptism of Jesus is the Indispensable Process for Redemption

<Matthew 3:13-17>

"Then Jesus came from Galilee to John at the Jordan to be baptized by him. And John tried to prevent Him, saying, 'I have need to be baptized by You, and are You coming to me?' But Jesus answered and said to him, 'Permit it to be so now, for thus it is fitting for us to fulfill all righteousness.' Then he allowed Him. When He had been baptized, Jesus came up immediately from the water, and behold, the heavens were opened to Him, and He saw the Spirit of God descending like a dove and alighting upon Him. And suddenly a voice came from heaven saying, 'This is My beloved son, in whom I am well pleased.'"

THE BAPTISM OF JOHN THE BAPTIST

What is repentance?

Turning back from the sinful life and believing in Jesus in order to be sanctified.

So many people in the world do not know why Jesus came to this world and was baptized by John the Baptist. Therefore let us talk about the purpose of the baptism of Jesus and about John the Baptist who baptized Him.

First, we should think about what led John the Baptist to baptize people at the Jordan. It is explained in Matthew 3:1-12 that John the Baptist baptized people to bring them back to God from sins by confessing their sins.

"I indeed baptize you with water unto repentance" (verse 11), and *"The voice of one crying in the wilderness: 'Prepare the way of the Lord, make His paths straight'" (verse 3)*. John the Baptist, clothed in camel's hair and carrying a bunch of locusts, cried out in the wilderness, preaching a baptism of repentance for the forgiveness of sins.

He cried out to people, "Repent, the Savior of humanity is coming; prepare the way for Him, make His path of salvation straight. Stop worshiping the gods of the Gentiles and receive the Lord in your heart."

Return from what? From worshiping idols and all the other evil deeds of a life full of sin. So what do we have to do? We have to be baptized into Jesus in order to be sanctified. John the Baptist cried out in the wilderness, "Be baptized by me. Be washed of your sins. The Savior, your Messiah, is coming to this world. He will take away all your sins as the sacrificial lamb of the Old Testament and wash away all your sins."

In the Old Testament, daily sins were passed on to the sin offering through the laying on of hands. The yearly sins of all Israel were also passed on to the goat by the high priest on the Day of Atonement, which fell on the tenth day of the seventh month every year (Leviticus 16:29-31).

In the same way, the sins of humankind had to be

passed on to Jesus through His baptism all at once so that they could be blotted out through Him. So John urged the people to come back to Jesus and be baptized by him.

The primary importance of the baptism performed by John the Baptist was repentance, which brought the people of Israel back to Jesus who was to come later. Repentance means to turn back from the life of sin and believe in the Messiah in order to be forgiven for all sins.

The people of Israel could be redeemed by hoping for the Messiah who would come later to wash away all their sins. Similarly, we are redeemed by believing in Jesus, who descended from Heaven 2000 years ago and washed away all the sins of the world. But the Israelites in the Old Testament abandoned the law of God, offered the wrong sacrifices and forgot the Messiah.

Because John the Baptist needed to remind them of the law of God and of the Messiah who would come later, he began baptizing people and eventually baptized Jesus at the Jordan.

Many people came to John and were baptized, repenting for worshipping idols and abandoning the law of God. There are three indispensible elements in the legitimate sacrifice—a live animal, the laying on of hands, and its blood. All the people of the world are saved by believing in Jesus.

When the Pharisees and Sadducees came to be baptized, John cried out to them, *"Brood of vipers! Who warned you to flee from the wrath to come? Therefore bear fruits worthy of repentance, and do not think to say to yourselves, 'We have Abraham as our father'"* (Matthew 3:7-9).

These Pharisees and Sadducees, groups of politicians and idol-worshipers, thought that they were God's people despite the fact they didn't believe in God's word. They believed in other gods and in their own thoughts.

When they came to John the Baptist to be baptized, he told them, "You should not offer wrong sacrifices but turn back from sin and truly believe that the Messiah will come and wash away your sins. You should believe this in your hearts."

To repent is to turn back from the wrong path. True repentance is to turn back from sin and false beliefs and to return to Jesus. It is to believe in the redemption of His baptism and His judgement on the Cross.

Thus, John the Baptist cried out to the people of Israel, who had abandoned the law of God and the sacrificial system, in order to convince them to return to God. It was the role of John the Baptist to bring people back to Jesus so that they would believe in Him and be saved from all their sins.

Do You Believe in Redemption through the Baptism of Jesus?

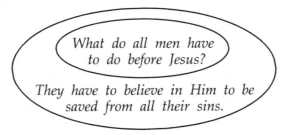

What do all men have to do before Jesus?

They have to believe in Him to be saved from all their sins.

The first thing Jesus did in His public ministry was to be baptized by John the Baptist. All the sins of the world were passed on to Him in this way.

Thus the baptism of Jesus was the beginning of God's salvation of humanity as well as the righteous act of Jesus that washed away all the sins of the world. God redeems all who believe in the truth that Jesus took away all the sins of the world through His baptism.

When Jesus came to this world and was baptized by John the Baptist, the gospel of the kingdom of Heaven began. The heavens were opened up with His baptism and as described in Matthew 3:15, it was exactly like the sacrifice of atonement described in Leviticus 1:1-5, 4:27-31 in the Old Testament.

Everything in the Old Testament has a mate in the New Testament and vice versa. *"Search from the book of the Lord, and read: not one of these shall fail; not one shall lack her mate"* *(Isaiah 34:16).*

BOTH THE OLD AND NEW TESTAMENTS SPEAK ABOUT THE ATONEMENT OF ALL PEOPLE'S SINS

Do we have to repent for our daily sins every day?

No. True repentance is to admit all one's sins and turn one's mind back to the baptism of Jesus in order to obtain redemption.

In the Old Testament, a day's sin was passed on to a sin offering by the laying on of hands. The offering would then bleed and be judged instead of the sinner. And the accumulated sins of the whole year were also be passed on to a sin offering by the laying on of hands, so that all people could be forgiven for the year's sin.

In the New Testament, in exactly the same way, Jesus Christ came and was baptized at the Jordan to take away all the sins of the world. Thus the word of God prophesied in the Old Testament was fulfilled.

John the Baptist, who baptized Jesus, was a servant of God who was sent 6 months prior to Jesus. He testified that Jesus took away all the sins of the world, saying in John 1:29. *"Behold! The Lamb of God who takes away the sin of the world!"*

John the Baptist passed the sins of the world on to Jesus by baptizing Him at the Jordan. In this way, the Lord made atonement for all the sins of humankind. All we have to do now is believe.

All the sins of the world were passed on to Jesus. The disciples of Jesus said in Acts 3:19, *"Repent therefore and be converted, that your sins may be blotted out, so that times of refreshing may come from the presence of the Lord."*

They were urging us to understand why John the Baptist baptized Jesus, why he told people to follow Him. He said, "Repent and be converted. Believe in the redemption of the baptism of Jesus. Be washed of your sins."

The Messiah came and washed away our sins all at one time by being baptized. All the sins of the world were passed on to Jesus in this way. Thus the Covenant of God was fulfilled with the baptism of Jesus, as it is recorded in Matthew 3:13-17.

"Then Jesus came from Galilee to John at the Jordan to be baptized by him. And John tried to prevent Him, saying, 'I have

need to be baptized by You, and are You coming to me?' But Jesus answered and said to him, 'Permit it to be so now, for thus it is fitting for us to fulfill all righteousness.' Then he allowed Him. When He had been baptized, Jesus came up immediately from the water, and behold, the heavens were opened to Him, and He saw the Spirit of God descending like a dove and alighting upon Him. and suddenly a voice came from heaven saying, 'This is My beloved son, in whom I am well pleased.'"

To fulfill the salvation of God, Jesus came to John to be baptized. John the Baptist was a special servant of God. Luke chapter 1 says that John was a descendent of Aaron, the first high priest. God had chosen John, a descendent of Aaron, because He wanted the representative of all humankind to fulfill all righteousness.

So, God had John born in the house of the high priest 6 months prior to the birth of Jesus. John the Baptist prepared the way for Jesus by crying out in the wilderness, "Repent, you brood of vipers! Repent and be converted. The Messiah will come. Be converted to Him, or He will cut you down and throw you into the fire. Believe in His baptism and His blood on the Cross. Repent and be baptized, then you will be redeemed."

The gospel of redemption is described clearly in Acts 3:19. When John the Baptist cried out about the sins of humankind, many were converted.

Because John passed the sins of the world on to Jesus, all the sins of mankind were blotted out at one time. Because John the Baptist testified that Jesus took away all our sins, we know we can be saved by believing in the gospel of redemption, the gospel of the water and the blood.

THE REASON WHY JOHN THE BAPTIST HAD TO COME BEFORE JESUS

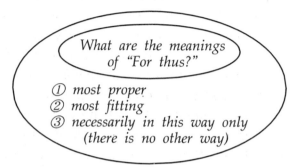

Those whose sins were washed away by believing in Jesus, the Savior, can confirm their salvation through the testimony of Matthew to the gospel of the baptism of Jesus. In Matthew 3:15-16, Jesus came to John and said, *"Baptize me."* And John answered, *"I need to be baptized by You, and are You coming to me?"*

It was John the Baptist who baptized Jesus, recognizing who He was. John was the servant of God who was sent to pass all the sins of humankind on to Jesus. Because Jesus came as the Savior to fulfill the prophecy of the Old Testament, He commanded John the Baptist to baptize Him in order to take all the sins of the world on to His head.

Why? Because Jesus is the Son of God Almighty, the Creator, and the Savior. He came to us in order to wash away all our sins. So, in order to save all people, He had to be baptized.

"For thus" Jesus was baptized by John the Baptist and washed away all our sins. He was judged on our behalf on the Cross. The baptism of Jesus was the testimony to our salvation. As God had promised in the Old Testament that all sins would be passed on to a sacrificial Lamb, the

Son of God became the Lamb and took all our sins upon Himself.

So both the laying on of hands in the Old Testament and the baptism of Jesus in the New Testament are the passing on of sins, and salvation and everlasting life is given to those who believe in the gospel of the water and the Spirit.

THE BAPTISM OF JESUS WASHED AWAY ALL OUR SINS

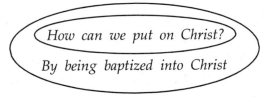

How can we put on Christ?

By being baptized into Christ

When Jesus wanted to be baptized, John the Baptist tried to prevent Him, saying, *"I need to be baptized by You, and are You coming to me?"*

But Jesus answered and said, *"Permit it to be so now, for thus it is fitting for us to fulfill all righteousness."* Permit it to be so now. Permit it. He told John, "You must pass the sins of all people on to Me so that I can bring to Me all those who believe in the gospel of the water of redemption. I will then be judged for all their sins so that all who believe in My baptism will be redeemed of all their sins. Pass on to Me the sins of the world through baptism so that all who come later will be redeemed of their sins all at one time. Therefore permit it to be so now."

Jesus was baptized by John the Baptist and the baptism of Jesus was in accordance with the righteous law of redemption of God. Because all sins were passed on to Jesus when He was baptized, we can be redeemed all at one time when we believe in Jesus and are baptized. Because He took on all our sins through the laying on of hands, died on the Cross on our behalf and now sits at the right hand of God, we can be saved by believing in the redemption of the water and the Spirit.

He is Jesus, who saved us from all the sins of the world. We can be saved by believing that Jesus took away all our sins and paid the wages of all our sins on the Cross. The baptism of Jesus was the beginning of the gospel of redemption.

The baptism of redemption is mentioned often in the Bible and the apostle Paul also says in Galatians that he was crucified with Christ because he was baptized into Christ and put on Christ. The apostle Paul talks about his faith in redemption through the baptism of Jesus and His death on the Cross.

"PERMIT IT TO BE SO NOW"

What was the role of John the Baptist?

His role was to pass all the sins of the world on to Jesus as the high priest of all mankind.

Jesus said, *"For thus it is fitting for us to fulfill all righteousness."* All righteousness means to blot out all sins through His baptism and make all people sinless in their hearts. *"Then he allowed Him."* Jesus was baptized at the

Jordan.

Just as the high priest laid his hands on the head of a goat, John the Baptist laid his hands on Jesus' head and passed all the sins of the world on to Him. John the Baptist was the high priest whose task was to pass all the sins of the world on to Jesus as the representative of humanity. "God, I pass all the sins of the world on to Your Lamb, Jesus." Thus all the sins of humankind were passed on to Jesus.

John the Baptist laid his hands on the head of Jesus, immersed Him in the water, and took his hands away when Jesus came up from the water. The baptism of Jesus made for the righteous salvation. Thus Jesus saved all humankind who believe in His baptism.

THE HEAVENS WERE OPENED AND A VOICE CAME FROM HEAVEN

From what time was the kingdom of Heaven opened?

From the days of John the Baptist (Matthew 11:12)

"When He had been baptized, Jesus came up immediately from the water; and behold, the heavens were opened to Him, and He saw the Spirit of God descending like a dove and alighting upon Him. And suddenly a voice came from heaven, saying, 'This is My beloved Son, in whom I am well pleased'" (Matthew 3:16-17).

When Jesus took away all the sins of the world with

His baptism, the heavens were opened to Him. Thus the Covenant of God which had been made several thousand years before was fulfilled through the baptism of Jesus at the Jordan.

Thus Jesus, as the Lamb of God, saved all the people of the world from their sins. All the sins of the world were passed on to Jesus and He fulfilled the will of God.

It is testified in John 1:29, *"Behold! The Lamb of God who takes away the sin of the world!"* Because all sins were passed on to Jesus, the Lamb of God, He walked toward the Cross at Golgotha after three years with that burden on His shoulders. After He took on all sins with His baptism, everywhere He went, He told those who received Him by faith that all their sins were forgiven.

In John 8:11, He told the woman who was caught in the act of adultery, *"Neither do I condemn you."* He could not condemn her because the One who had to be judged was Jesus Himself, who had taken on all sin. Thus He told all people that He was the Savior of sinners.

Because He, the Son of God, took away all our sins, every believer in the world can become sanctified. The heavens were opened up when He was baptized. The gates of the kingdom of Heaven were opened up and whoever believes in the baptism of Jesus can freely enter.

Jesus was Crucified after He Took away All the Sins of the World through His Baptism

How did Jesus bruise Satan's head?

By being resurrected from the dead after accepting the judgement for all our sins

Because all sins were passed onto His head, Jesus had to be judged on the Cross. He was deeply sorrowful and troubled when He thought about the agony He would suffer on the Cross. He prayed until His sweat became like great drops of blood. When He went with His disciples to a place called Gethsemane, He cried out, "O My Father, if it is possible, let this cup pass from Me" (Matthew 26:39). "I was baptized and took on all the sins of the world, but let Me not die for it." But God didn't answer.

On the Day of Atonement in the Old Testament, the sin offering had to be killed so that its blood might be sprinkled before the mercy seat by the high priest. In the same way, Jesus had to be crucified and God decided He could do it no other way.

The altar is the judgement of God and the blood of the sin offering is life. To sprinkle the blood seven times before and in front of the mercy seat means that all judgement is passed on (Leviticus 16:1-22).

Jesus prayed to God to let the cup pass from Him. But His Father didn't allow Him and Jesus finally said, "Not as I will, but as You will" (Matthew 26:39). He prayed to God to do as He saw fit. He finished praying and followed the will of His Father.

Jesus gave up His own will and obeyed His Father. Why? Because if He had not been judged after taking away all the sins of the world, salvation would have not been completed. He was crucified because He took away all the sins of humankind through His baptism. *"For the wages of sin is death, but the gift of God is eternal life in Christ Jesus our Lord" (Romans 6:23).*

God fulfilled the Covenant which said that He would send the Savior and save humanity through the laying on of hands, the baptism of Jesus. Jesus obeyed God's will and accepted judgement for us.

It was also the fulfillment of the prophecy in Genesis 3:15, *"And I will put enmity between you and the woman, and between your seed and her Seed; He shall bruise your head, and you shall bruise His heel."* God promised Adam to send the Messiah, a seed of Eve, and He would defeat Satan's power that made humankind a sinner and go to hell.

When we know and believe in the baptism of Jesus and His death on the Cross, all our sins are washed away and we are saved from judgement.

We have to have sound belief in our hearts when we consider the baptism of Jesus and His blood on the Cross. Believe it in your hearts, and then you will be saved.

THE BAPTISM OF JESUS IS THE BEGINNING OF THE HEAVENLY GOSPEL

What was the last commandment of the Lord before He ascended to Heaven?

He commanded His disciples to make disciples of all nations by baptizing in the name of the Father and of the Son and of the Holy Spirit.

The baptism of Jesus was the beginning of the gospel, and He saved all sinners with His baptism and blood. In Matthew 28:19, it is recorded, *"Go therefore and make disciples of all the nations, baptizing them in the name of the Father and of the Son and of the Holy Spirit."* Jesus told His disciples to testify that the Father and the Son and the Holy Spirit had saved all humankind from their sins and washed them all away through His baptism and His blood.

Jesus gave them the power to make disciples of all nations, to teach them about the baptism of Jesus, the baptism of redemption, the baptism that washed away all the sins of the world.

About 2000 years ago, Jesus came to earth in the flesh and was baptized by John the Baptist. With the baptism of Jesus, all the sins of the world, including all our sins, were passed on to Him.

How much sin was passed on to Him? How about the sins of tomorrow? He tells us that even the sins of tomorrow were passed on to Him. The sins of our children, those of all the generations, past, present and future, even those of Adam were passed on to Jesus.

How can there be no sin? How can we be without sin? Because Jesus took away all our sins and all the sins of the world with His baptism so that all believers could free themselves from sin and gain access to the Kingdom of Heaven.

"But he who does the truth comes to the light, that his deeds may be clearly seen, that they have been done in God" (John 3:21).

Jesus washed away all our sins with His baptism, His blood on the Cross, His death, and His resurrection. Therefore to believe in His baptism and His death on the Cross is to be saved from all sin. This is the faith of redemption.

When we believe in the baptism and the blood of Christ, we are saved. When we believe in Jesus correctly, are we the righteous or sinners? We are the righteous. Are we without sin even if we are incomplete beings? Yes, we are without sin. To believe in the baptism of Jesus and the judgement on the Cross is to have complete and proper faith.

TO BAPTIZE AND BE BAPTIZED IN THE NAME OF JESUS

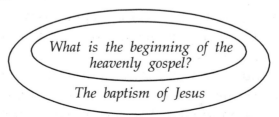

What is the beginning of the heavenly gospel?

The baptism of Jesus

Because people are incomplete beings, ministers baptize

those who believe in the baptism of Jesus and His blood to make them confirm their faith. The born again make sure their being saved by being baptized in the same manner of the baptism of Jesus as the proof of the faith.

The minister first prays with his hands on the head of a born again person, asking for the blessing of God so that this person will worship Him well until the end of his days. Then he baptizes him in the name of the Father and of the Son and of the Holy Spirit.

We are baptized on the basis of our faith in the baptism of Jesus and His blood. This baptism is to show that all sin was passed on to Jesus, that the baptized person died with Jesus and was resurrected with Him.

To be baptized is to proclaim one's belief in the passing of sins on to Jesus through His baptism, in being judged for one's sins alongside Jesus and in being resurrected with Him. It is to proclaim one's faith before the Father, the Son, the Holy Spirit, Satan, and one's brothers and sisters. It is to confess that one has been born again of water and the Spirit.

Those who believe in Jesus, knowing the true meaning of the baptism of Jesus and His blood on the Cross, are saved from all the sins of the world. Therefore they are baptized in the name of the Father and of the Son and of the Holy Spirit.

"Old things have passed away; behold, all things have become new" (2 Corinthians 5:17). Our old things have passed away and we have been born again as people of faith. To make it sure in our hearts, we are baptized. We are baptized into Jesus by believing in the baptism of Jesus.

LIFE AFTER BEING BORN AGAIN OF THE BAPTISM OF JESUS AND HIS BLOOD ON THE CROSS

> *What do the born again live for?*
>
> They live for the kingdom of God and His righteousness, preaching the gospel all over the world.

Life after being redeemed and born again must involve faith in the word of God. It should not be an emotional life in which one has to repent for daily sins every day. Rather, it has to be a faithful life in which we are assured every day that Jesus took away all our sins with His baptism.

All our sins were passed on to Jesus when He was baptized. He then lived for three years with this burden until He accepted the judgement for all our sins and was crucified.

Therefore we believers should have faith in the written word, not in mere emotions. If we fail to do so, we will only worry about our daily sins after we are redeemed and born again.

We have to discard the subjective viewpoint of sin and believe only in the gospel of the water and the blood. This is the life that the redeemed person should lead.

What did John the Baptist say about Jesus? He said, *"Behold, the Lamb of God who takes away the sin of the world"* *(John 1:29)*. He testified that Jesus took away the sins of today, tomorrow, and yesterday, all the way back to original sin.

Didn't He take away all those sins? Were not all those sins passed on to Jesus? The sin of the world includes all our sins of the past, the present, and the future. We have to confirm the gospel of redemption through the baptism of Jesus.

Those who believe in the truth of the baptism of Jesus and His blood shall be saved. Whoever believes in the baptism of Jesus has no sin in their heart.

However, many people think they still have sin because they are not aware that all their sins were already passed on to Jesus through His baptism. They are deceived by Satan. Satan whispers to them through their carnal thoughts. "You sin every day. How can you be without sin?"

They only have to believe in God to be without sin. But Satan tricks them into thinking they are sinners because they still sin. No one is with sin if he believes in the baptism of Jesus and His blood on the Cross.

Because we live in this world as insufficient and weak beings, we can never say we become righteous through our works and deeds alone. But we can say with faith that we are saved by the truth of the baptism of Jesus and His blood on the Cross. Once we understand that by believing in the baptism of Jesus and His blood, our hearts become sanctified, we know for sure that we have no sin.

"♫ I have been redeemed. You have been redeemed. We all have been redeemed ♫" It is such a joyous and happy feeling to live with the desire to preach the gospel to all and know that we are led by the Spirit.

Of course we believers sin every day but we have no sin. We have the baptism of Jesus and His blood in our hearts. Our hearts used to be filled with sin, but now that we believe in the baptism of Jesus, how can we remain sinful.

"This is the covenant that I will make with them after those days, says the Lord: I will put My laws into their hearts, and in their minds I will write them" (Hebrews 10:16).

Our hearts are free of sin. Jesus made it possible for us to be redeemed completely with His baptism and His death on the Cross. Salvation from sin stems from belief in the word of God.

WHOEVER BELIEVES IN THE BAPTISM OF JESUS AND HIS BLOOD ON THE CROSS CAN NEVER BECOME A SINNER AGAIN

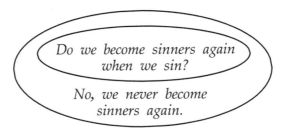

Do we become sinners again when we sin?

No, we never become sinners again.

When we did not believe in the baptism of Jesus and His blood, no matter how often we prayed for forgiveness, there was sin in our hearts. But when we came to believe in the true gospel, all our sins were washed away.

"Hey, how come are you so bright and cheerful these days?"

"You see, I don't have sin in my heart anymore."

"Really? Then I guess you can sin as much as you want now?"

"You know, man cannot help but sin. That's what man

is. But Jesus took away all sins with His baptism and accepted the judgement for them on the Cross. For this reason I now devote myself to serving the gospel in church. Romans chapter 6 says all of us should live like this. Since I no longer have sin in my heart, I want to do the righteous thing. We have to believe in the baptism of Jesus and in His blood on the Cross and preach the gospel throughout the world! When we believe in Jesus, our Master of redemption, we can never become sinners again. We have to believe in the eternal salvation of the baptism of Jesus and of His blood on the Cross. I am so full of gratitude!"

WHO RECEIVES THE SPIRIT?

> *What did John the Baptist testify about Jesus?*
>
> *He testified that Jesus was the Lamb of God who took away all the sins of the world, namely, sins of the past, the present and the future, even original sin.*

Whoever believes in the baptism of Jesus and His blood on the Cross receives salvation. How do we receive the Spirit? Acts 2:38-39 tells us the answer. *"Then Peter said to them, 'Repent, and let every one of you be baptized in the name of Jesus Christ for the remission of sins; and you shall receive the gift of the Holy Spirit. For the promise is to you and to your children, and to all who are afar off, as many as the Lord our God will call.'"*

To be baptized in the name of Jesus Christ means to

believe in the baptism of Jesus and be redeemed. Then the Spirit shall be given as a gift from God.

To be baptized in the name of Jesus Christ also means to become sanctified by believing in Christ's baptism and blood. When we embrace this belief, we are redeemed and become righteous. Believers become white as snow through the baptism of Jesus and His blood on the Cross.

"And you shall receive the gift of the Holy Spirit." When we firmly believe that all our sins were passed on to Jesus through His baptism and that He was judged for them with His death on the Cross, our hearts are washed clean. Our new lives begin when we believe in the baptism of Jesus and His blood and receive the gift of the Holy Spirit and become children of God.

"And you shall know the truth, and the truth shall make you free" (John 8:32). We should know the true meaning of the Lord's judgement on the Cross. The truth is that Jesus blotted out all our sins with His baptism and His death on the Cross. Redemption is given to us when we believe the truth.

THE BAPTISM OF JESUS REDEEMS US

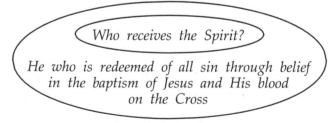

Who receives the Spirit?

He who is redeemed of all sin through belief in the baptism of Jesus and His blood on the Cross

The atonement for sin through the sacrificial system of the Old Testament represents the baptism of Jesus in the

New Testament. The baptism of Jesus is the very core of all the prophecies of the Old Testament. The counterpart to the laying on of hands in the Old Testament can be found in the baptism of Jesus in the New Testament.

All the sins of the world were passed on to Jesus through His baptism just as the sins of Israel were passed on to the scapegoat through the laying on of hands.

Do we have to believe in the baptism of Jesus to be saved from all our sins? Yes! We do! We have to accept the truth of the fact Jesus took away all the sins of the world through His baptism. If we do not believe in the baptism of Jesus, our sins cannot be passed on to Him. We must believe in order to make our salvation complete. Otherwise, we cannot become righteous.

Jesus saved all the sinners of the world in the most fitting and righteous way with His baptism. It could not have been done in a more fitting way. Because the baptism of Jesus was the process by which all sins were passed on to Him, we have to believe in it to have our hearts permanently cleansed of sin.

We should also believe that the blood of Jesus was the judgement for all our sins. Thus, all who believe in the baptism of Jesus and His blood on the Cross are saved from sin.

We have to believe in the baptism of Jesus in order to enter the kingdom of Heaven. This is the only way we can be delivered from all sin and escape just punishment.

The baptism of Jesus in the New Testament and the laying on of hands in the Old Testament are mirrors of each other. They are the connecting clasp and loop between the Old and New Testaments.

In the New Testament, John the Baptist came 6 months

before Jesus. When Jesus was baptized, it was *"The beginning of the gospel of Jesus Christ, the Son of God" (Mark 1:1)*. The gospel begins at the time Jesus took away all the sins of the world through His baptism.

The ministry of salvation of humankind was carried out through a chain of events: the birth of Jesus, His baptism, His death on the Cross, His resurrection, and His ascension to Heaven. When we know and understand and believe in the process of salvation in this chain of events, we are saved from all our sins. The baptism of Jesus was the beginning of the gospel while the blood on the Cross was its completion.

"The beginning of the gospel of Jesus Christ, the Son of God" (Mark 1:1). We cannot omit any one of His righteous deeds —His baptism, His blood on the Cross, His resurrection, His ascension, and His Second Coming— from the gospel of the Son of God.

Jesus came to this world in the flesh and washed away all the sins of humankind with His baptism, this was the beginning of the heavenly gospel. If even one of these were missing, the heavenly gospel would not be complete.

Therefore, if someone is to be born again, he has to believe in Christ's baptism and His blood. These days, many people do not believe the truth of the baptism of Jesus and His blood. They think the baptism of Jesus was merely a ritual. This is a serious misconception. Anyone who believes in Jesus must also believe in His baptism and blood.

How can our sins be washed away simply by praying for forgiveness? All our sins were passed on to Jesus when He was baptized by John the Baptist. There was no other way for Him to take on the sins of humankind.

We have to be born again of water and the Spirit to

enter the kingdom of Heaven. There can be no redemption without the water of baptism, the blood on the Cross, and the Spirit. Only someone who has been born again can see God, as Jesus said to Nicodemus in John 3:5. True salvation comes to us only when we believe in the baptism of Jesus and His blood.

CAN WE BE SAVED WITHOUT THE BAPTISM OF JESUS?

How did Jesus become our Savior?

By taking on all our sins through His baptism

If we were to omit from the Lord's public ministry the fact that Jesus came to this world and took away all our sins through His baptism, or overlook the holiness of Jesus, who was born to the Virgin Mary, or neglect to believe in the Cross of Jesus, Christianity would became merely a superstitious religion that leads believers to chant "forgive me, forgive me, forgive me" like Buddhists do in their temples.

To omit the baptism of Jesus would mean that our sins were not passed on to Him. Our faith would be worthless, making us no different from the debtor who claims that he paid off his debts in full when in fact he paid nothing at all. It would make us all liars. If a debtor said he had paid off all his debts when in fact he had done nothing of the sort, he would still be a debtor in fact and in conscience.

Jesus washed believers clean with the water of His baptism and made them children of God. Jesus took away all the sins of the world through John the Baptist, so that all believers could be sanctified. When we know and believe this, our hearts become clean forever.

Thank God for His grace. Luke 2:14 says, *"Glory to God in the highest, and on earth peace, goodwill toward men!"* Our faith in the water and the blood of Jesus brings us complete salvation and makes us children of God. The baptism of Jesus and His blood saved us and whoever believes in these two things is saved.

Nothing can be omitted from His works. Some only believe in the blood, saying the apostle Paul boasted of nothing but the Cross. But the baptism of Jesus was included in His Cross.

We can see in Romans chapter 6 that Paul was baptized into Christ and died with Christ. And also in Galatians 2:20, *"I have been crucified with Christ; it is no longer I who live, but Christ lives in me; and the life which I now live in the flesh I live by faith in the Son of God, who loved me and gave Himself for me."*

And in Galatians 3:27-29, *"For as many of you as were baptized into Christ have put on Christ. There is neither Jew nor Greek, there is neither slave nor free, there is neither male nor female; for you are all one in Christ Jesus. And if you are Christ's, then you are Abraham's seed, and heirs according to the promise."*

To be baptized into Christ means to believe in all the things He did in this world, His baptism and His blood on the Cross. To believe in the baptism of Jesus and His blood is to believe in the truth that Jesus already blotted out all our sins nearly 2000 years ago. There is no other way that brings us salvation.

WE ARE SAVED BY GOD WHEN WE BELIEVE IN THE BAPTISM OF JESUS AND HIS BLOOD ON THE CROSS

Can our sins be washed away just by praying for forgiveness?

No. Forgiveness of sin is possible only through our belief that all sins were passed on to Jesus when He was baptized by John the Baptist.

"For with the heart one believes unto righteousness, and with the mouth confession is made to salvation" (Romans 10:10).

"For as many of you as were baptized into Christ have put on Christ" (Galatians 3:27). Our faith leads us to be baptized into Christ, to put on Christ, and to become children of God. When Jesus came to this world and was baptized, all our sins and the sins of the world were passed on to Him.

Our faith has led us to be one with Christ. We died when He died. We were resurrected when He was resurrected. Now because we believe in the baptism of Jesus, His blood, and His resurrection, His ascension, and His advent, we can enter the kingdom of Heaven and live forever.

When people believe in the blood of Jesus alone, they cannot but suffer from the sin that remains in their hearts. Why? Because they neither know nor accept the meaning of the baptism of Jesus, which took away all their sins and cleansed their sinful hearts, making them as white as snow for all eternity.

Do you believe in the baptism of Jesus and His blood that saves you from all your sins? Please believe in this unalterable truth. Without belief in the baptism of Jesus, your faith is in vain. Without faith in the baptism of Jesus, you cannot be redeemed of your sins; you are engaged in unrequited love.

Those who only believe in the Cross say, "Jesus is my Lord, my Savior, who died on the Cross for me. He rose again from the dead and testified to His resurrection for 40 days before ascending to Heaven and now sits at the right hand of God. I believe that He will come a second time to judge us and I pray that Jesus will change me completely so I can meet Him. Oh, my beloved Jesus, my Lord."

They ask for the forgiveness of their sins and hope to be without sin, but there is sin in their hearts. "I believe in Jesus but I have sin in my heart. I love Jesus but I have sin in my heart. I cannot say, 'Please come to me, my bridegroom' because I have sin and I cannot be sure of my salvation. So I hope Jesus will come when I am well prepared and only after I pray harder and repent harder. I love Jesus with all my heart but cannot dare to face Him because of the sins in my heart."

If Jesus were to ask such people, "Why do you think you are not complete?"

They would answer, "Lord, I know I am not righteous because I sin every day. So please call me when you call the sinners."

They do not know that God, the Creator and the Judge, will neither accept sinners nor make them His children.

The bridegroom came and solved all the problems of sin for the bride, but because the bride was not aware of this fact, she was tormented. When we think we are sinners because we have sinned with the flesh, we do not have faith in God. When we neither know nor understand the truth of the word of God, the sin in our hearts keeps multiplying.

Why do some people suffer from the sin that remains in their hearts?

Because they neither know nor accept into their hearts the meaning of the baptism of Jesus, which took away all their sins.

The bridegroom took away the sins of the world. Where? At the Jordan when He was baptized. Those who do not believe this are still sinners. They remain defiled brides.

The groom asks the bride, "How can you love Me when you are not My bride? Before you call Me your bridegroom, all your sins must be washed away."

Can we be redeemed without the baptism of Jesus? No! We are created in the image of God, so we seek justice in our hearts, and our consciences try to be just. But it is impossible for us to think we are sinless if our hearts have not been cleansed. Only when we accept and believe in the baptism of Jesus can we truly say that we have no sin and we are righteous.

Our consciences can never become sanctified if we consider ourselves to be without sin when in reality we have sin in our hearts. Nor can God accept us under these circumstances. God never lies.

God told Moses to take a census of the Israelites to count them and pay Him a ransom for their lives. The rich were not to give more than a half shekel and the poor were not to give less. Everyone had to pay a ransom.

Therefore, how can someone become sanctified if he does not believe in Jesus who paid him a ransom for his life? Such a person continues to have sin in his heart.

When we believe only in the blood of Jesus, we have sin in our hearts and have to confess that we are sinners. But when we believe in the gospel of His baptism and the Cross together, we can truly state that we have no sin. Salvation and eternal life are ours.

THE BLASPHEMY AGAINST THE SPIRIT

What kind of sin condemns man to hell?

Sin against the Spirit, in other words, not to believe in the baptism of Jesus

Romans 1:17 says, *"For in it the righteousness of God is revealed from faith to faith."* The righteousness of God is revealed in the gospel. Jesus Christ came to this world and washed away all our sins with His baptism and His death on the Cross. The baptism of Jesus and His blood is the power of the gospel. Jesus washed away our sins once and for all.

To believe means salvation and not to believe means

eternal hell. Our Father in Heaven sent His only begotten Son Jesus to this world and had Him baptized for the atonement of our sins. Thus, he who believes in Him can be cleansed of all his transgressions.

The only sin remaining in this world is the sin of not believing in His baptism and blood. Not believing is blasphemy against the Spirit and a sin that shall be judged by God, condemning the non-believe to hell. It is the gravest sin of all. Any of you who commits this sin must repent and be redeemed by believing in the baptism of Jesus. If not, you will be ruined forever.

Are you saved with the testimony of redemption through His baptism and blood? Have you received the testimony of John as it is written in John 1:29, *"Behold! the Lamb of God who takes away the sin of the world!"* Do you believe in the baptism of Jesus and His blood as it is written in Hebrews 10:18, *"Now where there is remission of these, there is no longer an offering for sin."*

God certifies those who believe in the baptism of Jesus and His blood in their hearts. God makes them His children. Those who believe in the baptism of Jesus and His blood are redeemed through the righteous love of Jesus.

Whoever God sent speaks the words of God, but those who are of the earth, who have not been sent by God, preach in accordance with their own thoughts. There are many on this earth who preach the word of God, and those who have been sent by God speak of the baptism of Jesus and His blood.

But those who preach their own words are only expressing their own thoughts. They say, "We are redeemed of original sin, but each has to repent his daily sins." They say we have to become sanctified gradually.

But can a person be sanctified on his own? Can we become sanctified on the strength of our own merits and through our own efforts? Are we sanctified because God washed away all our sins, or because we tried to achieve redemption on our own?

The true faith is what sanctifies us. Can we make coal white by washing it a thousand times? Can we make black skin white with lye? No amount of soap or lye can wash away our sins, and our own righteousness is like a dirty rag. Do we become righteous by believing in the baptism of Jesus and His blood or by believing only in the blood on the Cross?

The true faith comes out of the water of Jesus' baptism and the blood on the Cross. Salvation does not come as a result of our own efforts. Only our faith in the baptism of Jesus and His blood frees us from sin and makes us righteous.

The Father has given all people into His Son's hands, and those who believe in Him shall have everlasting life. To believe in the Son means to believe in redemption through His baptism and blood. Those who believe shall have everlasting life as a child of God. Those who are saved live on forever at the right hand of God.

Faith in the baptism of Jesus and His oneness with God is also faith in the Spirit. The word of truth allows us to be born again. We are saved by believing in the baptism of Jesus and His blood.

Have faith. To believe in the baptism of Jesus and His blood is to earn redemption. Have faith in the true gospel and obtain the forgiveness of sin. ✉

SERMON 8

Let Us Do the Will of the Father with Faith

The next day John saw Jesus coming toward him, and said, "Behold! The Lamb of God who takes away the sin of the world!" (John 1:29).

Let Us Do the Will of the Father with Faith

<Matthew 7:21-23>
"Not everyone who says to Me, 'Lord, Lord,' shall enter the kingdom of heaven, but he who does the will of My Father in heaven. Many will say to Me in that day, 'Lord, Lord, have we not prophesied in Your name, cast out demons in Your name, and done many wonders in Your name?' And then I will declare to them, 'I never knew you; depart from Me, you who practice lawlessness!'"

MAYBE I AM THE ONE...

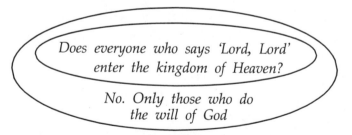

Does everyone who says 'Lord, Lord' enter the kingdom of Heaven?

No. Only those who do the will of God

Jesus Christ says, "Not everyone who says to Me, 'Lord, Lord,' shall enter the kingdom of heaven, but he who does the will of My Father in heaven." These words have struck fear in the hearts of many Christians, causing them to work hard to do the will of God.

Most Christians think the only thing they need to do is to believe in Jesus to enter the kingdom of Heaven, but Matthew 7:21 tells us that not every one who says to Him, 'Lord, Lord,' will enter the kingdom of Heaven.

Many who read this verse are driven to wonder "Maybe I am the one." They try to convince themselves, "No, Jesus must have meant the unbelievers." But the thought remains in their minds and keeps nagging at them.

So, they hang on to the latter part of the verse which reads, *"but he who does the will of My Father in heaven."* They hang on to the words, *"does the will of My Father"* and think that they can do that by paying the tithe faithfully, praying at the break of dawn, preaching, doing good deeds, and not sinning . . . and they try so hard. It makes me feel so sorry to see them.

Many people make mistakes because they do not understand this verse. Therefore I would like to explain this verse clearly so that we may all know the will of God and live by it.

First, we must know that the will of God is for His Son to take away the sins of all people and thus free us from sin.

In Ephesians 1:5, it is written, *"God has predestined us to adoption as sons by Jesus Christ to Himself, according to the good pleasure of His will."*

In other words, His intention is for us to know the true gospel that Jesus Christ washed away all our sins, thus allowing us to be born again. He wants us to be born again of water and the Spirit by passing all our sins on to His Son, Jesus. This is the will of God.

JUST FOR SAYING, "LORD! LORD!"

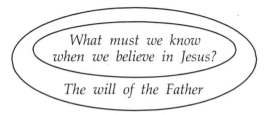

*What must we know
when we believe in Jesus?*

The will of the Father

*"Not everyone who says to Me, 'Lord, Lord,' shall enter the
kingdom of heaven, but he who does the will of My Father in
heaven" (Matthew 7:21).*

We ought to understand the Father's will in two ways.
First, we should know that it is His will that we obtain
forgiveness for our sins and become born again of water
and the Spirit. Second, we should work on the basis of
that faith.

It is His will to blot out the sins of all people on the
earth. Satan brought about the fall of our ancestor Adam
through sin. But the will of our Father is to wipe out all
the sins of man. We should understand that it is not our
Father's will for us to offer the tithe faithfully and offer
prayers at the break of dawn, but to save us all from sin.
It is His will to save all os us from drowning in a sea of
sin.

The Bible says that not everyone who says 'Lord, Lord'
shall enter the kingdom of Heaven. This means that we
should not just believe in Jesus, but know what our Father
wants for us. It is His will to save us from sin and the
judgment of hell, knowing that the legacy of Adam and
Eve means that we cannot help but live in sin.

THE WILL OF GOD

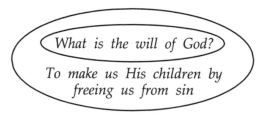

What is the will of God?

To make us His children by
freeing us from sin

Matthew 3:15 says, *"For thus it is fitting for us to fulfill all righteousness."* Thus it was to fulfill God's plan that Jesus came to this world to save us all from sin. The will of God was fulfilled when Jesus was baptized by John the Baptist.

He wanted to save us and make us His children. In order to do that, His Son had to take away all our sins. It was His will to make all people His children. So He sent His own Son to take away the sins of all people who had fallen into Satan's clutches. It was His will to offer the life of His own Son for all people so that they could become His children.

When Jesus was baptized and died on the Cross, the will of God was fulfilled. It is also His will for us to believe that all our sins were passed on to Jesus when He was baptized and that He took the judgment for all our transgressions through His death on the Cross.

"For God so loved the world that He gave His only begotten Son" (John 3:16). God saved His people from sin. To do so, the first thing Jesus did in His public ministry was to be baptized by John the Baptist.

"But Jesus answered and said to him, 'Permit it to be so now, for thus it is fitting for us to fulfill all righteousness.' Then he allowed Him" (Matthew 3:15). It was the will of God that Jesus came to this world, took away all the sins of the world through His baptism, died on the Cross, and was resur-

rected.

We should know this clearly. Many people read Matthew 7:21 and think that it is His will for us to serve the Lord, even to the point of death, by offering all our worldly possessions to build churches.

Fellow Christians, we who believe in Jesus should first know the will of God and then do it. It is wrong for you to dedicate yourself to the church without knowing His will.

People ask themselves what else can there be except to live in faith within their orthodox churches. But I myself studied Calvinism in the Presbyterian Church and was raised under an adoptive mother who was as religious as any veteran pastor. I learned in the so-called "orthodox church".

The apostle Paul said that he could also boast that he was from the tribe of Benjamin and studied the Law under Gamaliel, who was a great rabbi at the time. Before Paul was born again, he was on his way to arrest those who believed in Jesus. But he found faith in Jesus on the road to Damascus and became righteous through the blessing of being born again of water and the Spirit.

WE HAVE TO KNOW THE WILL OF GOD BEFORE WE CAN DO IT

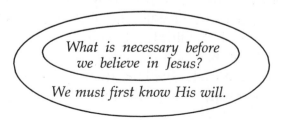

What is necessary before we believe in Jesus?

We must first know His will.

Our sanctification is the will of God. *"For this is the will of God, your sanctification: that you should abstain from sexual immorality" (1 Thessalonians 4:3).* We know that it is the will of God that we be completely sanctified through the water and the Spirit and live in faith all our lives.

If there is anyone who believes in Jesus but still has sin in his heart, he is not living in accordance with the will of God. Following His will requires that we be sanctified through the salvation found in Jesus. To know this is to do the will of God.

When I ask you, "Do you still have sin in your heart even though you believe in Jesus?" and your answer is yes, then clearly you do not yet know the will of God. It is the will of God that we should be sanctified and saved from all our sins through faith in the water and the Spirit.

Once there was a man who had obedient sons. One day he called the eldest, who was also the most obedient, and said, "Son, go to the village across the field . . ."

Before he finished speaking, the son said, "Yes, father" and was gone. He didn't wait to find out what he was supposed to do. He just went.

His father called after him, "Son, it is all very well and good that you are so obedient but you should know what I want you to do."

But the son said, "It is all right, father. I will obey you. Who can obey better than I?"

But of course he came back empty-handed. He had no way of doing his father's will without knowing what it was he wanted. He just blindly obeyed.

We could be like him if we do not know Jesus Christ. Many devote themselves, follow theological doctrines, offer the tithe faithfully, pray all night, fast . . . all without knowing the will of God.

When they die with sin in their hearts, they are turned away at the gate of Heaven. They were so eager to do the will of God but didn't know what God wanted.

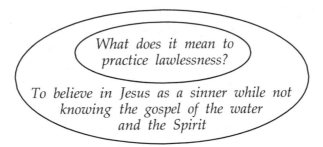

What does it mean to practice lawlessness?

To believe in Jesus as a sinner while not knowing the gospel of the water and the Spirit

"Many will say to Me in that day, 'Lord, Lord, have we not prophesied in Your name, cast out demons in Your name, and done many wonders in Your name?' And then I will declare to them, 'I never knew you; depart from Me, you who practice lawlessness!'" (Matthew 7:22-23)

There are things God wants us to do and there is faith He demands of us. He wants us to believe that Jesus took away all our sins. Many prophesy, cast out demons, and do wonders in His name without knowing the truth of the water and the Spirit.

Doing wonders means building many churches, selling all one's possessions to donate to the church, offering one's own life for the Lord, among their things.

To prophesy in His name means to be a leader. Such people are like the Pharisees who boast of living according to the Law while antagonizing Jesus. This also applies to would-be orthodox Christians.

To cast out demons is to exercise power. They are all so enthusiastic in their faith, but the Lord will tell them in the end that He does not know them. He will ask them how can they know Him when He does not know them.

The Lord says, *"And then I will declare to them, 'I never know you; depart from Me, you who practice lawlessness!'"* On that day, crowds of people will cry out to Him, "Lord, I believe. I believe that You are my Savior." They will say they love Him but they have sin in their hearts. The Lord calls them the practitioners of lawlessness (the sinners who are not delivered) and will tell them to depart from Him.

On that day, those who died without being born again will cry out before Jesus. "I prophesied, built churches and sent out 50 missionaries in Your name."

But Jesus will declare to those sinners, *"I never knew you; Depart from Me, you who practice lawlessness!"*

"What do You mean? Don't You know that I prophesied in Your name? I served in the church for many years . . . I taught others to believe in You. How can You not know me?"

He will answer, "I never knew you. You who claim to know Me yet have sin in your heart, depart from Me!"

It is lawlessness before God to believe in Him with sin in one's heart or not to believe according to His law of salvation. It is lawlessness not to know His will. It is lawlessness to try to do His will without knowing it or not to know the blessing of being born again of water and the Spirit. It is also lawlessness to follow Him without obeying His will. Lawlessness is a sin.

THE WILL OF GOD IN THE BIBLE

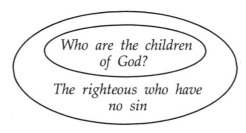

*Who are the children
of God?*

*The righteous who have
no sin*

It is His will for us to believe in the gospel of being born again of water and the Spirit. The true gospel fosters our rebirth. It is also His will that we live for the gospel as His children. We should know the will of God, but so many do not know the gospel of being born again of water and the Spirit.

When I ask people why they believe in Jesus, many say they believe in Jesus in order to be saved from their sins.

I ask, "Then, do you have sin in your heart?"

They say, "Of course, I do."

"Then, are you saved or not?"

"Of course I am."

"Can a sinner who has sin in his heart enter into the kingdom of Heaven?"

"No, he can't."

"Then, are you going to the kingdom of Heaven or into the fires of hell?"

They say they are going to the kingdom of Heaven, but can they? They will go to hell.

Some think that because they believe in Jesus, they can enter into the kingdom of Heaven even if they have sin in their hearts and that it is the will of God for them to do so. But God does not accept sinners into the kingdom of Heaven.

What is the will of God? It says in the Bible that the will of God is for us to believe in His Son, to believe in the blessing of being redeemed through the baptism of Jesus and His blood on the Cross.

Those who believe in the blessing of being born again of water and the Spirit become His children. It is our glory to become His children. His children are righteous.

When God calls us righteous, does He regard a sinner-Christian as righteous? God can never lie. So before Him, you are either a sinner or a righteous person. There can never be 'considered to be without sin.' He calls only those who believe in the gospel of the water and the Spirit to be sanctified.

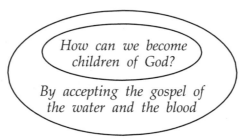

How can we become children of God?

By accepting the gospel of the water and the blood

Because God passed all the sins of the world on to His Son, even His own Son had to be judged on the Cross. God could never tell a lie. He says, *"The wages of sin is death" (Romans 6:23).* When His Son died, the darkness fell on the earth for three hours.

"Jesus cried out with a loud voice, saying, 'Eli, Eli, lama sabachthani?' that is, 'My God, My God, why have You forsaken Me?'" (Matthew 27:46)

Jesus took away all the sins of the world through His baptism to save all people from their sins. He took away the sins of humanity, knowing that He had to be crucified and forsaken by God, His Father. So God judged His own Son for the sins He took away at the Jordan and turned His face from His Son for three hours.

"But as many as received Him, to them He gave the right to become children of God, to those who believe in His name" (John 1:12).

Are you children of God? We are the born again because we have accepted the gospel of being born again of water and the Spirit. Those who are born again of water and the Spirit are righteous. Now we have all become righteous.

"If God is for us, who can be against us?" (Romans 8:31). When a righteous man calls himself righteous before God and the people, those who are not redeemed tend to judge him. So the apostle Paul says, *"Who shall bring a charge against God's elect? It is God who justifies"* (Romans 8:33). God wiped out all our sins through Jesus and called us sanctified, righteous, and His children. He gave us the right to become glorious children of God.

Those who are born again of water and the Spirit are His children. They live with Him eternally. They are no longer just creatures in this world but children of God who belong to Heaven.

Now that they are righteous children of God, there's no one who can bring a charge against them, judge them, or separate them from God.

We have to know the gospel of the water and the Spirit in order to believe in Jesus. We have to know the Bible. It is essential that we know and believe the will of God in order to be able to carry it out according to His will.

IT IS THE WILL OF GOD THAT SINNERS BE BORN AGAIN OF WATER AND THE SPIRIT

Why did God send His Son in the likeness of sinful man?

To have all sins passed on to Him

It is the will of God that we become redeemed and born again of water and the Spirit. *"For this is the will of God, your sanctification" (1 Thessalonians 4:3).*

It was the will of God to send His Son so that all sins would be passed on to Him and we could be saved. This is the law of the Spirit that allows us to be born again of water and the Spirit. It freed us from all sins.

We are redeemed. Now can you all recognize the will of God? It is His will to redeem us all. He doesn't want us to compromise with the world but rather to believe only in His words and worship Him alone.

It is also the will of God that those who have been born again testify the gospel and live in the church, devoting themselves to the work of bringing other souls back to God.

We sin not because we want to, but because we are weak. But Jesus took away those sins. God passed all the sins of the world on to Jesus through John the Baptist. He sent His own Son for that purpose and had him baptized by John. We are saved by believing in this. This is the will of God.

IT IS THE WILL OF GOD FOR US TO BELIEVE IN JESUS, WHOM HE SENT

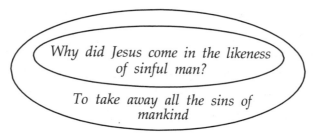

Why did Jesus come in the likeness of sinful man?

To take away all the sins of mankind

The Bible says doing the will of God is to believe in Him whom He sent. *"Then they said to Him, 'What shall we do, that we may work the works of God?' Jesus answered and said to them, 'This is the work of God, that you believe in Him whom He sent.' Therefore they said to Him, 'What sign will You perform then, that we may see it and believe You? What work will You do? Our fathers ate the manna in the desert; as it is written, 'He gave them bread from heaven to eat'"* (John 6:28-31).

People told Jesus that God had given Moses a sign when he was on the way to Canaan, giving the Israelites the manna from Heaven, and as a result they believed in God (John 6:32-39). People asked Jesus, *"What shall we do, that we may work the works of God?"*

Jesus answered that they should believe in Him to do the work of God. If we are to do the work of God, we have to believe in the works of Jesus Christ. It is the will of God for us not only to believe and preach the gospel but to live it.

God commands us, *"Go therefore and make disciples of all the nations, baptizing them in the name of the Father and of the Son and of the Spirit, teaching them to observe all things that I have commanded you"* (Matthew 28:19-20).

Jesus clearly tells us to baptize in the name of the Father and the Son and the Spirit. Everything He did for His Father and the Spirit is contained in His baptism. When we understand that, we can believe in God and see everything Jesus did in this world and how the Spirit testified to that.

Jesus was sent by God to testify to the gospel of the water and the Spirit. Therefore only when we believe in the word of God and His servant can we be saved.

TO DO THE WORK OF GOD

What is the purpose of our lives?

To do the will of God by spreading the gospel all over the world

If we are to do the work of God, we must first believe in the gospel of the baptism of Jesus and His death on the Cross. It is the work of God to believe in Him whom God sent. In order to believe in Jesus, we should first believe that He saved us with the water and the blood.

The will of God is accomplished in us when we believe in Jesus and preach the gospel. In this way we do the work of God. He told us that only those who believe in the blessing of being born again of water and the Spirit can enter the kingdom of Heaven.

Let us all take our places in the kingdom of Heaven by recognizing the following essential truths. Recognizing the true will of God, by knowing and believing that all our sins were passed on to Jesus with His baptism. Live for the expansion of His kingdom. Finally, preach the gospel until the day you die.

Fellow Christians! Those who believe in the gospel of the water and the Spirit are the ones who do the work of God. It is the work of God to believe in Him whom God sent. It is doing His will to believe that all sins were passed on to Him whom God sent and that Jesus Christ is our Savior.

The work of delivering man from sin was accomplished when Jesus was baptized at the Jordan and died for all of us on the Cross. The second part of the work of God is to believe in Him whom God sent, to believe in the Savior who took away all the sins of the world, and to preach the gospel throughout the world.

Now we who are born again should live and preach the gospel to the end of the world.

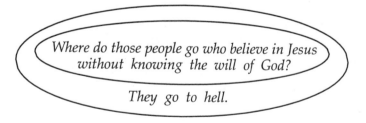

Where do those people go who believe in Jesus without knowing the will of God?

They go to hell.

"Many will say to Me in that day, 'Lord, Lord, have we not prophesied in Your name, cast out demons in Your name, and done many wonders in Your name?' And then I will declare to them, 'I never knew you; depart from Me, you who practice lawlessness!'" (Matthew 7:22-23)

This passage tells us clearly who are the sinners before God and who are the practitioners of lawlessness.

There are so many who are not born again among those

who say 'Lord, Lord.' They are in pain because they still have sin in their hearts. So they cry out to God, calling, 'Lord, Lord,' in a half complaining manner, ill-befitting true prayers of worship.

They believe their consciences will be cleansed if they cry out in prayer, but it is impossible because sin remains in their hearts. They pray in the mountains, crying out in anguish, as if God was far away. When we do not have complete faith, we tend to call out 'Lord, Lord' more often.

In some churches in which the congregation is not born again, they pray with so much enthusiasm that the pulpit breaks down.

But we can see in the Bible that not all those who call out 'Lord, Lord, enter into the kingdom of Heaven. Only those who believe in the gospel of the water and the Spirit have the faith that leads them to do the work of God.

The Bible tells us that it is lawlessness to call out His name with sin in one's heart. Have you ever been to mountain prayer meetings? Some old female deacons cry and cry, calling out His name because they have neither met Jesus in truth, nor accepted the Spirit in their hearts, nor become born again of water and the Spirit. They call His name so urgently because they live in permanent fear that they will go to hell.

Suppose that someone who had devoted his life to serving the church as a missionary or a pastor was ultimately discarded by the Lord. To be abandoned by a parent or a spouse would be enough to break anyone's heart, but having been abandoned by God, the King of kings, the Judge of our souls, where would we go?

I hope this will never happen to any of you. Please listen and believe in the gospel of the water and the Spirit.

It is the will of God for us to be born again and live within the gospel of the water and the Spirit.

We Christians have to truly believe in the gospel of the water and the Spirit and draw strength from the truth of the Bible. Only then can we be saved from the judgment of God. ⊠

Testimony of Salvation

Testimony of Salvation

Brother Lee, Jin-hee

It has been 30 years since I started believing in Jesus. In other words, I have believed in Jesus all my life. At my mother's urging, I went to early morning services, children's services and even the regular grown-up services. Gradually I got to know God and believed in Him. I witnessed several unusual phenomena, miracles and an exorcision of the devil. While my faith grew every day, I also found myself sinning before God on a daily basis. I had lewd thoughts and committed many sins in my heart.

The Bible says, "Whoever looks at a woman to lust for her has already committed adultery with her in his heart." I was committing adultery every day of my life and could not stop myself no matter how much I tried. I also craved honor, felt envy, arrogance, selfishness and murder in my heart. Just as it is written in Romans 7:24, I was a wretched man and could not be delivered from the law of sin and death. The apostle Paul clearly stated in Romans 8:1, "There is therefore now no condemnation to those who are in Christ Jesus, who do not walk according to the flesh, but according to the Spirit. For the law of the Spirit of life in Christ Jesus has made me free from the law of sin and death." I thought at the time this confession of the born again person did not apply to me, who was still a 'condemned man' and who could not stand proudly before God.

I hated myself so much that sometimes I felt like committing suicide. I had to do something, so I tried my best to go before God through my good deeds. I participated in numerous revival meetings, Bible seminars, mission training meetings, mountain prayer meetings, all-night prayer meetings and fasting prayers. But my heart was still not filled. I was afraid because I still had sin in my heart. Matthew 7:21 says, "not everyone who says 'Lord, Lord' shall enter the kingdom of God, but he who does the will of My Father in heaven." Therefore, I thought no matter how often I applied myself to attending large church gatherings, doing devotional works and experiencing miracles, I would be abandoned by Jesus owing to the sin in my heart.

I was especially afraid when I committed grave sins, and I could find no peace no matter how much I prayed in repentance. I would think of 'being born again of water and the Spirit,' but I had no idea how to do this. I asked people around me and read many books, but I still couldn't find the answers. I was told to just have faith that Jesus redeemed us through His death on the Cross. But, this belief could not erase the sins on my conscience nor remove the fear in my heart.

I read "Liberation Theology and the Community Movement" and wholly sympathized with it. It said if Christians don't act on their faith, people would no longer believe in us. Therefore, believers should form a community in which to live like the people of the early church, setting examples by their works and preaching the gospel. I was unable to be washed of my sins but wanted to be recognized through my actions, so I decided to join in this community movement. I had to serve in the army first, but my mind was unchanged upon my discharge from the military. In the mean time, I had the chance to meet a servant of God. He knew the state of my spirit even before he got to know me. He asked me "Do you have sin in your heart?" I felt my heart jump at the question. It was so much to the point that I could not answer. From that time on, through him, I learned how to be born again of water and the Spirit, how my sins could be washed away as clean as snow, through the words of God.

I came to know how man could be atoned through the sacrificial system and how, according to the law, Jesus offered Himself for the perfect redemption. I learned that the laying on of hands in the Old Testament was the shadow of the baptism in the New Testament, and that the offering without blemish was Jesus while the blood of the Old Testament was His Cross. Above all, I learned that because I had only believed in the Cross of Jesus, I still had sin in my heart. When I realized all my sins were passed onto Jesus when He was baptized, I could be sure that I no longer had sin in my heart (Matthew 3:13-17, John 1:29).

When I believed in the Cross of Jesus without His baptism, my faith was only half complete. That was why I still had sin in my heart and could not be born again. Jesus gave us the complete redemption. So now there is no longer an offering for sin (Hebrews 10:18). By believing in this complete word of the gospel, I could be born again as a completely righteous Christian. I am without sin now not because I have not sinned, but because all my sins were passed onto Jesus through His baptism.

Hallelujah! Praise the Lord. "There is therefore no condemnation to those who are in Christ" (Romans 8:1).

I now have complete faith like the apostle Paul. "And you shall know the truth, and the truth shall make you free" (John 8:32). We have to know the truth. We should not just believe, but know what the truth is before believing in it. I wish all who read this will learn the truth and believe it, be born again of water and the Spirit and be free from sin. It is so wonderful to believe in the gospel. Now I can truly believe in God and know what it means to live in faith. I hope the same thing will happen to everyone. I praise and thank the Lord with all my heart. ⊠

HAVE YOU TRULY BEEN BORN AGAIN OF WATER AND THE SPIRIT?

PAUL C. JONG

Among many Christian books written about being born again, this is the first book of our time to preach 'the gospel of the water and the Spirit' in strict accordance with the Scriptures. Man can't enter the kingdom of heaven without being born again of water and the Spirit. To be born again means that a sinner is saved from all his lifelong sins by believing in the baptism of Jesus and His blood on the Cross. Let's believe in the gospel of the water and the Spirit and enter the kingdom of heaven as the righteous who have no sin.

- To purchase this book, visit Amazon.com
- Email : newlife@bjnewlife.org

The Holy Spirit who Dwells in Me

A Fail-safe Way for You to Receive the Holy Spirit

Paul C. Jong

In Christianity, the most significantly discussed issue is salvation from sins and the indwelling of the Holy Spirit. However, few people have the exact knowledge of these two things, while they are most important issues in Christianity. Nevertheless, in reality people say that they believe in Jesus Christ while they are ignorant of redemption and the Holy Spirit.

Do you know the gospel that makes you receive the Holy Spirit? If you want to ask God for the indwelling of the Holy Spirit, then you must first know the gospel of the water and the Spirit and have faith in it. This book will certainly lead all Christians worldwide to be forgiven of all their sins and to receive the Holy Spirit.

The Righteousness of God that is Revealed in Romans

Our LORD
Who Becomes the
Righteousness
of God
(I)

PAUL C. JONG

The words in this book will satisfy the thirst in your heart. Today's Christians continue to live while not knowing the true solution to the actual sins that they are committing daily. Do you know what God's righteousness is? The author hopes that you will ask yourself this question and believe in God's righteousness, which is revealed in this book.

The Doctrines of Predestination, Justification, and Incremental Sanctification are the major Christian doctrines, which brought confusion and emptiness into the souls of believers. But now, many Christians should newly come to know God, learn about His righteousness and continue in the assured faith.

This book will provide your soul with a great understanding and lead it to peace. The author wants you to possess the blessing of knowing God's righteousness.

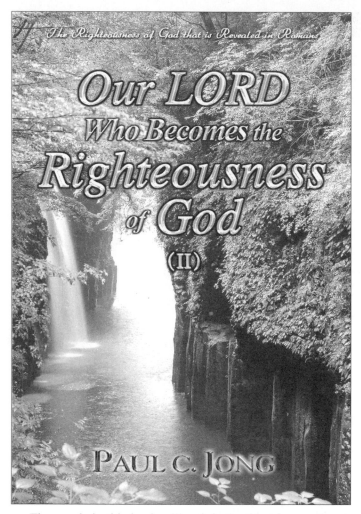

The Righteousness of God that is Revealed in Romans

Our LORD
Who Becomes the
Righteousness
of God
(II)

PAUL C. JONG

The words in this book will satisfy the thirst in your heart. Today's Christians continue to live while not knowing the true solution to the actual sins that they are committing daily. Do you know what God's righteousness is? The author hopes that you will ask yourself this question and believe in God's righteousness, which is revealed in this book.

The Doctrines of Predestination, Justification, and Incremental Sanctification are the major Christian doctrines, which brought confusion and emptiness into the souls of believers. But now, many Christians should newly come to know God, learn about His righteousness and continue in the assured faith.

This book will provide your soul with a great understanding and lead it to peace. The author wants you to possess the blessing of knowing God's righteousness.

Paul C. Jong's Christian book series, which is translated into English, French, German, Spanish, Portuguese, Swedish, Italian, Hindi, Malayalam, Japanese, Chinese, Taiwanese, Mongolian, Vietnamese, Indonesian, Tagalog, Russian, Czech, Polish, Hungarian, Romanian and Turkish, is also available now through e-book service.

E-book is digital book designed for you to feel a printed book on screen. You can read it easily on your screen in your native language after download the viewer software and a text file. Feel free to visit our website at http://www.bjnewlife.org for e-book service, and you can get the most remarkable Christian e-book absolutely for free.

And, would you like to take part in our project of having our free Christian books known to more people worldwide? We would be very thankful if you link your website to our site so that as many people as possible get an opportunity to meet Jesus Christ through our literature.

Please visit our site at http://www.bjnewlife.org/english/nlmbanner.html to take our banners. In addition, we would be also very grateful if you introduce our website to the webmasters around you to add our link to the sites of interested parties.

The New Life Mission
Contact: John Shin, General Secretary
E-mail: khshin99@kornet.net